# GOVERNING GLOBAL BANKING

# Global Finance Series

Edited by
John J. Kirton, University of Toronto, Canada, Michele Fratianni, Indiana
University, U.S.A. and Paolo Savona, LUISS Guido Carli University, Italy

The intensifying globalisation of the twenty-first century has brought a myriad of new
managerial and political challenges for governing international finance. The return of
synchronous global slowdown, mounting developed country debt, and new economy
volatility have overturned established economic certainties. Proliferating financial
crises, transnational terrorism, currency consolidation, and increasing demands that
international finance should better serve public goods such as social and
environmental security have all arisen to compound the problem.

The new public and private international institutions that are ememrging to
govern global finance have only just begun to comprehend and respond to this new
world. Embracing international financial flows and foreign direct investment, in both
the private and public sector dimensions, this series focuses on the challenges and
opportunities faced by firms, national governments, and international institutions,
and their roles in creating a new system of global finance.

*Also in the series*

**Sustaining Global Growth and Development**
**G7 and IMF Governance**
Edited by Michele Fratianni, Paolo Savona and John J. Kirton
ISBN 0 7546 3529 5

**Governing Global Finance**
**New Challenges, G7 and IMF Contributions**
Edited by Michele Fratianni, Paolo Savona and John J. Kirton
ISBN 0 7546 0880 8

**Global Financial Crime**
**Terrorism, Money Laundering and Offshore Centres**
Edited by Donato Masciandaro
ISBN 0 7546 3707 7

# Governing Global Banking
## The Basel Committee and the Politics of Financial Globalisation

DUNCAN WOOD
*ITAM, Mexico*

## ASHGATE

Published by
Ashgate Publishing Limited
Gower House
Croft Road
Aldershot
Hants GU11 3HR
England

Ashgate Publishing Company
Suite 420
101 Cherry Street
Burlington, VT 05401-4405
USA

Ashgate website: http://www.ashgate.com

**British Library Cataloguing in Publication Data**
Wood, Duncan
    Governing global banking : the Basel Committee and the
    politics of financial globalisation. - (Global finance)
    1.Basel Committee on Banking Supervision 2.Banks and
    banking, International - Management 3.International finance
    I. Title
    332.1'5

**Library of Congress Control Number** 2004062398

ISBN 0 7546 1906 0

Printed and bound by Athenaeum Press, Ltd.,
Gateshead, Tyne & Wear.

# Contents

# Foreword

In the popular imagination, 'globalisation' is often something which intrudes uninvited into the lives of the ordinary citizen or state. One of the most visible mediums are international organisations and international markets. Almost everyone has heard of the International Monetary Fund (IMF) and the World Bank, as well as the World Trade Organization (WTO). The prominent role which the IMF has played in global economic governance in recent years has led to a broad (though not deep) understanding amongst the general public of its functions. Criticisms from non-governmental organisations (NGOs) and from the developing countries, which both benefit from and pay the cost of IMF structural adjustment policies, has led to an often vocal campaign against the Bretton Woods Institutions, which includes the World Bank. The 'Battle of Seattle' put the WTO into the popular imagination as lying at the forefront of 'globalisation.'

But who has heard of the Basel Committee on Banking Supervision? If one were to attempt a protest against the Basel Committee, it would be cancelled for lack of interest in and understanding of this institution's crucial role in global governance. Yet this offshoot of co-operation among the Group of Ten (G10) central banks arguably plays a far more central role in the integration and management of global financial markets than the IMF, and most certainly surpasses the World Bank (though their effects on the developing world should not be underestimated). The WTO, with its member-state-based and decentralised authority structure, is far from the interventionist globalising bogey of popular and NGO understanding. Global trade remains far less liberal than financial markets, and the WTO can only do what its members wish. It has no power of its own.

But Basel matters, and it matters a lot. The Basel Committee sets the rules on banking supervision and capital adequacy for all banks with international transactions in G10 markets. G10 country banking institutions easily account for over 80% of global transactions. The financial institutions of other countries require a presence in G10 markets in order to have access to global markets. Thus the Basel Committee effectively sets the rules for everyone. Even Cuban banks are supervised in line with Basel standards and capital adequacy levels, and Cuba is hardly renowned for its acceptance of globalisation. As ownership structures have shifted to the advantage of banks, the global securities and insurance industries have become part of the Basel process. Basel sets these rules in one of the most discreet policy processes which ever cut across borders. It does so in a policy process which involves extensive consultation with some of the most powerful private interests in the global economy. But almost never does the setting of international supervisory norms involve legislation or equivalent consultation with national parliaments. This has its benefits in terms of efficiency of the decision-making process and the ability of the Committee to reach delicate compromises. Yet it does raise questions about the accountability of the policy process.

This is an important period for global financial governance. Crises abound, markets are responding nervously (at best) to the fallout of the events of 11th September and the ongoing turmoil in the Middle East. The Japanese banking crisis and rumours of growing and similar problems in Germany threaten even developed countries with spillover and contagion. Systemic risk and its management is the order of the day for public and private sectors alike. 'Global' means risk, and risk takes many forms which can have an impact on the financial system. One way or another, we are all involved, because our pensions, our securities-backed mortgages, and our insurance policies all depend on successful risk management by financial institutions. The buck stops at Basel.

In this sense, it is high time that someone produced a book-length treatment of the Basel Committee from its origins to the present day. It is excellent timing that this study should emerge when the Basel II capital accord (so long in gestation) has recently been signed although the details of its implementation still need to be worked out. In the agreement the new 'market-based' approach to supervision and risk management are apparent. This book captures well the characteristics of this hybrid public-private policy process, making up for the inadequacies of earlier, more state-centric treatments: because Basel, as a process, is not about states. It is about bankers and their supervisors. It also goes well beyond the technically garbed accounts of law or economics, putting politics back squarely where they belong. Agreements forged by the Committee affect the transaction costs and competitiveness in global markets, with a differential impact on different types of institutions and national markets. Political conflict there is, though well disguised indeed.

Thus Basel is about more than getting the technicalities right. It is about making them acceptable to the industry, to governments, and, ultimately, to the public, all of whom rely on supervisory processes for a working financial and monetary system. And finally, successful risk management makes globalisation possible. So the Basel process cuts two ways: it helps manage risk, but also underwrites it by providing at the global level what domestic supervisory and legal systems do at the national level.

Thus Basel is where it's at, even if its work has remained largely unknown until now. Read on!

Geoffrey Underhill
Chair of International Governance
University of Amsterdam

# Acknowledgements

My thanks must go, first of all, to John Kirton for inviting me to contribute to this series of books. I also owe him a huge debt of gratitude for the patience he has shown in waiting for the manuscript to emerge.

Thanks to Kirstin Howgate at Ashgate for her good humour and willingness to listen to my excuses.

To Madeline Koch for being there all through, for prodding me when necessary and for mediating.

My thanks, of course, to Geoffrey Underhill for contributing the foreword to this book. It was Geoffrey who first inspired my interest in IPE and things financial, which eventually led to this book.

My sincere gratitude goes to all who reviewed the manuscript of this book, anonymously or otherwise, and for their comments that have made the book better than it would otherwise have been. I am particularly grateful for advice and comments received from Tony Porter, Randall Germain and Benjamin Cohen.

Rafael Fernandez de Castro has been immensely supportive of me during my professional life at ITAM and for this and his friendship I am deeply grateful.

I also owe a debt of thanks to ITAM and to the Asociación Mexicana de Cultura; in particular to Arturo Fernández and to José Ramón Benito for all their support during my time there.

Lastly, thanks to all the research assistants who have helped me over the years: Gabriela Valero, Carla Hammond, Monica Otero, Alfonsina Peñaloza, Mónica Diaz. Mónica Ibarra suffered through the editing and the creation of the index for this book; in lieu of a beatification, I can only offer her my sincere gratititude.

# List of Abbreviations

| AMA | Advanced Measurement Approaches |
|---|---|
| BCBS | Basel Committee on Banking Supervision |
| BCCI | Bank of Credit and Commerce International |
| BIS | Bank for International Settlements |
| BoE | Bank of England |
| BoJ | Bank of Japan |
| ERM | Exchange Rate Mechanism |
| FATF | Financial Action Task Force |
| FBSEA | Foreign Bank Supervision Enforcement Act |
| FDIC | Federal Deposit Insurance Corporation (US) |
| FDICIA | Federal Deposit Insurance Corporation Improvement Act |
| FFIEC | Federal Financial Institutions Examination Council (US) |
| FRB | Federal Reserve Bank (US) |
| FSA | Financial Services Authority (UK) |
| FSI | Financial Stability Institute |
| G7 | Group of Seven |
| G8 | Group of Eight |
| G10 | Group of Ten |
| GAB | General Agreement to Borrow |
| HLI | Highly Leveraged Institution |
| HST | Hegemonic Stability Theory |
| IAIS | International Association of Insurance Supervisors |
| IBRD | International Bank for Reconstruction and Development |
| IBS | International Banking Standard |
| IET | Interest Equalization Tax |
| IFA | International Financial Architecture |
| IFI | International Financial Institution |
| IIF | Institute of International Finance |
| ILSA | International Lending Supervision Act |
| IMF | International Monetary Fund |
| IOSCO | International Organisation of Securities Commissions |
| IPE | International Political Economy |
| IRB | Internal Ratings Based |
| ISDA | International Swaps and Derivative Association |
| KYC | Know Your Customer |
| LDC | Less Developed Country |
| LLR | Lender of Last Resort |
| LTCM | Long-Term Capital Management |
| M&A | Merger and Acquisition |
| MNE | Multinational enterprise |

| MOF | Ministry of Finance (Japan) |
| NAFTA | North American Free Trade Agreement |
| NGO | Non-Governmental Organisation |
| OCC | Office of the Comptroller of the Currency (US) |
| OECD | Organisation for Economic Co-operation and Development |
| OGBS | Offshore Group of Banking Supervisors |
| OPEC | Organisation of Petroleum Exporting Countries |
| OTS | Office of Thrift Supervision (US) |
| PCA | Prompt Corrective Action |
| QIS | Quantitative Impact Study |
| RCA | Regulatory Capital Arbitrage |
| SME | Small and Medium Sized Enterprise |
| SPV | Special Purpose Vehicle |
| TNC | Transnational Corporation |
| VFCR | Voluntary Foreign Credit Restraint |
| WTO | World Trade Organisation |

*To my boys, Sam and Jack,*
*without whom this book would have been much easier to write*

Chapter 1

# The Regulation and Supervision of International Banking

## Introduction

The end of the Bretton Woods system, precipitated by the unilateral decision of the United States government in August 1971 to end its commitment to exchange gold for dollars at $35 an ounce, brought about a fundamental change in the management of the international economy. Though some have referred to the post-Bretton Woods arrangements as a 'non-system', the international economy was hardly left rudderless. New institutions were created to govern the world economic system, and the Bretton Woods institutions themselves took on new functions.

Certainly the 1970s appeared to many to be a decade characterised by an ad hoc approach international economic management by the great powers, but there were initiatives that have proved more permanent than others. Two such examples can be found in the G7/8 and the Basel Committee on Banking Supervision (BCBS). In the first, the major economic powers of the western system came together in an attempt to shape the global economy and to smooth their mutual relations, while in the second, the largest states in the world financial system joined together to prevent and manage the crises that emerged in the post-Bretton Woods era.

This book examines the development of the second of these two post-Bretton Woods institutions, the Basel Committee, studying its creation, achievements and its prospective role in the 21$^{st}$ century. I argue that the Committee has become one of the central organs of global economic governance, being both a locus of financial decision-making, and a facilitator for co-ordinating the actions of other international financial institutions (IFIs). The Basel Committee has been able to expand its area of focus from merely banking supervision to playing an integral role in shaping the rules of the international financial system for the new millennium.

In doing so the Committee has been pushed forward by the appearance of new challenges in banking regulation brought about by the evolution of the international banking marketplace. But the work of the Committee has been limited and shaped by political forces operating at both domestic and international levels. The dynamic relationship between regulators and the markets they seek to oversee is therefore in large part determined by the interplay of particular and national interests.

This is not, of course, the first study of the Basel Committee. The examinations by Kapstein (1989, 1991, 1992) and Porter (1993) did much to introduce the Basel Committee to the political science and international relations communities. Porter's work in particular is of importance as it examines the interaction between the Committee and the market it is meant to regulate. More recently, work by Nabors and Oatley (1998) and by Simmons (2001) have pointed to the importance of politics at both national and international levels in explaining the development of the Committee. Recognising this, the present study seeks to evaluate the importance of political processes in explaining the evolution of the Basel Committee at the dawn of the 21$^{st}$ century as a central institution of global governance.

## Central Questions

In order to evaluate the development and significance of the Basel Committee this book is guided by six key areas of inquiry:

1.  What success has the Basel Committee attained?
2.  How does the work of the Committee interact with the international banking market?
3.  What are the driving forces behind negotiations in the Committee?
4.  How does the Committee function as an organ of global governance?
5.  How does the Committee relate to the other organs of global economic governance?
6.  What is the future and what challenges lie ahead for the Committee?

The answers to these questions are essential if we are to fully understand the nature and role of the Basel Committee, an institution that became one of the central players in the financial dramas that marked the end of the 20$^{th}$ century and the beginning of the 21$^{st}$. Rapid and far-reaching change in the international financial system since the 1970s has made financial stability an issue that sits close to the top of the international agenda at the turn of the century, and a crucial theme for global governance. As a promoter of financial stability, of safety and soundness in the international system, the Committee has established itself as a body that demands the attention, no longer only of academics and specialists, but of top economic policy makers around the world.

## Hypothesis

The argument contained in this inquiry is firstly that the evolution of the Basel Committee has been driven by the need of banking authorities in the major economies to respond to challenges that have arisen from changes in the marketplace. As private financial institutions have sought out new profit opportunities, in many cases they have adopted risky practices, practices that pose a threat to the safety and soundness of the international banking and financial systems.

In turn the banking supervisors from the world's major national financial systems have cooperated with each other through the Basel Committee to formulate mechanisms for the exchange of information, the determination of supervisory responsibility and the creation of minimum standards. These moves have had two effects. First, they have strengthened the ability of national authorities to supervise their banks in both their national and international activities. Second, banks have responded to these new supervisory developments by engaging the Committee in a dialogue that seeks to refine its agreements to minimize their effect on bank profitability, competitiveness and efficiency.

In the 1990s the Basel Committee embraced a methodology in the international harmonization of standards that involved close consultation with the private sector. This new approach was driven both by the increasing complexity of banking and finance and by the belief that clumsily formulated standards threatened the profitability of banks and the stability of national and international banking systems.

The consultation process, carried out in such a public manner, has created both efficiencies and inefficiencies. First it has allowed for the banking industry to become closely involved in the making of banking policy at the international level and has resulted in the use of bank expertise in developing policies that will be acceptable to and workable by banks themselves. On the other hand, however, over time it has greatly complicated the process of international negotiation for new rules and has greatly lengthened the bargaining period necessary to conclude agreements.

This dynamic leads to the central hypothesis that guides this study. The shape of international banking regulatory and supervisory agreements will be determined by three main factors. First, the changing landscape of the international banking market will play a defining role in national regulators' attempts to impose a harmonized international approach. The dynamic relationship between regulation and the market, and the perennial attempts by private actors to evade costly regulatory and supervisory control, will clearly be a factor of central importance. Second, outcomes of international banking supervisory negotiations will be shaped by the process of bargaining that occurs at different levels, among particular and national interests. Though the evolution of the market creates the need for international cooperation between banking authorities, the possibilities for successful cooperation are inevitably limited by the results of multi-level bargaining, at national and international levels. Third, outcomes will be determined by the distribution of power in the international economy, and by the exercise of leadership within the system. Power will therefore emerge as a key element in this study, as will the concepts of leadership and 'spoiling' behaviour. These factors do not exist in isolation, but interact to produce patterns of negotiation whose explanation requires an international political economy approach.

## The Findings

There can be little doubt that the international financial system has changed drastically since the mid-1970s when the Basel Committee was created. Fundamental changes in the structure of the international system, in the nature of its dominant actors, and in the methods used to extend credit and mobilise money make the system of the early $21^{st}$ century seem a very distant cousin to that of the immediate post-Bretton Woods years. Nonetheless, the Committee has continued to respond effectively to new problems and crises in that system by co-ordinating the actions of national supervisory authorities and by adapting policies already in place. Rather than fading into obscurity as the system has changed, the Basel Committee has grown in importance, constructing for itself a niche as the central body for the co-ordination of national banking regulation and supervision. Indeed the continued success of the Committee in a changing world has brought it an expanded role in recent years as new issues and problems have become apparent to national decision-makers.

The success of the Committee has been limited. The Basel Committee clearly has not eliminated crises from either national or international banking systems. Nor has the Committee established itself as an interventionist organisation that directly regulates and supervises banking activity across the world. However, the existence and work of the Basel Committee has contributed greatly to the stability and soundness of the international financial system, responding to new developments in that system and working towards solving existing and future problems and challenges to its stability.

How has the Committee been able to do this? The Basel Committee has been successful because it has responded effectively to new developments in the organisation and activities of the international banking market. As the market has changed, so has the work and structure of the Committee. This responsiveness has been key to the success of the Committee. As such, it represents an excellent case of the dynamics of political economy, of the interaction between public authority and the private market. This relationship and interaction is truly dynamic, for as the Committee has moved to institute new regulatory and supervisory standards in one area in order to improve safety and soundness in the system, so the international market in banking services has created new areas of activity that challenge that self-same safety and soundness.

But how can the limited success of the Committee be explained? While there are many institutions involved in the business of global economic governance, there are few that have adapted so well to the changing international structure. The IMF spent many years seeking a new role for its itself in the aftermath of the Bretton Wood's system, while its sister institution, the World Bank, has seen its importance greatly reduced by the new realities of the international economy. The success and failure of the Basel Committee to date can be explained by three factors in the nature of the Committee:

1.   the will of powerful states to create an agenda for cooperation and coordination;

2.  the influence of private actors in the policy process at the national level; and,
3.  the capacity of the Committee to avoid or overcome conflict between its members.

Each of these factors has played a significant role in ensuring the continued success of the Committee. They highlights some of the most important differences between the Basel Committee and other major international institutions.

The third factor is of vital importance. Politics is central and essential to an adequate understanding of the functioning of any international institution, regime or organisation. The BCBS is no exception. The bargaining process, mediation of interests, political manoeuvring and the use of power have all been vital in the development of the Committee. It is true that the Committee's removal from the hurly-burly of everyday politics, its image as an institution involved in dry and esoteric work, and the overall lack of public knowledge or even awareness of its existence, greatly aided the cooperative efforts it undertook in the past. But the presence of deep divisions within the Committee at various points in its history has significantly complicated the project of harmonizing approaches to banking regulation. Indeed ideological divisions have emerged in the Committee (between the Anglo-Saxon states on the one hand and the continental European states on the other) that have posed a very real challenge to the cooperative effort. Moreover, the growing visibility and increasing international profile of the Committee may pose a threat to its continued success, as more and more actors become involved in debates at the national and international levels over the Committee's work.

It is thus essential to avoid the pitfall of viewing the Committee as merely an epistemic community engaged in the academic discussion of technically elevated topics of banking supervision and regulation. One must instead address the politics within the Committee, and the clashes of interest that have periodically marked its development.

## Importance and Logic of Regulation and Supervision in National and International Systems

What are the purposes of banking regulation? Though such systems vary in the form that they take in different countries, the aims of regulation are essentially similar. The central goal of regulation and supervision is to promote the safety and soundness of the financial system in order to prevent a systemic crisis that would threaten not only the financial system, but also the economy as a whole. The primary role of financial authorities and their regulatory and supervisory activities is not to prevent the failure of individual financial institutions, although at times, if the institution is big enough, or its obligations far-reaching enough, this may be the same thing as preventing systemic failure. Ultimately financial authorities must be willing to provide emergency financing to institutions whose failure would threaten the system as a whole, either as a Lender of Last Resort (LLR – see below) or in the form of a government bank take-over or rescue. Often it is the largest financial institutions that receive such injections of public money. It is in such cases one hears talk of an institution being 'too big to fail'.

However, rather than provide such emergency financing, national authorities around the world try to prevent systemic crisis by putting in place regulations that minimise the level of systemic risk, and by supervising the activities of banks. This is a preferable alternative to the high-cost of bank bailouts, which ultimately must be funded by the public purse.

One central point is the difference between regulation and supervision. Though this book deals with both elements, it is important that a distinction is made between the two. Regulation refers to the legal framework governing both market entry and market activities, while supervision refers to the oversight of banks' activities by the banking authority. In some states financial jurisdiction is split between bodies responsible for regulation and supervision. In Japan for example, responsibility is divided between the Ministry of Finance (MOF), which applies regulations to the nation's banks, and the Bank of Japan (BoJ), which is responsible for supervision (though some is also carried out by the MOF). A similar situation exists in the United Kingdom (UK), where responsibility is divided between three bodies. While the Bank of England (BoE) is responsible for the overall stability of the financial system, monitoring the monetary system and infrastructure such as the payments system, and the Treasury covers the institutional structure and legislative framework of regulations, the Financial Services Authority (FSA) is the body mandated with regulating and supervising financial activity on a day-to-day basis.

In the US the picture is considerably more complex: leaving aside banking at the state level, national banks must deal with three main regulators, namely the Office of the Comptroller of the Currency (OCC), the Federal Reserve Board (FRB), and the Federal Deposit Insurance Corporation (FDIC), each of which puts forward regulations and engages in supervision of banking activities.[1] Regulatory overlap is considerable and there have long been calls for a rationalised regulatory and supervisory system.

A financial system rests on one major support – confidence. Indeed, the roots of the word 'credit' point to this as it derives from the Latin, *credere*, to believe. If the regulatory authority is unable to maintain confidence in that system amongst consumers, the system will be thrown into crisis; 'a financial system requires a stable and credible legal framework to retain the public confidence that is essential for its functioning' (Schuijer, 1992, p.86). Much more is at stake than merely the health of the financial system itself. For the entire economy, and hence society, relies on the ready supply of liquidity that flows through the banking industry. As Cohen has written, the industry is 'exceptionally influential – in effect providing the oil that lubricates the wheels of commerce' (Cohen, 1986, p.299). Thus the supervisor's interest in preventing systemic failure is immense.

The first, and most important, aim of banking regulation and supervision is the prevention of a crisis affecting the stability of the financial system as a whole.

---

[1] In addition to these three main bodies, there exist the Federal Financial Institutions Examination Council (FFIEC), the Office of Thrift Supervision (OTS), and a host of state-level agencies.

Sundararajan and Balino (1991, p.3) describe a financial crisis as 'a situation in which a significant group of financial institutions have liabilities exceeding the market value of their assets, leading to runs and other portfolio shifts, collapse of some firms, and government intervention.' Of course, the business of banking and finance involves the assumption and correct gauging of risk: without it, financial intermediation would achieve minimal returns and capitalism would stagnate. However, if this risk is not gauged and managed correctly, there exists a threat not just to the institution involved, but also to the entire banking system. Regulatory authorities must supervise the activities of banks and put in place mechanisms and regulations that minimise the possibility of one (or several) bank's assumption of risk threatening the stability of the system as a whole.

Linked to this first function is that of the role of lender of last resort. In the event that existing regulations and supervision are insufficient to prevent the failure of a financial institution (or several institutions), and there is the possibility of the crisis spreading from one institution to others, the regulatory authority must provide temporary liquidity assistance to the institution/s in question. By temporarily supporting the insolvent institution, the lender of last resort aims to maintain confidence in the financial system as a whole.

Of a similar nature is the function of deposit insurance, which has come to be a standard aspect in the banking systems of advanced market economies. By insuring investors' bank deposits up to a certain limit ($100,000 in the US, for example), the regulators' goal is to prevent runs on banks in times of financial instability. Of course there is always the risk that financial institutions will rely too heavily on the knowledge that the lender of last resort will bail them out in the case of insolvency (or that the deposit insurance system will protect their investors), and expose themselves to liabilities that promise a high return, but also high risk. This dilemma is known as the moral hazard problem. This is what links the lender of last resort and deposit insurance functions to the first aspect of regulation: the regulator 'cannot acknowledge its residual responsibility for the stability of the financial system unless it engages in oversight of financial institutions to ensure sound practices and prevent excessive risk taking' (Bryant, 1987, p.120).

The regulation and supervision of financial institutions does not impinge merely on the health of the financial system but on that of the economy as a whole. Moreover, a direct corollary of the control of the banking industry in advanced market economies is control of the payments system. Without an effectively functioning payments system, commerce would rapidly grind to a halt. Moreover, the operations of banks play an integral role in that system and thus, though 'there is no logically inevitable correlation between commercial banking and the provision of the payments mechanism', (Bryant, 1987, p.121) their health and stability is crucial in today's economies.

These macroeconomic goals of regulation coexist with other, microeconomic concerns. These aim at the protection of depositors,[2] the prevention

---

[2] Though it can be identified as a micro-economic concern, the protection of depositors, under such programs as the Federal Deposit Insurance Corporation in the United States, and

of monopolies or promotion of competition in the banking industry, and, in some countries, the protection of national financial institutions which are threatened by foreign competition. Though these microeconomic concerns are not as fundamental to the health of the financial system and the economy as the first three outlined above, they are nonetheless areas to which much regulatory attention has been directed.

These regulatory goals point to a crucial aspect of authority-market relations. In the area of banking, the role of authority is to ensure the maintenance of the *sine qua non* of the business of banking that is confidence. Without consumer confidence, banks would be unable to function. Thus it is in the interest of banks to comply with regulations aimed at its maintenance. However, because of the centrality of financial affairs in the health of the economy as a whole, it is also in the interest of regulatory authorities to ensure the health of banks without hindering their ability to provide liquidity to industry and commerce. This equation means that regulation is best devised and applied with the co-operation of the banking industry, which has given rise to a special relationship between banks and the authorities that regulate them. This relationship will become apparent when the work of the Basel Committee is examined in closer detail.[3]

Thus far this analysis has referred exclusively to the activities of financial authorities at the national level. But at the level of the international financial system, many of the same principles apply. One major difference is that there is no single political authority mandated with the oversight of the international system. The international financial regulatory and supervisory regime is made up of many different national and regional financial authorities. This stands in stark contrast to global financial markets. Although it is important to recognise that the global financial system operates through the activities of national financial centres (such as London, New York and Tokyo), the high level of interdependence between these centres and the ability of market operators to move capital almost instantaneously and at relatively low cost between them has created a unified global market in finance.

The contrast between national regulators and a global financial marketplace creates serious tensions and problems for practitioners of financial regulation. First, financial firms can take advantage of differences between national regulatory systems, moving money around so that they can evade regulation. Second, responsibilities for regulation and supervision of internationally operating firms are often unclear. Who, for example, should supervise the activities of a German bank operating in New York? Should the Federal Reserve assume responsibility, or should it be the task of supervisory authorities in Germany? The third problem is related to the second and concerns contagion. Because of the

---

the Deposit Protection Scheme in the UK, is similarly aimed at maintaining depositor confidence in the financial system.

[3] This does, of course, raise the issue of regulatory capture, in which financial authorities are, to some degree, controlled by the institutions they are trying to regulate. The close relationship between regulator and regulated is a problem in all industries, but in finance the relationship has traditionally been very tight.

highly interdependent nature of global finance, a financial crisis in one national system can rapidly spread to others. What can financial authorities do to reduce the risk of contagion?

The fourth and final problem concerns the competition between financial centres, the revenues that national economies receive from their activities, and the pressure applied by financial firms to national authorities to reduce regulatory and supervisory burdens. Because financial firms, unlike corporations involved in heavy industry for example, have a relatively low level of fixed costs, in theory it is possible for them to pick up and move to another financial centre if the firm is not happy with the regulatory and supervisory environment in which they have to operate. Governments and financial authorities recognise that a substantial portion of the economy (and tax revenue) depends upon the success of the national financial centre and its ability to draw firms from all over the world. In the face of widespread threats (even implicit) by financial actors to leave one centre for another offering lower regulatory and supervisory costs, national authorities standing alone are likely to reduce their level of intervention/interference. Globally this can lead to a downward spiral, or a 'race to the bottom'.

The purpose of financial regulation at both national and international levels is to prevent system-wide crisis that would threaten the broader macro-economy. At the international level, however, there is no lender of last resort that can be called upon to inject emergency financing into the financial system. The creation of an international LLR was an option that was contemplated, and roundly rejected, both in the 1970s after the fall of the Bretton Woods system, and again in the late 1990s in the aftermath of the Asian financial crises. Nor does there exist an international authority capable of implementing global financial regulations and standards. The creation of such an authority has proven unpalatable to national governments, rising as it does the spectre of direct external interference in domestic economic affairs.

Instead of either an international LLR or a global authority, there is a need for national authorities to join together in a regime and co-ordinate their actions. By doing so it is hoped that significant gaps in the regulation of the international financial activity will be filled, and that the scope for regulatory arbitrage will be reduced. Such collective action presents its own challenges and problems. But the story of the Basel Committee shows that, under certain circumstances and given the right motivation, national authorities are able and willing to put in place internationally recognised standards that make a significant contribution to the safety and soundness of national and global financial systems.

## The Contribution of This Book

This book provides a political economy-based study of the work and achievements of the Basel Committee on Banking Supervision by addressing issues of power, leadership, the influence of private actors and the dynamic relationship between regulators and the markets they seek to control. This study contains a number of assumptions about the relationship between public authorities and private markets, and about the nature of the international system.

The development of political economy and of international political economy as areas of study have shown that the interaction between authority and the market brings an ever-changing balance of authority and power between states and markets (and also among states). These same states and markets, as well as international economic and financial organizations, should be viewed as genuinely social structures - that is they display the attributes of hierarchy, social interaction, cooperation, the advocacy of certain beliefs and ideas, self-perpetuation, and competition. This competition between states, to further both the national and particular interests, continues to be a driving force in the relations between states.

Since the end of the Second World War, states have made a series of decisions that have resulted in the liberalisation of financial markets. This increased market freedom has brought results that threaten not only state sovereignty, but also the economic security and the stability of the international financial system. In response to this tendency, states, although they remain the dominant form of social structure in the international political economy, are finding that the control of financial markets carries too great a cost if it is attempted unilaterally. International cooperation, therefore, has become a necessary policy tool to bring about effective and meaningful control of international finance, without sacrificing national competitiveness.

Effective cooperation and coordination requires international leadership if it is to be successful. This leadership, if it comes, will be given by the dominant authority in the international political economy, namely the government of the United States. However, in the negotiations that lead to cooperative agreements, the US has consistently sought to defend its national interests, and the interests of key domestic actors, often at expense of private actors in other states. This means though leadership may emerge at crucial moments from the dominant power to secure international agreement, it is also likely that this country will act as a 'spoiler' to alter the outcome of negotiations in its favour, and in the favour of its domestic actors.

This reality raises questions about the viability of such international cooperation, reflecting some of the issues seen in regulation at the national level. The direct involvement of domestic actors in the process of supervisory policy-making at the international level greatly complicates the conclusion of mutually acceptable agreements and, over time, and tends to aggravate the problem of regulatory capture.

This work then situates itself firmly within the disciplines of political science, international relations and international political economy. It attempts to understand the Basel Committee, not as an autonomous international regime, but as the nexus of powerful interests that compete for influence over the process of international banking regulation. The power of certain states means that their national constituencies will see their interests more than adequately represented in the Committee, while smaller, weaker members will be forced to adapt to the preferences of the dominant states.

## The Political Economy of International Banking

The political economy of banking has been an important area of study since Bagehot. Throughout the 20th century banking was recognised by analysts of politics, political economy and international relations as key to understanding questions of power, prosperity and stability. Naturally enough, differing perspectives on the political economy of banking have emerged, ranging from those highly critical of the privileged position held by banks and bankers in domestic and international systems, to those, such as the Cato Institute, who have persistently argued for a freer hand for the banking community. Within the discipline of international political economy (IPE), the judgement on international banking has been overwhelmingly critical, although its scholars have never failed to recognise the central place of banking in the stability of the international system.

Because of this, since the 1930s the management of international banking has been a focus for students of IPE, and the factors that limit or promote effective governance have consistently been central concerns. Power has been identified as a principal factor, while leadership and collective action have also been recurring themes. The influence of the banks themselves, as well as other important private financial actors, over the policy process, has been an issue of vital import.

The following sections, therefore, examine two principal questions from a theoretical perspective. First it looks at the international banking systems in terms of stability and its proclivity to crisis. In general the international political economy literature suggests that the market in international financial services tends towards instability and crisis. This impacts directly on the second issue, that of management of the system to minimize both the frequency and the harmful effects of turbulence. The potential for effective management of the system is, of course directly affected by the factor of power and by the dynamic between authorities and the actors they seek to regulate.

## The Debate Over International Banking

The rapid expansion of finance from the national to the international and then global levels was a common area of interest for scholars of IPE in the 1980s and 1990s. Different perspectives emerged, from those who claimed that states and public authorities still exert considerable control over the system (Pauly, 1988) to those who have seen an integrated global financial system dominated by private actors (O'Brien, 1992).

Perhaps the pivotal issue in the political economy of international banking has been the tendency of the system towards instability, turbulence and crisis, and the explanations that have been put forward for that tendency. Economists such as Kindleberger (1978) and Galbraith (1993) have recognised the inherent tendency of international finance towards instability, examining the system in historical perspective and pointing out the proclivity of markets to tend towards 'manias, panics and crashes'. According to these authors, the elements of herding, euphoria and human nature all play a role in pushing financial markets towards crisis and instability. Their work suggests that crisis is not only unavoidable in free financial markets, but also that irrational expectations made each crisis a traumatic and unexpected event. Of particular importance is the idea that each occurrence of euphoria is seen as a novelty, with financial markets re-inventing themselves in such a way as to make each crisis entirely unpredicted by market participants (though not by seasoned observers).

This perspective has come to dominate discussions of international financial markets in international political economy circles, creating an overwhelming atmosphere of dread and scepticism over the future of international banking. Repeated, and increasingly frequent, financial crises since the early 1970s have produced a series of works in IPE that view the market as dangerously turbulent and threatening to the stability of the economy and society at both national and international levels. The nature of the market has come to be seen in terms of irrational behaviour and even more irrational outcomes from the market. Strange's description of the international financial system first as a casino (1986), and then as a system of 'mad money' (1998), encapsulated many of the concerns of the 1980s and 1990s, that public authorities had lost control of the market and that a small group of comparatively young men were gambling with the economic future of entire nations, and indeed of the international system. The concept of 'casino capitalism' would become a catchphrase for students of the political economy of international finance for the next decade. Key to this understanding of the contemporary international financial system was the idea that governments had allowed the progressive, and at times rapid, liberalisation of financial markets through decisions and 'non-decisions'. Explicit in Strange's analysis of the liberalisation process is the idea that states pursued financial market liberalisation for reasons of economic competitiveness and power. Implicit is a suggestion that powerful financial actors helped to propel the process through domestic political pressure, and that financial liberalisation has in turn increased their political influence.

In a 1993 book concerning the relationship between politics and finance at the global level, Cerny poses a question fundamental to understanding the importance of the international financial system. Put simply, he asks:

> to what extent do the actors operating within the transnational financial structure have the capacity to act independently of constraints from other structures – especially states – and to use the resources available to them to pursue autonomous organizational goals bypassing the constraints embedded in the state and/or the states system? (Cerny, 1993, p.156)

Cerny's answer leaves little doubt that states, in particular the US, are steadily losing their capacity to control the actions, and consequences thereof, of actors and organizations in the international financial system. In other words, the trans-national financial structure has attained a high, and still growing, level of structural autonomy. Cerny (p.157) goes so far as to decry the neo-realists for clinging to 'the catch-all concept of regimes to keep the state in the driver's seat at the transnational level'. The rising power of private actors within the international financial system poses a threat to the stability of that system.

The recurring theme, then, in studies of international finance, that the market and private actors, left to their own devices, will ultimately produce turbulence and crisis in the international economy, is central to understanding the tone and direction of these studies. The inability of financial actors to control themselves, a fact established over a period spanning hundreds of years, it is consistently argued, thus necessitates firm management achieved through interstate cooperation. Understanding the nature of such cooperation, whether it is voluntary, coerced or through convergence of interests and perspectives, forces one to study issues and themes that are clearly located within the realms of political science and political economy.

## Power and International Banking

Kapstein's various publications on the Basel Committee (1989, 1991, 1992, 1994) have focused on different aspects of international financial cooperation. One theme, however, that has appeared in his work is that of the exercise of power, both positive and negative, in the Committee. His story of the Basel Accord of 1988, elaborated upon later in this book, highlights the importance of elements of power and coercion in the area of international banking cooperation. What is missing from his work, however, is a theoretical appreciation of the different ways in which power can be exercised in the international banking system. This section aims to explore the different manifestations of power in international banking, and its connection first to leadership and then to political will.

More recently, Simmons's study of attempts to harmonize international capital market regulation (2001) has stressed the hegemonic position of the United States and the powerful position held by the United Kingdom as central factors in their ability to achieve international agreements. The present book develops Simmons's concern for relative and structural power, and for the element of leadership, hegemonic or otherwise.

The study of the exercise of power has always been central to International Relations (IR) theory, from Thucydides to Morgenthau to Gilpin. Indeed, some still see the study of international affairs as Morgenthau described, namely the struggle for power and peace. However, many of the early examinations of power centred on military capabilities and the use of force, which produced a rather unidimensional understanding of the concept. The debate began to get far more interesting with the growth in the sub-discipline of IPE in the 1970s. Here various dimensions of the concept received attention, as writers examined the many different aspects of power, be they military, economic, ideological or financial. What, then, is power? Realist theorists traditionally defined power as agent X's ability to get agent Y to do something agent Y would not otherwise do. Morgenthau (1967, p.24), though recognising that the meaning of power is not fixed, gave its definition as 'anything that establishes and maintains control of man over man'. The rise of strategic studies in the 1950s and 1960s narrowed the common usage of the term power to mean force, with writers such as Schelling and Kahn focusing on the power of nuclear weapons. Hedley Bull's (and others') investigations into the balance of power served to confirm this tendency. It is clear that such understandings derived directly from the experiences of the Cold War and the preoccupation of society and academia with military prowess. Yet these definitions missed out on much of the subtlety that can be applied to theoretical examinations of power.

Waltz's version of neo-realism that emerged in the late 1970s seemed to provide a new departure for realist thought, and consequently for the concept of power. Unfortunately, though it seems at first glance a far more sophisticated theory, and includes other elements (such as economics) in its calculations, structural realism fails to escape the narrow confines of its realist precursor in its treatment of power.

Nye's (1991) study of power, however, is much more enlightening and provided discipline of IR with a definite step forward in this regard. In pondering the future of American leadership of the international system, Nye examines the various faces of power and finds two main distinct forms. The first he calls 'command power', which closely resembles the established, realist definition of power outlined above. This, Nye recognises, can rest on either threats or inducements. The second face of power, though, is far more interesting. 'Co-optive power' he defines as (1991, p.31):

> an indirect way to exercise power. A country may achieve the outcomes it prefers in world politics because other countries want to follow it or have agreed to a system that produces such effects. In this sense, it is just as important to set the agenda and structure the situations in world politics as it is to get others to change in particular situations....Co-optive power can rest on the attraction of one's ideas or on the ability to set the political agenda in a way that shapes the preferences that others express.

This understanding shows the unavoidable link between the issues of power and leadership.

A similar distinction between two different types of power has been made by Strange. Alongside the traditional, realist definition of power (i.e. as the ability of agent X to get agent Y to do something agent Y would not other wise do) which she refers to as 'relational power', Strange (1988, p.25) posits the existence of what she calls 'structural power'. This is 'the power to shape and determine the structures of the global political economy within which other states, their political institutions, their economic enterprises, and (not least) their scientists and other professional people have to operate'. This means more than merely setting agendas or deciding the rules of the economic game; Strange holds that structural power refers to the ability to mould the international economic and political environment and thus control the manner in which agents (be they states, international organizations, businesses, or individuals) interact.

This definition of power is clearly of great utility when both international banking and the balance between authority and markets are addressed. Strange recognises the international financial system as one of the four pre-eminent structures in the international political economy. Furthermore, if structural power concerns the ability to shape and mould the environment in which interstate activity occurs, the issue of how such power affects the relationship between authority and the market must be examined, the market being a significant part of that environment.

Having questioned how control over structure might translate into political and economic power, the ability of states to convert potential power into realized power should also be addressed. Nye's examination of power devotes some attention to this issue, though he is dealing primarily with relational power and with the conversion of power resources such as military or economic strength. (Nye, 1991, p.27) Nonetheless, his attention to the concept of power conversion may be equally useful in an examination of structural power. For, unless a nation state is able to mobilise domestic support and the political will necessary to act on its structural power, that power is of little use.


## Leadership in International Finance

Many of the same issues that arose in the previous examination of the concept of power also arise in discussions of leadership. The focus, over the past thirty years, in studies of this concept, has fallen on the theory of hegemonic stability. Hegemonic stability theory (HST), though, is of little use to contemporary studies of the international political economy in its commonly held formulation. This does not mean, however, that there is nothing to be salvaged from the debates surrounding this theory, and thus it merits attention.

Kindleberger's original formulation of HST (1973) dictated that a stable, liberal international economic system required the leadership or hegemony of one power. Taking his lead from the Gold Standard and Bretton Woods systems originating in British and American leadership of the international system respectively, Kindleberger (1973, p.37) posited that 'for the world economy to be stabilized, there has to be a stabilizer, one stabilizer'. The theory gained currency throughout the 1970s and 1980s as it was applied to what was seen as declining US hegemony. In the process, much attention was given to the concept of hegemony.

Block's (1977) examination of the exercise of US hegemony in the sphere of international monetary and financial affairs lends another new dimension to existing formulations. He emphasises an interpretation of international monetary arrangements 'as social creations that tend to reflect and maintain the distribution of power among nations and classes' (p.ix). Block, while reinforcing the belief in the importance of leadership for the stability of the international system, also puts forward an interpretation of US actions between 1961 and 1971 that portrays the US as a negligent, sometimes predatory lead nation. Rather than enforcing the principles of the Bretton Woods system, Block's account (1977, p.203) shows that 'step by step the US either broke the rules of the old order or forced other countries to break them'.

Again questioning the traditional understanding of power as relational, Strange (1987) examines US power over the four primary structures of the international political economy. Strange's conclusion is that declining US hegemony is a myth, but most importantly, by studying US power in each of these four structures, her analysis opens the way for examination of leadership in different sectors of the international system. Structural power emerges as a fundamental element in the present study, not only on the part of the US but also its primary supporter in this area, the UK.

After twenty-odd years of debate and research on HST, the paradigm had, by the 1990s, come to be seen in some quarters as a tired topic offering little in the way of new research opportunities. However, the end of the Cold War and renewed US predominance in economic and military spheres served to revitalise the debate. Lake (1993) breathed new life into this area of study by adopting a novel approach that breaks HST down into its constituent parts. Though his attempts to measure and quantify are a little over-zealous and threaten to lead to the neglect of other unquantifiable factors in authority-market dynamics, his recognition of two sub-theories within HST provide an interesting way forward. Lake identifies both leadership and hegemony theories within the parameters of HST, and demands renewed investigation into the importance of leadership in the functioning of the international economy.

Although Lake's study focuses on trade policy preferences, the distinction he proposes between hegemony and leadership is one that can be usefully employed in the following examination of post-Bretton Woods financial politics. Lake (1993, p.469) suggest that while '*leaders* may use coercion...', *hegemons* must use it', and stresses the role of power 'in creating and maintaining international economic openness'. The point here is clearly that although a hegemonic state has little choice about enforcing openness and stability in the international system, to remain a leader, a state does not necessarily have to act similarly in all situations. Even the briefest of examinations of US economic policy since 1970 will show that leadership is a far more appropriate term than hegemony.

Leadership studies broaden the parameters of the enquiry and should rule out endless debates over the presence or not of 'true' hegemony. A focus on leadership can be issue specific, may include nations not usually recognised as leading powers, and need not neglect ideological or consensual dimensions. Such a perspective should broaden comprehension of the workings of international organizations and structures alike. The lead nation seeks to create cooperative institutions designed to facilitate the effective functioning of the international economy. A usable definition of leadership, then must include a recognition of this factor. As Lake (1993, p.466) points out:

> It is always possible to define any state that effectively produces stability as a 'leader' and any state that does not as a 'non-leader'. Indeed, it is a fairly common tendency in the literature. But in the end, of course, this sleight-of-hand produces not an explanation but a tautology. The task before us is to move beyond behavioral definitions of leadership and to define the necessary and sufficient conditions for the production of the international economic infrastructure.

A more specific definition of leadership comes from Ikenberry in a 1996 article on the future of American dominance of the international system. Defining leadership as 'the ability to foster cooperation and commonalty of social purpose among states' (1996, p.386), he outlines three manifestations thereof: structural, institutional and situational leadership. Structural leadership 'refers to the underlying distribution of material capabilities that gives some states the ability to direct the overall shape of world political order' (1996, p.389). Institutional leadership, on the other hand, 'refers to the rules and practices that states agree to, that set in place principles and procedures that guide their relations' (1996, p.391). Lastly, Ikenberry defines situational leadership as 'the actions and initiatives of states that induce cooperation quite apart from the distribution of power or the array of institutions. It is more cleverness or the ability to see specific opportunities to build or reorient international political order...that makes a difference' (1996, p.395).

Although the first dimension of leadership is most commonly associated with the United States, the second understanding is that which most closely fits the experience of the US within the Basel Committee. Of course the three manifestations of leadership should not be viewed in isolation; for example, it should be obvious that structural leadership enhances the ability of the state to provide institutional leadership.

All of this raises, however, another, more intriguing question, one that is most appropriate for the exercise of US power and leadership. What happens when the leading country acts, not as a leader by promoting cooperation and the provision of public goods, but rather in ways that smack more of coercion and unilateralism?

## Leading Country Spoilership

Lake's discussion of international leadership in the 1990s was preceded a decade earlier by his examination of US foreign economic policy in the late 19th and early 20th centuries. In that piece (1983) he analysed the international sources of American foreign economic policy and concluded that the major causal factor in shifting the US from a protectionist to a liberal foreign trade posture was the distribution of power and its position in the structure of the international system. But within that discussion Lake identified four categories of states: hegemons, supporters, free riders and spoilers. What Lake means by hegemons is clear. Free riders are the smaller states in the system who benefit from international cooperation without having to contribute to its maintenance. Supporters are middle-sized states that, while not possessing sufficient power to lead, can contribute to the long-term management of the system. Spoilers, however, are middle-sized powers that free ride and thus are highly disruptive to the process of cooperation.

It is worth asking however, whether hegemonic states can also behave as spoilers during certain periods. This would involve the hegemonic state shifting costs to other, middle-sized states, and protecting domestic economic interests at the expense of its international obligations. There are a number of ways in which a hegemonic or leading country could do this. It could negotiate cost-sharing with its allies. As will become increasingly likely, however, the hegemon will force other states to bear the costs of international cooperation. A third alternative is to skew international cooperation so that it benefits the hegemon's interests at the expense of the interests of other states.

At times the hegemonic power *must* use coercion in order to guarantee stability in the international system. However, it is also possible for a hegemonic or leading country to use its power, be it structural or institutional, to act not as a leader but in a more negative fashion. The dominant power can use its capabilities to derail cooperation and policy coordination, or to shift the costs of leadership onto middle-powers.

In the 1980s this idea was propagated by Conybeare (1987) when he wrote of the hegemon ceasing its benign behaviour and becoming more 'predatory'. A predatory hegemon is one that shifts the costs of macroeconomic adjustment to its less-powerful allies. This implies that the hegemon is attempting to free-ride on the other members of the system. Predatory hegemons, Conybeare argues, are likely to occur during periods of hegemonic decline, when the costs of providing public goods are increasing relative to the benefits received by the hegemonic power. Conybeare makes specific reference to US foreign trade policy in the 1980s. But the same patterns of behaviour can be seen in American international monetary policy in the 1960s when the US demanded greater contributions from the Europeans and Japanese in maintaining the Bretton Woods exchange rate system.

By the early years of the twenty-first century, it is difficult to argue that the US is in a period of hegemonic decline. However the US has now begun to turn to tactics of 'hegemonic spoilership' in international banking negotiations in order to benefit its domestic economic interests ahead of its commitments to international stability. Possessing both structural and institutional power resources, the United States is able to both coerce other states into accepting its preferred rules and norms, and to limit the options available to them.

## Domestic Sources of Leadership and Spoilership Behaviour

Throughout studies of the political economy of international finance, scholars have noted the dynamic relationship that exists between public and private spheres, and between authorities and the actors they seek to regulate. The preferences and interests of private actors have consistently been a limiting factor in international negotiations in the international economy in general, and specifically in international finance and banking. At the domestic level, the close relationship between regulatory authorities and the markets they seek to control exacerbates this tendency in banking, and has led to questions about regulatory capture. The trade-off between creating efficient regulation that takes private actor interests into account and reducing the probability of market failure and financial crisis is a delicate balance to achieve. As Goodhart et al. (1998, p.7) have noted, 'the boundary between appropriate accommodation of practitioner objectives on one side, and regulatory capture on the other, inevitably becomes blurred'. Kane (1977) has specifically referred to the attempts by certain financial actors to pressure regulators to impose new restrictions on other actors enjoying a competitive advantage. This same dilemma marks the relationship between private actors and national negotiators in international banking regulation regimes.

The rising power of private finance and its growing influence over the world's economic destiny has been addressed by a number of scholars and writers who see the system increasingly shaped by the preferences of private actors. While earlier writers looked at the question of public control of monetary and financial affairs in the international system, examining the 'money mandarins' (Wachtel, 1986), the more recent focus on private actors raises questions of legitimacy and democratic control of the future of finance. Pauly (1997), for example, asks 'who elected the bankers?', focusing on the delegation of 'authority to actors in private markets' (p.18), as well as the development of international organisations such as the IMF. Helleiner's historical examination of the development of post-war international financial and monetary affairs traces the resurgence of private financial actors and the inability or reluctance of states to restrain them through coordinated attempts to re-regulate the system. Germain (1997), on the other hand, looks at the importance of major international financial centres in the global organisation of credit and the consequent fragility of the system. This emphasis on financial centres, combining the public and private organisation of credit, is important in that, like Pauly's work, it shows how governments and private actors cooperate in the governance of global finance. Porter's 1993 study of the private organisation of international banking and security markets (looking at the Basel Committee and the International Organization of Securities Commissions) and the link to public mechanisms of policy coordination was enormously important in establishing a connection between the capacity of the market to organise itself and the willingness of governments to provide inter-state alternatives. Similarly, Underhill's work on international finance (1997) has stressed the importance of examining questions of state-market relations and public-private cooperation and conflict. Examining the emergence of order (and disorder) in financial markets, Underhill's work is significant in pulling together official and market-based forms of organisation in international finance. Underhill's work is also important for the way it places special emphasis on the ability of powerful private actors to set the agenda for negotiations in international finance.

The relationship between domestic constituencies, lobby groups and elites on the one hand, and governments and foreign economic policy on the other is a well-established area of inquiry in international relations. Most famously Robert Putnam has talked of 'two-level games' in which states conduct negotiations at both the international and domestic levels. These twin sets of bargains, which may be simultaneous, impact upon each other in a dynamic fashion, and create the potential for transnational as well as international bargaining patterns. They complicate international negotiations. They also make possible new bargaining strategies and approaches for states.

Kahler (1993) applied the logic of Putnam's model to negotiations between two developing countries, Somalia and Jamaica, and the IMF. In his study Kahler emphasises internal struggles, both within the IMF and the states concerned, as a determining factor in the negotiations. The utility of this approach, however, has yet to be applied to the area of the harmonization of international banking regulations and supervision. Although the present work does not conduct a methodical investigation into the patterns of two-level bargaining in the Basel Committee, it does stress the importance of domestic politics, in particular those of the dominant state in the Committee, the United States, and its attempts to skew international cooperative agreements in favour of domestic constituencies.

This element brings into question the legitimacy of banking regulatory processes in general, and of the Committee in particular. Porter's work (2000) on the issue of legitimacy in international finance is informative here as it links it to considerations of power, to effective rule-making and to representation. In the present work the legitimacy of the regulatory process, and of the Basel Committee as international representative of that process, must be challenged due to the strong influence of private market actors in determining policy outcomes. This is not to say that all private actor involvement in regulation is unwarranted or worrying. Clearly consultation is a vitally important element in crafting effective and efficient regulatory frameworks that do not result in excessive regulatory burden. However, regulatory capture that compromises the objective of regulation, by necessity, calls into doubt the legitimacy of the process and indeed, of the institution itself.

## The Structure of This Study

Adopting a largely historical approach, this book traces the evolution of the Basel Committee from its origins in the 1970s into the early years of the $21^{st}$ century. This examination supports the argument that the BCBS has moved to close holes in the international supervisory net in response to new banking practices and structures, but also that the interplay of conflicting interests, and at times ideologies, has limited and shaped outcomes within the Committee.

Chapter two explores the origins of the Committee in the dramatic changes that took place in the system of international banking in the 1960s and 1970s. It describes the make-up and goals of the Committee and its status as an international organisation. This chapter establishes the BCBS as an institutional response to market developments, in this case the dramatic internationalisation of private banking.

Chapter three addresses the theme of policy coordination through the Basel Concordat, looking at the problems of regulatory and supervisory control in a world of internationalised finance. It looks at the debates over the agreement and the various revisions through which it has passed since the mid-70s. The Concordat went a long way towards establishing supervisory responsibility among national authorities overseeing banks operating in many different jurisdictions, thus countering one of the most important challenges posed by international banking. But it did not prevent Basel members from knowingly abrogating the spirit and letter of the Concordat. Such actions have led to further revisions of the agreement.

In the fourth chapter the first Basel Accord on capital adequacy is examined from its origins in the Latin American debt crisis, through interstate negotiations to the final signing of the accord in 1988. This Accord is the most important contribution and achievement of the BCBS thus far. The story of the capital adequacy agreement demonstrates so many of the elements of international relations that have affected the international harmonization of banking supervision. In this story power, leadership and national interest all play key roles in determining the final outcome.

Chapter five addresses and evaluates the impact of the Capital Accord on the market in international banking services, on national banking authorities in key countries, and on the Committee itself. It shows how the Accord, both positively and negatively, helped to reshape the business of international banking and the supervisory process in the 1990s.

In the sixth chapter the activities of the Basel Committee in the 1990s and early years of the $21^{st}$ century are examined. This is a period during which the Committee established itself as one of the central organs of global economic governance. The Committee played a key role in the reshaping of the international financial architecture in the second half of the 1990s and worked closely alongside international organisations such as the IMF and the G7/8.

Chapter seven returns to the issue of bank capital. It examines the various revisions that were made to the original Capital Accord and the negotiations for a second Basel accord, or Basel II. Although the Committee has always closely consulted with the private sector before implementing its agreements, it is here that the beginnings of a truly dynamic and interactive relationship between the BCBS and banks is seen. For in the various revisions of the 1988 capital accord the private sector has played a pivotal role in shaping the guiding concepts behind the renegotiation of the agreement. More importantly, the process of revising the accord has brought to the fore many of the tensions underlying the new air of cooperation between banking authorities and the institutions they oversee. The Committee has come to see its mandate as one that incorporates much more than piecemeal efforts to stabilise the system. Instead Basel II is an attempt to lay out the framework for a far more comprehensive approach to banking supervision and quest for international banking stability and soundness. The attempt shows the interplay between politics and international cooperation in banking supervision.

Chapter eight confirms, in conclusion, that the Basel Committee on Banking Supervision is a highly political body. Though the Committee has frequently been idealized as purely technical, as an esoteric body of specialists engaging in technocratic deliberations over the future of the international banking system in a political vacuum, the reality is that politics has marked almost every step of its evolution and work.

# Chapter 2.

# The Origins of the Basel Committee

## Introduction

Although the immediate origins of the Basel Committee are to be found in the systemic changes taking place in international finance in the 1970s, the organisational roots of the committee were created more than 40 years earlier. In the chaos following the US stock market crash of 1929, the world's oldest surviving international financial organisation was created to handle a very specific problem. The Bank for International Settlements, however, evolved into much more than originally projected. A process of central bank co-operation began that was to lead eventually to the creation of the Basel Committee.

This chapter describes the origins of the BCBS and, more importantly, stresses that the Committee emerged during a period in which the internationalisation of private banking and finance posed a profound challenge to the capacity of national regulatory and supervisory authorities to maintain control and oversight of financial institutions and systems. In this way the creation of the Committee must be seen as a response to a change within the market, a market which had been strictly controlled in most nations following the Second World War.

That theme is central to the argument of this book and it suggests two things. The first is that, following the breakdown of Bretton Woods, national financial authorities would be caught in a perpetual game of 'catch up', doomed to respond to developments in financial markets rather than pre-empting them. Although some might argue that this is a positive thing for market freedom and economic liberties, it does severely limit the scope for authorities to prevent crises and minimize systemic instability. Whether or not such prevention is possible or even desirable is a debate best left to others, but it is clear that the balance between authority and the market has been fundamentally altered by the ability of private finance to operate simultaneously from multiple nations and even to escape the attention of national regulators and supervisors completely through the Euromarkets.

Second, the chapter suggests that cooperation is fundamental in meeting the challenges of internationalised private finance. Both ad hoc and institutionalised forms of cooperation are seen in this chapter, both being necessary to first manage, then seek to prevent, the outbreak of financial crises at the international level.

The chapter begins by looking at the creation of the parent institution of the BCBS, the Bank for International Settlements and the need for institutionalised cooperation between central banks in the 1930s in response to the financial crisis of that time. Next it examines the nature of financial regulation in the period following the end of the Second World War under the Bretton Woods system, when a majority of governments decided that private finance should be restricted to the national level and public authorities should control the international. There follows a description of the internationalisation of finance in the post-war period and the emerging challenge of the Euromarkets, which set the basis for the banking crises that arose in the mid-1970s, the subject of the next section. This section is key in explaining the need for the consequent internationalisation of banking authorities seen in the creation of the Basel Committee that is the focus of the remainder of this chapter.

Though most of this chapter has a historical focus, and the history concerned extends back as far as the end of the Second World War, it is necessary to show that the Committee arose as an international response to a long-term process of structural change in the international political economy. That change has fundamentally altered the balance between states and markets, and has heightened the need for international cooperation to match an international banking market that is in constant flux.

**The Bank for International Settlements**

The inter-war years have traditionally been described as a period of deep international instability, of systemic weakness and most famously, as 'the Twenty Years Crisis' (Carr, 1946). It marked the true end of the 19<sup>th</sup> century and the emergence of the troubled reality of the mid-twentieth century. The profoundly weak international financial system was continually threatened by the cycle of war debts and reparations. The problem of German war reparations (of around 20 billion marks) created by the Versailles treaty and the Dawes Plan remained unsolved throughout the 1920s, with the German government continuously protesting that it was unable to maintain its payments to Paris and London. Paris and London in turn depended on this capital to repay the billions of dollars borrowed from the United States during World War One. With the German economy in the depths of recession and experiencing the trauma of hyper-inflation, the only thing that allowed the flow to continue was the supply of capital stemming from the world's foremost financial centre of the time, New York. As long as New York bankers were willing to channel funds into German government bonds, the cycle of payments could continue. Capital from the US flowed to Berlin, Berlin in turn made its war reparations to Paris and London, and these two capitals repaid their war debts to the US. As a cycle, it seemed virtuous to many of the day; in fact it was to change rapidly into a vicious cycle in which capital stalled and the world economy plunged into crisis.

It was the trauma of the stock market crash of 1929 that effected this change. As the speculative bubble of the 1920s burst, individuals, corporations, and most importantly banks panicked and rushed to sell their rapidly-dwindling assets. Banks had been key players in the stock market bubble because they had not only lent money to speculators (both individual and corporate) but had also engaged in speculative activities themselves. Several histories of the great crash, written by political scientists and political economists, relate the feeling of chaos and despair that marked the period (Levien, 1997; Sobel, 1968; Brennan, 2000). The short- and medium-term international effects of the crash are also well-known, thanks to the work of Kindleberger (1986) and others. There can be little doubt that the events of 1929 created the perfect conditions for the rapid descent in economic autarky and tension, and the eventual worldwide conflagration that would begin in 1939.

Shortly after the crash, it became apparent that the cycle of war loans and reparations was unsustainable. As capital flows from New York slowed down, the governments of Germany and Austria found themselves unable to continue making their payments to Britain and France. Germany sought a renegotiation of the debt and between 1929 and 1930 the Young Committee, headed by Owen D. Young of the United States, drew up a new schedule for reparations payments that gave Germany 58 and a half years to spread out the debt. The plan greatly reduced Germany's annual payments, and this reworking of the problem of reparations seemed to offer hope that the international financial system could regain stability.

In order to administer the plan, a new international financial institution was required, and in 1930 the central banks of the Young Plan countries came together to form the Bank for International Settlements (BIS). Acting as trustee for the Young Plan, the BIS was also intended as a mechanism to facilitate central bank cooperation on other matters of international importance, and indeed it was this side of the institution's work which quickly became central, after the Hitler government in Germany defaulted on the unpaid debt.

The BIS was created with a dual nature. First it must be noted that it is funded through issued share capital in the same way as a limited company. However, under the Hague Agreements, the BIS acquired the legal status of an international organization governed by international law, giving it all the necessary faculties to carry out its functions. In the post-World War II period the BIS became a key actor in the international economy as the US sought cooperation in the management of the Bretton Woods system from its European and Japanese allies.

## The Post-1945 Internationalisation of Finance

Following World War I, almost all flows of international finance had been come from private sources. The representatives of the allied powers present at the Bretton Woods conference in 1944 blamed these private flows of capital for the economic instability that had propelled the world economy into chaos and autarky in the 1930s and sought, through the new agreement, to institute a system by which capital flows would be strictly controlled (Gardner, 1980).

The details of the Bretton Woods agreement have been given greater attention by many authors but it will suffice for now to say that the framers of the accord created a system in which international financial flows were 'the servant, not the master, of human desires' (Gardner, 1980, p.76). Believing that a stable system of exchange rates was the key to an effectively functioning economy, the planners designed restrictions that allowed flows of capital only through official channels. Indeed, the IMF and World Bank were created to be *public* international financial organizations, intended to monitor and maintain a stable financial and exchange rate system.

In this way freedom in capital movements was to be sacrificed to provide the conditions under which national economies and world trade could flourish. It is vital to take note that this was seen as being a real trade-off: the post-war planners did not believe international economic growth and stability to be possible without severe constraints on the free movement of capital between nations. Pauly makes the rationale clear:

> The reluctance of governments to match trade liberalization with financial liberalization is understandable. Capital is inherently mobile, but labor is not. If a national population is subjected to bracing international competition through trade flows, countervailing financial flows might be necessary to cushion the effects, both economic and political. Especially under a system designed to minimize movements in exchange rates, governments needed tools to facilitate necessary adjustments to international payments imbalances. The ability to direct national savings toward national investments appeared to be the necessary concomitant to a liberal trading system with fixed exchange rates. (Pauly, 1993)

Thus for the good of human society and national policy autonomy, governments asserted their dominance over the market.

The Bretton Woods agreement has traditionally been viewed as an international economic accord negotiated by national governments. Indeed the Bretton Woods accord is generally accepted in the IPE literature as having been the result of a bargain struck between the new world leader, the US, and that which preceded it, namely the UK. Yet non-state actors also played a significant role in the development of the accord and strongly disputed the eventual outcome. Eric Helleiner's examination (1994) of bank-government negotiations on the Bretton Woods treaty shows that private actors representing the market, in constituency and idea, exerted significant pressure on the US government during the negotiations. Indeed, Helleiner's observations help us to conceptualise this period in the fashion that Polanyi had put forward, as a sea-change in the balance between political authority and the market in international finance.

Private financial actors, in particular the New York banking community had few problems with the proposals for a World Bank. To most it seemed a logical solution to reconstruction and development projects, such as canals, dams, etc., from which the private sector would shy away. The objections on the part of US bankers lay more with the IBRD's sister institution, the IMF. This opposition, on the part of private financial actors in the US, to the IMF stemmed from three major differences of opinion between themselves and the Bretton Woods planners over capital controls. According to Helleiner, the bankers did not object to the proposals only based on a cold calculation of self-interest. They appear to have been driven equally by differences of opinion over the principles the bankers saw underlying the Bretton Woods proposals.

The first difference focused on the role of disruptive and unproductive financial flows. While anathema to Keynes and White, by the New York banking community they were seen as a reflection of inappropriate interest rate management. Secondly, speculative flows of capital, perceived as damaging and a constraint on national policy autonomy by Keynes and White, were seen as the agents of market discipline by some bankers. What's more, to many in the US banking community, it seemed that 'the IMF would relax or even replace the discipline that the market should impose on borrowing countries' (Frieden, 1987). Lastly, there was a perception in private financial markets that capital controls were in some way incompatible with free and democratic government, reminding many of the Hitlerian/Schachtian monetary system.

These objections brought only minor alterations to the Bretton Woods accord and, despite the best efforts of the New York financial community, the final agreement still bore a strong resemblance to the original proposals put by Keynes and White in their early drafts (Helleiner, 1994). This meant severe constraints on the free flow of private capital between national economies. It is vital to remember that the actions of the market, in particular speculative movements of capital, were held to be largely responsible for the breakdown of the international economy in the 1930s. Furthermore, as Block (1977) points out, the IMF 'had come to embody the hopes of many for a rationally ordered international economy. It was a symbol of America's good intentions on the international front'. Due to these perceptions on the part of national policy-makers (and, just as importantly, US voters), the subordinate position of private financial markets created by the Bretton Woods agreement is hardly surprising.

The Bretton Woods system of organising international finance gave authority for the international movement of capital to two bodies, the World Bank and the IMF. The New York bankers objected to the function of the IMF as they wanted for themselves the role of providing short-term financing to states experiencing balance of payments deficits. Though they didn't get their way in this regard, the New York banking industry did succeed in influencing the development of the international financial and monetary systems. First, they acquired a great deal of influence over the future shape of the IMF through the National Advisory Council on International Monetary and Financial Problems which guided IMF affairs in the early years of its existence. Second, the 1951 decision to grant the Federal Reserve control over US monetary affairs gave American bankers a central position in the US, and thus global, monetary systems. Third, capital controls were made voluntary, rather than obligatory, by the Bretton Woods agreement.

The true application of the Bretton Woods system of organising international monetary relations was delayed until 1958 as a result of the immense problems of restoring the European post-war economies. The Fund and World Bank were severely under-funded relative to the liquidity needs of the post-war western economies. Any country receiving Marshall Aid from the US was rendered ineligible to draw from the IMF so that the Bretton Woods system of rules existed only on paper for the first 13 years of the post-war era. Finance, however, remained 'public' rather than private; the

Marshall Plan and US military spending provided liquidity to the global economy. And this public, or official, finance performed the task of post-war reconstruction extremely well; similar success would undoubtedly have been beyond the capabilities of private financial markets.

However, the Bretton Woods system of organizing international financial affairs that was agreed to in 1944 existed in the presence of strict capital controls in most states. The post-war planners put strong restrictions on the movement of private capital across national boundaries. By subjugating market activity in the cause of international monetary stability, the post-war planners built a dyke that would be gradually worn away by the efforts of that market, and as Strange (1986) has argued, by the decisions and 'non-decisions' of powerful states. The earlier opposition of the New York banking community to the IMF and the idea of capital controls during the Bretton Woods negotiations was rewarded by the American government choosing not to impose capital controls on money leaving the US.

## The Internationalisation of Finance and the Rise of the Euromarkets: 1958-1971

The decades of the 1950s and 1960s are often portrayed as the 'golden years' of economic growth and stability, and this is commonly attributed to the success of the Bretton Woods system. However, the agreement signed in New Hampshire in 1944 was crippled by the ineffectiveness of the IMF and World Bank until the 1950s. More important than the Bretton Woods system was simply the supply of credit flowing from, first, the US government through the Marshall Plan and military spending, and then from US corporations expanding into Europe through acquisitions of European companies. The internationalisation of US multinational enterprises (MNEs) also served as the prime mover of the growth of private international finance in the late 1950s and 1960s. As Pauly explains:

> The expanding activities of MNEs themselves significantly compromised the capacity of governments to maintain capital controls. Leads and lags in invoicing and payments, transfer pricing practices, access to funding sources in a range of markets, and the ability to shift some operations to different regulatory jurisdictions - all helped undercut the efficacy of controls (Pauly, 1993, p.141)

International financial markets grew to the extent that, by the end of this period, they were challenging not only the political authority of weaker states such as Italy and the UK, but also of the strongest state in the international financial system, the United States. During this stage in the internationalisation of private finance, the influence of the market grew, not only in the extent of its activities, but also in the extent to which the idea of the market became accepted amongst political authorities as the dominant form of economic organization.

The rapid growth in private international finance from 1958 to 1971 is largely the story of the rise of the Euromarkets. As a result of US regulatory policies aimed at halting the flow of US dollars into the international monetary system, this amorphous entity grew in size and importance to the extent that daily transactions dwarfed global trade.

The Euromarkets were created in the early 1950s as a way for communist governments in the Soviet Union and China to protect their dollar holdings. As Wachtel (1986, p.94) writes, 'After the Chinese Revolution in 1949, the United States took steps to freeze Chinese accounts in American banks. To evade this move, the Chinese moved their dollar accounts into a Russian-owned bank in Paris, the *Banque Commerciale pour l'Europe du Nord*' and the Soviet Union quickly followed the Chinese example. However, the Euromarkets came of age when American banks turned to offshore lending as a means of circumventing the Kennedy administration's restrictions on foreign lending by US banks. As successive US governments tried to stem the outflow of dollars by imposing capital controls, these same controls served as a catalyst for the internationalisation of private finance.

The government of the United Kingdom also played a key role in promoting the development of the Euromarkets. In 1951 trading was allowed to reopen on London's commodity markets. This decision was integral in the rebirth of London as a financial marketplace that would rival New York by offering less regulation and thus fewer hindrances to market participants. With a viable alternative to the more strictly regulated New York financial market, American banks would in future be able to take advantage of London to escape US regulatory controls. This development set the scene for the rapid internationalisation of banking that would come in later years.

Secondly, in 1958, the Bank of England made the decision that established controls over outward capital flows from the UK did not apply if those flows were denominated in a currency other than sterling. This was a clear attempt by the UK regulatory authorities to increase the City's share of global banking business by attracting US banks to London. Strange (1988, pp.104/105) explains the importance of this development:

> Briefly the Eurodollar market developed because of two inviting gaps in government controls over the power of banks to create credit. The American regulatory system installed during the 1930s had tried to prevent short-term funds being too large or too mobile by making it illegal for banks in the US to pay more than minimal interest on short-term deposits. But the rule did not apply to interest paid on dollar deposits with US banks' branches in London. The Bank of England, meanwhile, even after 1958, still kept strict controls over British foreign investment and over financial transactions in *sterling*, other than payments for trade transactions. But it was decided that it was safe to allow British and foreign banks in London to raise and lend money and conduct all forms of financial business, not in sterling but in *dollars*, because it could not jeopardise the British balance of payments. Thus the Eurodollar loan became a new unregulated growth point in the international financial system; and the faster their bankers followed them to London, and later to other Euro cities.

This dynamic shows the factor of regulatory arbitrage at its most simple and most effective. Regulatory arbitrage, put simply, is the attempt by market participants to profit from differences in regulation between national markets. In essence, market players in an open system are able to 'shop around' for the best business environment in which to conduct their business. This phenomenon plays to the disadvantage of any authority that chooses to execute and enforce controls that are stricter than those in rival markets, and is a clear example of a case where the market has been able to defy national political authorities. The growth of the Euromarkets relied on such differences between national regulatory systems.

1958 also saw the return to convertibility of the major European currencies. Though this was immensely beneficial to the growth of the global economy, the decisions taken by European governments to make these currencies convertible brought detrimental consequences, both national and international, as a direct result of currency speculation. The speculative 'struggle between governments and private banks for control over the international monetary system' (Wachtel, 1986, p.103) began with the return to convertibility in 1958, and spurred the growth of banks' international operations, the rise of the Euromarkets, and the eventual market challenge to the authority of states over the international economy.

In very basic terms, the Euromarkets involve the borrowing and lending, by private financial actors, of funds denominated in currencies other than those of the actors host nations. For example, a French bank in London may lend $X million (US) to a firm operating out of Hamburg. Alternatively, an Italian bank in Frankfurt may lend £Y million to an American multinational seeking to purchase a British company. However, in the early days of the Euromarkets, this international network of banks was used primarily by governments and corporations to buy and sell foreign exchange, and is also known by the name 'Eurocurrency markets' (Johnson, 1983).

Nonetheless, the most important facet of the Euromarkets is that they promoted the continued use of the US dollar as an international currency. US multinationals were able to continue their expansion into Europe and the rest of the world by borrowing funds on the Euromarkets. The total amount of Eurodollars, that is funds denominated in US dollars but held outside the United States, came to first rival, then far exceed the American domestic money supply. In effect, what has happened is that a huge pool of dollars has accumulated outside of the US that is immediately available for use by banks, corporations and governments.

The Euromarkets appeal to these consumers for differing reasons. Bank interest in the Euromarkets derives mostly from the opportunity to expand loan operations beyond the scope of funds deposited in their branches. Banks can borrow readily from the Euromarkets, at an interest rate lower than that in the domestic economy, and then re-lend that money at a higher rate. Corporations have found the Euromarkets to be a boon for several reasons. First, MNEs are able to circumvent any national restrictions on outward flows of capital by borrowing outside the country. Second, by turning to the Euromarkets, corporations operating abroad may avoid restrictions on local borrowing by foreign-owned entities. Third, as with banks, corporations can generally obtain cheaper financing through the Euromarkets. Fourth, there is a greater availability of funds in the Euromarkets than in a single national economy. Fifth, the Euromarkets offer a wider range of borrowing instruments which allows corporations greater flexibility in their financing options. Lastly, corporations turn to the Euromarkets to supply their need for foreign exchange.

Ironically, the growth of the Euromarkets has been substantially aided by business from governments themselves. Governments may turn to the Euromarkets over domestic financial institutions for a variety of reasons some of which mirror those of banks and corporations. But the three most important reasons (Quinn, 1975) for government Euro-borrowing are:

1.  to finance balance of payments deficits;
2.  to fund short-term foreign borrowing by longer-term borrowing; and
3.  to borrow substantial sums of money without raising the domestic interest rate.

What makes these markets so interesting to the student of international political economy, and moreover, so attractive to international borrowers, is that they lie beyond the reach of any of the world's national regulatory regimes. The genesis and growth of the Euromarkets lay in attempts to evade national regulatory restrictions and this remains the *raison d'être* of the markets. Frieden (1987, p.90) has called the Euromarkets a 'banking Twilight Zone' that, much like the Internet, 'belongs to no nation, is governed by no country's laws, and is subject to little or no regulation'. And, just like the Internet, the Euromarkets have radically changed the way international banks and national political authorities conduct their respective businesses.

The Euromarkets have also fostered cooperation between banks. This centres on the manner in which banks have banded together to arrange mega-loans for both sovereign and private borrowers. Syndicated Euromarket loans have developed throughout the life of the Euromarkets. Their most recent incarnation consists of loans 'put together typically by a small management group of banks, who recruit a larger group of banks to participate once the deal is negotiated' (Frieden, 1987, p.105).

The absence of regulation in the Euromarkets, combined with the fact that Eurocredits involve immense amounts of money, means that banks operating through the Euromarkets are able to offer greater returns to investors and lower rates of interest to borrowers. However, in addition to the lower costs of Eurobanking, there is another phenomenon of interest resulting from the huge sums of money available to international banks on the Euromarkets. This is that these immense financial resources, tied to no one international financial system, yet linked to them all, play havoc with national regulatory attempts to control both the money supply and the value of the national currency.

To understand how the available credit in the Euromarkets has reached such proportions, one must grasp the one of the basic principles of banking. The sheer size of the Euromarkets derives from a simple facet of all banking, namely the multiple expansion of money. This process, as it works in US domestic banking with an official reserve requirement of around 20 percent, is neatly explained by Wachtel:

> For every dollar deposited in a bank, about 20 cents is held by the bank as a reserve and the balance of 80 cents is available to be lent out to borrowers. The 80 cents lent out by the bank provides dollars to its loan customers who probably will turn around and deposit this 80 cents either in the bank from which the money is borrowed or in some other bank. Now a new account of 80 cents has been created in the banking system, and again the bank has to hold 20 percent of this (16 cents) in reserve and can lend out a new 64 cents...After the second round, for example, banks as a total system have $1.80, and after a third round $2.44 - the original dollar, the 80 cents after the first lending cycle, and 64 cents after the second. The first dollar deposited, in effect, turns over each time a portion of it is lent out and re-deposited to create new deposits

in the banking system. The process does not go no indefinitely because of the reserve requirement. At each stage in the cycle, a smaller amount is availaable (sic) to lend out, and quickly credit expansion atrophies as smaller and smaller amounts are available for new lending. (Wachtel, 1986, pp.102-103)

Unlike national financial systems, however, there exists no reserve requirement in the Euromarkets, for there is no authority to impose one. Thus the multiple expansion of money in the Euromarkets could feasibly continue without limit. Now the banks operating in the Euromarkets do retain reserves, but these operate as a much smaller percentage of the moneys deposited with them, and consequently the multiple expansion of money in the Euromarkets has created a vast pool of available credit.

The rise of the Euromarkets was but one form (though the most important) that the internationalisation of private finance took in this period. For this period also saw the progressive internationalisation of banking activities through the extension of branches in other countries. Most marked was the internationalisation of American banks as they sought to aid established corporate clients in their growing international business. Mark Casson (1990, p.27) has identified the economic motives for the multinationalisation of banking as benefits from vertical integration, location, communications, monopolistic advantage and network linkages; 'motives analogous to similar motives operating in manufacturing but which manifest themselves differently because of the importance of local rather than global monopolistic advantage'. However, there was also considerable foreign bank penetration of the American domestic banking market, a phenomenon which was to encourage changes in the way that US banks conducted their affairs.

## The Consequences of International Private Capital

The gradual internationalisation of banks and the amount of credit available through the Euromarkets have proved to be of immense value to the global economy yet have also acted as a destabilising force. For, through this international financial network, vast sums of capital seek out the greatest rate of return, moving seemingly effortlessly to the location where it is required. Such mechanics have helped spur international economic growth, and may be seen to have helped bring to maturity the economies of certain developing countries. But the ready availability and vast amounts of Eurocredit act as a double edged sword.

For these huge amounts of capital moving rapidly around the international economy often exert a truly destabilising force on national macroeconomic management. Not only do international financial markets react immediately to every policy announcement, ministerial statement or release of annual, quarterly or monthly statistics, but market actors also engage in speculative activities that often have little connection to the health, or otherwise, of the national economies concerned.

Speculation became established as a feature of international finance as early as 1964, which saw a series of speculative attacks against the pound sterling. This was not the first time that the pound had come under attack in international financial markets since the end of the war, but the renewed onset of speculation in 1964 marked the beginning of a period in which the markets would increasingly win out over national policy goals. From November 1964 to November 1967, three sets of speculative attacks finally succeeded in bringing the official exchange rate of sterling down from $2.80 to $2.40. In the process the Bank of England was forced to spend $5.2 billion, vainly trying to stave off the market's assault.

Such speculative flows are precisely the phenomenon that Keynes and White had sought to prevent in their formulation of the Bretton Woods agreement. However, the rise of the Euromarkets permitted a form of private financial interaction that was unforeseen by the framers of Bretton Woods. Not only had the post-war planners neglected the possibility of a completely unregulated pool of capital freely moving around the global economy, they could not have imagined a pool as large as that of the Euromarkets.

With the pound's devaluation, speculative pressures turned to the US dollar. The market, according to its nature, sought the maximum return available and saw such a possibility in exerting pressure on the dollar. It must be remembered that speculation by financial actors with access to amounts as large as those in the Euromarkets does not involve just 'betting' on the possible devaluation of the targeted currency. Rather, the goal is to apply enough pressure to the currency in question that a devaluation will be unavoidable for that currency's issuing authority. Believing that a devaluation in the pound is coming, banks (and corporations) sell sterling on the Eurocurrency markets, and buy other currencies which are perceived to be stronger, such as German marks or Swiss francs. The combination of these actions applies downward pressure to the pound, and upward pressure to the other currencies concerned. When the Bank of England eventually gives in and devalues the pound, these market players can transfer their money back into sterling, with a considerable net gain. This is not merely an automatic economic process; speculation involves a veritable struggle between the market and political authority.

The speculative forces that turned against the US dollar from 1967 onwards brought another round of capital controls, but the continued worsening of the Vietnam conflict in January 1968 meant that such measures merely temporarily delayed the speculative campaign. In spite of the efforts of both the Johnson and Nixon administrations, the combined attacks by international financial markets on the dollar slowly weakened the US regulatory authorities' resolve to counter the will of the market.

## Banking Regulation in the 50s and 60s: The Erosion of Authority

It is appropriate that the focus of this section falls mainly on the regulatory authorities of the United States for, until 1971, the US government remained by far the pre-eminent regulatory structure in the international political economy. The Bretton Woods system, and the capital controls that it encompassed, retained the firm ideological allegiance of state policy makers at this time. The 1959 Radcliffe Report in the UK is an ideal example of this phenomenon for it 'supported the maintenance and even extension of post-war direct controls while the clarity of its exposition forcefully suggested that rapid market developments could quickly make these recommendations invalid' (Pringle, 1992, p.14). It must be remembered that the Bretton Woods system rested on the legitimacy of US leadership, and the 'belief that the system had legitimacy and respectability was very important in sustaining it' (Pringle, 1992, p.95). At the same time, however, the need to enhance national economic competitiveness drove states to liberalise their national financial systems.

The restoration of European currency convertibility was just one of the key decisions made by political authorities in this period that spurred the internationalisation of banking. However, before addressing these other issues, it is worth noting that authorities in the US began the 1960s with an effort to stabilize that system. Robert Roosa, as Under Secretary of the Treasury, headed up the Kennedy administration's efforts to strengthen the international monetary and financial systems. Initiatives such as the forming of the Gold Pool and the General Arrangement to Borrow (GAB) in 1961 demonstrated in practice both Roosa's and the Kennedy administration's ideological commitment to shoring up the stability of the Bretton Woods system. Less well-known, but just as significant, were Roosa's personal efforts aimed at strengthening international financial cooperation through reciprocal agreements created between the industrialised nations' central bankers (Roosa, 1967). Most important of these was the setting up of swap arrangements between the central banks which would help national authorities obtain official credit in times of currency speculation. Of particular interest with regard to Roosa's efforts is that he intended them to reinforce US predominance of the system, and rejected any efforts that involved multilateral economic power-sharing with the allies. As Block (1977, p.181) explains, this rejection stemmed from his belief 'that any plan that diminished the dollar's role as an official reserve would endanger its role as a key currency in international trade and finance'.

Roosa's endeavours to bring stability to the international monetary system failed to achieve their desired end, however, and by the middle of the decade attention turned to a problem that was to dominate international economic policy for the next two decades. The growth of the US deficit threatened confidence in the stability of the international monetary system through the well-documented phenomenon of the Triffin Dilemma, which had clearly permeated policy circles by the mid-1960s. In a series of attempts to halt the growth of dollars held outside the United States, it can be seen that the US authorities in fact encouraged the growth of the Euromarkets as a source of dollars for the global (and US) economy. It would be going too far to suggest that successive US administrations foresaw that the consequence of these policies would be the strengthening of the market's grip over international finance. It would be hard to believe, though, that decisions such as the implementation of the Interest Equalization Tax (IET) were taken without acknowledging that US banks would switch their business operations to an overseas base, namely the Euromarkets.

Regulatory decisions such as the imposition of the IET in 1963/4 and the Voluntary Foreign Credit Restraint (VFCR) program in 1965, when combined with the limits placed on interest rates by Regulation Q, constituted an attempt by the administration to encourage inward investment in the US by American firms instead of looking abroad for potentially greater returns. As Odell (1982, pp.363-364) writes, at a more fundamental level, they represented a choice of:

resisting the market...rather than executing or promoting a depreciation, partly because Kennedy and Johnson administration leaders did not accept the diagnosis that pointed to devaluation or floating.

The VFCR measures fell woefully short of halting or even slowing the growth of dollars held outside the US, however, because they did not apply to funds loaned from foreign branches of US banks (Dale, 1984, p.22). This was presumably done so that US banks would not lose business to banks from other countries. In addition, the Federal Reserve gradually exempted most short-term deposits from the Regulation Q interest rate ceilings until, as Dale (1984, p.24) writes, by 1973 'Regulation Q ceased to be a major influence on the Eurodollar market'.

US banks responded to these regulatory impediments by shifting a large part of their business operations to London. In a move typical of the emerging dynamic between regulator and the regulated, US banks took full advantage of the opportunity to conduct their business comparatively unrestricted in the City of London, a situation that existed due to the British authorities' desire to restore London as a financial centre. By making loans in Eurodollars through their London branches, US banks circumvented both US and UK regulatory restrictions on their affairs. What made these activities all the more significant in the expansion of the Euromarkets was that US banks used not only Eurodollars deposited in their foreign branches; they also transferred funds drawn from deposits made in the United States.

Another form of US resistance to the market came in the support given by the Federal Reserve to the UK government in its ongoing fight against currency speculation. In the 1964 sterling crisis, for example, the Federal Reserve was integral in arranging a loan from the major central banks. By defending the pound against the whims of the market, the US authorities hoped to stave off a potential run on the dollar. As Block (1977, p.188) writes:

> The Fed's willingness and eagerness to help was based on the perception that the dollar's fate was linked to the pound's, so that every possible measure should be taken to defend the pound's parity.

Though the attempts by the Kennedy and Johnson administrations to stem the outward flow of capital from the United States only pushed more and more US banks to increase their activities in the Euromarkets, the ideology behind them was centred in an unfailing belief both in the ability of state authorities to correct systemic inadequacies, and in the central role to be played by the state apparatus of the US. Later administrations would not hold such unwavering conviction in either but would look instead to the market as a cure-all for the malaise affecting the international monetary and financial systems.

Part of the irony of the US authorities' attempts to halt capital outflows is that a large part of the responsibility for the growth of the US deficit lay not at the door of private US banks and multinationals. Instead the dollar overhang originated primarily in the expansionary domestic policies of the Kennedy and Johnson administrations and in the massive outflow of official funds due to the Vietnam war.

Several writers have commented on the consequences of this phenomenon for global inflation and the stability of the Bretton Woods system. But few have noted that huge amounts of these dollars both came from, and found their way into, the Euromarkets and thus helped boost the internationalisation of finance:

> Thus from the mid-1960s the new international money markets granted President Johnson an initially ample supply of credit to finance the Vietnam War.....(which) fuelled a further expansion of Eurodollar credit which was then used to finance massive speculation against the dollar. (Pringle, p.97)

The Euromarkets are unregulated; it is there that the free market ideal finds its clearest expression, free from the intervention of authority. It must not be forgotten that the actions of political authorities were integral in bringing about this state of affairs.

In addition to regulating American banks' activities to reduce the flow of funds leaving the United States, US banking authorities also focused on the issue of foreign bank penetration of the US market. The 1967 Zwick Report of the Joint Economic Committee of Congress studied the extent of foreign bank penetration of the US market and examined the manner in which American banks were treated abroad by foreign regulatory authorities. This report constituted the first step in a policy debate that would take 11 years to resolve.

The findings of the Zwick Report 'supported the view that such (foreign bank) operations on the whole benefited the American economy and balance of payments' (Pauly, 1988, pp.30-31). More importantly the report stressed that by extending national treatment to foreign banks operating in the United States, US authorities would be able to regulate an increasing share of the market in international banking services. The report was not merely advocating openness, as Pauly is anxious to stress. Instead, it showed how US authorities could best cope with the consequences of, and thus benefit from, the opening up of the US financial services marketplace.

It is clear, however, that throughout the 1960s and early 1970s the idea of the market as a superior alternative to state planning or *dirigisme* gradually took hold of US policy makers. John Odell's study of US international monetary policy over this period recognizes the power that ideas held in the economic policy process. Of particular importance is the grasp that the Triffin Dilemma came to have in regulatory circles. But it is also apparent that the market began to exert a powerful ideological influence at this time. It has already been noted above that the policies of the Kennedy and Johnson administrations stemmed from an ideology that saw the US authorities as central in the organization of the world's money and finance. Odell (1982, p.64) goes so far as to say that the policy circles in these administrations 'were more suspicious of unhindered free market forces - in general and especially in the foreign exchange market - than were the officials who followed them in the 1970s'.

The first example of this change in belief system actually occurred in the closing months of the Johnson administration. In March 1968 the US government announced that the price of gold for private purchasers would henceforth be determined by the free market. This abdication of authority increased the grip of the market on international monetary affairs and set the stage for a further extension of market influence. It was only a matter of a few years before the market was put forward as a cure for all of the Bretton Woods system's monetary and financial ills.

In the interim the United States authorities had to face a growing currency crisis that threatened the stability of not only the dollar, but the entire Bretton Woods system. This crisis was instrumental in turning the tide against proponents of fixed exchange rates. International currency markets had turned their speculative powers against the pound between 1964 and 1967 and in this period the Federal Reserve forwarded the Bank of England financial support through the swap arrangements set up by Robert Roosa. The motive was clear - as long as speculation failed to compel a devaluation of sterling, the brunt of these forces would not be turned against the dollar.

In November 1967, the British authorities submitted to market pressures and devalued sterling from $2.80 to $2.40. This event heralded an onslaught against the dollar, a concerted market campaign to force a devaluation that culminated in the 1971 devaluation. As speculation increased against the dollar, an ideology supporting the market as an alternative to state control gradually became entrenched in policy circles in the US. Odell's account of the spread of ideas supporting for currency floating demonstrates that in the late-60s political backing grew for limited floating, although the early years of the Nixon administration saw few omens of the 1971 watershed that was to follow. The reason for this was simply that Nixon was more concerned with the US relationship with both China and the USSR than he was with international monetary and financial affairs.

The Nixon administration as a whole, however, brought with it into office an ideological predisposition against government control of the economy and for increased market influence and the potential benefits of currency speculation. There was limited resistance - Arthur Burns continued to oppose the idea of floating until 1973. But the administration provided a fertile breeding ground for theories supporting floating exchange rates, particularly those expounded by Milton Friedman, a key advisor to the Nixon cabinet. Odell (1982, pp.310-311) points out that George Schultz and Herbert Stein were both followers of Friedman. It is for this reason that, when Nixon could no longer afford to ignore the issue of the US deficit, the events of August 1971 are not, in retrospect, at all surprising.


**The Market Triumphs: 1971-73**

The speculative pressures that built against the dollar from 1968 to 1971 were a major contributing factor to the August 1971 decision by the Nixon administration to de-link the dollar from gold, impose a 15 percent import surcharge and institute domestic wage and price controls. The import surcharge was to act as a bargaining chip with America's economic allies in an effort to persuade them to allow a devaluation of the dollar.

This period of the post-war development of international finance was by far the most chaotic. The opening three years saw the transition from a managed to a floating system of exchange rates; that is a system governed by the market. This was not a natural progression from one level of financial development to another; the market drove and nurtured the change from the former system to that which replaced it. As Moffitt (1983, p.71) puts it, 'the midwife in the transition from a govt-dominated regime to a market-oriented one was massive speculation against the dollar in the currency markets'.

There are few other periods of financial and monetary history that show the ongoing dialectic between political authority and the market as clearly as this, for it involved a true struggle for primacy between the West's two opposing forms of economic organization. Moffitt (p.71) describes the significance of this period most dramatically:

> The transition from a government-dominated monetary system to a market-oriented system was not a smooth one. It was marked by a series of monetary crises and upheavals that were among the most tumultuous in history. Essentially these were the manifestations of a struggle between governments and the private banks for control over the international monetary system. The showdown between governments and the banks came during the currency crises of 1972 and 1973.

And a showdown it proved to be, for the speculative forces that had aligned themselves against the dollar in the final years of the 1960s had been merely a prelude to the onslaught that occurred between 1971 and 1973. Private banks by now knew what their collective resources were capable of achieving through speculation, and the currency realignments set at the Smithsonian in 1971 acted only as a temporary holding action in the defence of the dollar.

By the middle of 1972 speculation had turned again to the pound sterling and, despite the Bank of England spending $2.6 billion in its defence in one week, the British government bowed to market pressure and was forced to let the pound float, that is let the world's financial markets decide its value relative to other currencies. As in 1967, as soon as speculative pressure eased on the pound, it increased on the dollar, forcing the US authorities into another dollar devaluation in February 1973. This struggle, though it was to be in vain, was a titanic one, as Moffitt (p.75) describes:

> The second devaluation hardly made a dent in the speculation. The speculators had the dollar on the ropes and they wanted blood. On March 1, barely two weeks after the devaluation, a new wave of dollar selling hit Europe, forcing the Bundesbank and other central banks to spend nearly $4 billion to defend the dollar.

Nonetheless, the coordinated actions of Western central banks failed to hold off the seemingly inexorable force of the market. The world's financial markets were closed on March 2 and remained so for 17 days. By the time they reopened, the decision had been made to hand over responsibility for setting relative currency values to the market and from this point on the world's currencies have floated freely against each other.

The assumption amongst national regulators was that 'devolving' responsibility for exchange rates to the market would drive currencies to their 'natural' relative prices and thus significantly reduce speculation. It certainly relieved national authorities of the burden of deciding amongst themselves the correct rates of exchange. The prescribed cure, however, merely aggravated the patient's symptoms.

## Banking Regulation in the Post-Bretton Woods World

National authorities faced three options in looking to the future of banking regulation. The first was to tighten regulations and restrict banks' activities to the point where there would be little chance of a systemic threat. The second option lay in removing existing regulations on banks, in the belief that the market would most efficiently regulate itself. It should be remembered that this ideology had been a driving force in the US decision to abandon fixed rates. The third option was to improve cooperation between regulatory authorities in the world's major financial centres in the expectation that an enhanced exchange of information would reduce the chances of major market failures in the future.

The first of these policy choices would clearly have been a disaster. By the early 1970s the global economy was already dependent on rapid and ready international financial flows, and a heavy-handed restriction of banking activities would likely have resulted in a severe liquidity crisis. As Schuijer (1992, p.86) puts it:

> if regulators overemphasize the need to prevent grave disruptions of the financial system by a stringent regulation of financial institutions, they run the risk of stifling competition and thereby removing these institutions' incentives to outdo their competitors' efficiency.

However, a blend of the second and third options was seized upon by regulators over the next ten years as a possible solution to the problems facing the international financial system.

It is appropriate that some time is devoted here to explaining the (continuing) moves towards the deregulation of financial markets across the industrialised nations. While there is insufficient space to examine each country in turn, general trends can be identified by examining the case of the United Kingdom. Though some have seen financial deregulation as a headlong rush towards the free market, it has in fact been tempered by a concurrent extension and formalization of banking supervisory practices. The main thrust of deregulation since the mid-1970s has been to de-compartmentalize the financial services industry. This has meant the removal of regulations governing both the extent of services that financial firms can offer, and the geographical locations in which they can be offered. Most important has been the move to allow banks to engage in non-traditional financial activities. Banks have gained increased access to capital markets, allowing them to decrease their traditional dependence on the intermediation of deposits. A corollary of this has been the emergence of competition for this traditional business from non-bank financial firms. Indeed, increased competition has been offered as the main justification in the de-compartmentalization of finance.

Yet competition has played a role not only within national financial markets, but also among them. For national authorities have, for the past 20 years, been engaged in what may be seen as 'competitive deregulation'. In the drive to attract firms to financial centres, authorities came to see deregulation as the incentive needed to put, say, London ahead of Frankfurt as the first choice for a banking firm. It is clear that in the late 70s and early 80s tax and (de-)regulatory incentives were successful in building the strength of some financial centres; indeed it has been argued that a 'country's willingness to provide implicit regulatory subsidies to financial services firms affects the international division of labor and the distribution of wealth' (Kane 1988, p.368). This deregulation would have posed a threat to both national and international financial systems had it not been for the simultaneous trend towards more formal supervision of banking activities. Phil Cerny (1993, pp.169-170) offers an additional rationale for deregulation which is compelling. He claims that deregulation was/is attractive to states because:

1.  'it can appear to be a non policy...the removal of regulations'; and,
2.  'unlike the multilateral decision-making processes embodied in the IMF or GATT, the decision to deregulate can be - and generally is - a unilateral one. This was a crucial advantage in an international system where consensus (had broken down)'.

The most obvious case of this two-track approach may be seen in the United Kingdom. After the shock of the Secondary Banking Crisis of 1973-75, the Bank of England began to formalize its prudential oversight of the British banking system. The Banking Act of 1979 accomplished both this formalization and allowed for new areas of banking supervision by the Bank. It also served to implement the 1977 First Banking Directive put in place by the European Community. The 1979 Act is of particular interest as it coincided with the end of exchange controls in the British financial system and the beginning of a progressive deregulation of UK banking that continues today. It has been called a turning point in UK banking regulation because it went a long way towards ending the old system of 'gentlemen's agreements' that had long characterised the relationship between regulator and regulated in the British banking system. Indeed the Act formalized the system of supervision and for the first time required that deposit-taking institutions be licensed by the Bank of England. For example, banks operating in the British Isles were required for the first time to provide detailed statistical reports and allow for close on-site inspections and interviews by the supervisory staff of the Bank of England. These powers were added to in the 1987 Banking Act.

## Banking Under the Non-System and Emerging Crisis

The market's response to floating exchange rates was to intensify, rather than diminish, the drive for speculative profit. The foreign exchange (forex) divisions of all major banks grew dramatically in size and importance, and forex activities accounted for an increasing proportion of bank profits. For, with the new situation in which exchange rates fluctuated from, minute to minute, day to day, banks found for themselves a new role in helping business and thus turning a profit. In addition to providing foreign currency to corporations engaging in foreign trade and investment, banks also acquired the role of organising hedging actions for these corporations.

To protect themselves against unforeseen fluctuations in foreign currencies, international business turned to futures contracts as a way of eliminating some of the instability that now plagued the world's financial markets. But banks were adding new business practices to their arsenal of financial instruments. In addition to the traditional business of financial intermediation (the borrowing and lending of money), many banks were becoming involved in activities that sought to profit from risk. Almost all of the larger international banks had become involved in foreign exchange trading; however many of the larger banks had come to see foreign exchange trading not only as a business practice that could be used to hedge against risk, but also as a speculative activity to bring in off-balance sheet profits at a time when profits in other divisions of the banking business were under pressure due to rising levels of competition.

Banks quickly discovered that the profits to be made from providing the service of hedging against instability were small compared to those derived from other speculative activities linked to floating exchange rates. Now, as has already been noted, speculation was not a new phenomenon in international financial markets; during the currency crises of 1964-67 (sterling), 1968-71 (dollar), 1972 (sterling), and 1973 (dollar) the banks had learned that there were huge profits to be made from it. However the floating rate system made potentially profitable currency speculation an everyday affair. No longer did the speculator have to wait for (or rather precipitate) a currency crisis; with a floating exchange rate system considerable fluctuations became commonplace *and* could be brought about through the actions of a few large market players.

The process behind the growth in currency speculation in the years following the end of Bretton Woods is neatly explained by Strange:

> Under such conditions of uncertainty, countries, corporations and banks all did what they could to reduce their vulnerability. They hedged their bets, as the gamblers would say. They bought or sold foreign exchange forward, dealt in commodity futures and then in financial futures. The one group that profited - with the rare exception of the few that went bust - were the financial operators. Banks made profits as never before. Financial business boomed and created new jobs and new opportunities for tipsters, researchers, commentators and others catering for the growing demand for information and advice. Competition between the banks accelerated the process of financial innovation. (Strange, 1988, p.108)

Most large banks increased their forex operations after 1973 and this increased the instability that was to plague the foreign exchange markets for the rest of the decade. Many banks now derived considerable profits from their forex operations; however, the banking community as a whole was soon to learn that massive currency speculation by leading banks can be perilous, not just for those banks whose speculative activities backfire, but for the entire international financial system.

Due to the progressive internationalisation of financial institutions and increasingly sophisticated communications technology, the world's major national financial markets had, by the early seventies, become interlinked in a fashion hitherto unimaginable. This process of internationalisation continued throughout the 1970s, creating a truly global financial system.

These two developments in international finance, namely interlinked financial markets and increasingly risky business practices, combined in 1974 to bring the international system close to disaster. First, in May of that year, the Franklin National Bank of New York crisis erupted, a crisis due in large part to overly risky forex speculation by the bank and overly lax supervision by US banking authorities. This failure sent an immense shock wave throughout the global banking community due to Franklin's size, importance in foreign exchange markets and its international operations. Foreign exchange trading suffered a more serious blow in June 1974 with the failure of Bankhaus I.D. Herstatt of Cologne.

The tale of Franklin National Bank is one of the more sordid in the history of US banking and highlights many of the problems associated with the modern international banking system. A long-established regional bank, in the 1960s it tried to expand nationally and then internationally, and became involved in a number of highly risky practices. In the latter part of the decade the bank began an aggressive international strategy that involved opening branches in Nassau and London. Simultaneously, Franklin National expanded its foreign currency activities to take advantage of the increasing levels of volatility in international currency markets. Much of this activity was undertaken in order to offset losses that were emerging from its domestic business. Franklin National, in an attempt to establish itself as a major bank in the US market, had taken on large numbers of loans to borrowers of questionable credit. While the loan portfolio expanded, its quality deteriorated rapidly, raising the eyebrows and the attention of the office of the Comptroller and of the Federal Reserve. In 1965 Franklin had been identified as a problem bank and was once again deemed thus in 1970. At the same time US regulatory authorities did little to prevent Franklin from undertaking new activities and expanding its international reach (Spero, 1980).

A key event in the eventual unravelling of Franklin's business occurred in July 1972 when the bank was bought by Michele Sindona, an Italian financier with a mysterious background and a reputation for aggressive business expansion. Sindona significantly overpaid for his controlling interest in Franklin National, and was eager to recuperate his investment by encouraging the bank's management to pursue more aggressive strategies. A central element in this strategy was increasing foreign currency dealing under the management of Carlo Bordoni, Sindona's colleague who had a less-than-respectable reputation amongst forex dealers (Spero, 1980). Taking advantage of lax, and in some cases non-existent, internal controls, Franklin traders rapidly established huge positions in Eurocurrency markets. This would have been an uncomfortably risky practice in banks with long-established forex divisions; in Franklin National there were many inexperienced traders who were given license to falsify profit-loss reports. It was a recipe for disaster.

The combination of lax internal controls, fraudulent behaviour, regulatory failure, and over-exposure in foreign currency market eventually led to huge losses on the part of Franklin National. Compounding this situation was the turmoil in international currency markets as the dollar first strengthened and then rapidly weakened vis-à-vis other major currencies. Very soon word got out that Franklin was in trouble on its contracts. By 1973 several major banks refused to trade with Franklin in fear of a default, and Franklin's freedom of movement to sign forward contracts was greatly reduced. Interestingly, other banks operating in foreign currency markets seemed better informed of Franklin's activities than the US authorities charged with overseeing the bank. and it was ultimately these same actors who raised concerns with US regulators (Spero, 1980). On May 1, 1974 the Federal Reserve denied Franklin's request to buy Talcott National Corporation, citing Franklin's status as a problem bank. With this announcement, Franklin's financial problems became public, and as word spread of Franklin's losses, market confidence in the bank rapidly deteriorated and investors sold off Franklin shares. At the same time customers began withdrawing their money from Franklin's overseas branches. Franklin's share price dropped rapidly and it became obvious to the bank's administration, national regulators, and other market actors that Franklin's situation was untenable (Spero, 1980). The bank was closed by US regulators as they sought a resolution to Franklin's problems and a process of international consultation and cooperation began between national regulatory authorities.

Franklin became an international problem for several reasons. First because of the size of the bank and the threat of a knock-on effect on other banks. Second, because of the dire conditions present in the US and international economies, with stagflation and other problems connected to the OPEC oil price hike, and the blow to international banking confidence that the failure could deal. Thirdly, because of the bank's dealings in foreign currencies, and because of its involvement in the Eurocurrency markets, both problems that threatened levels of confidence in international markets and raised the issue of defaults on forward contracts.

The international implications of Franklin's failure were revisited and greatly compounded when the full implications of unrestricted international banking became painfully clear to banking authorities in June 1974. Bankhaus I.D. Herstatt, a small private German bank, was closed by German banking authorities at the end of the German financial business day. This was still only 10am in New York. Thus at the close of business in Germany, US banks had transferred dollars to Herstatt but the German bank was unable to meet its liabilities. Until this time, regulators and banks had foreseen the problem of a bank not meeting its forward liabilities, but had not contemplated default on spot transactions.

Both the Franklin and Herstatt crises demonstrated how in the new international financial system of the post-Bretton Woods world, interdependence now defined the relations between not only private financial actors, but also between the authorities that regulate their activities. The crises necessitated emergency, ad hoc measures aimed at coordinating actions between national regulators and forced authorities to recognize that their national reach no longer sufficed in a world of highly mobile international private capital.

The importance of foreign exchange markets in a global economy marked by extensive international trade and the presence of huge MNEs cannot be overstated. The succession of the Herstatt crisis on the heels of Franklin National's failure severely disrupted the smooth functioning of these markets, so much so that, within a matter of weeks, total world foreign exchange trading had declined by almost two-thirds (Spero, 1980, p.112).

Nor were Franklin National and Herstatt the only two major bank crises of that year. The secondary banking crisis in the UK posed a serious threat to the stability of the British financial system, a threat that was to bring new thinking to the business of banking regulation in the City (Moran, 1984). Furthermore, banks across the US and Europe were experiencing severe financial problems for a variety of domestic and international reasons, including the dismal state of the Western economies at the time, and the problems associated with currency instability affected almost all the major banks. The prospect of a run of bank failures, a consequent massive contraction of global liquidity and the end of easy access to foreign currencies forced national banking authorities to reassess their domestic regulatory regimes. However the banking industry's seemingly legion problems only temporarily dampened bankers' taste for risky operations. Within a couple of years, currency speculation had again become a major source of revenue for the major banks.

## The Creation of the Basel Committee

The need for an international body coordinating national banking regulatory systems was made abundantly clear by the 1974 crises at Franklin National and Herstatt banks. These failures highlighted the way in which, in a truly interdependent global financial system, a crisis in a bank in one national system could easily and rapidly spread to become a system-wide, international problem. An internationalisation of regulatory response was clearly required, unless regulators were willing to reinstate severe capital controls.

The Franklin National crisis alone required international cooperative moves to prevent a string of bank failures. These moves took the form of ad hoc cooperation among the central bankers of the US, Japan and the European countries. Central bank cooperation, as mentioned above, has a long history going back to the 1920s, and the central bank governors had been meeting at monthly intervals since 1960 at the Bank for International Settlements to discuss economic and monetary affairs. Such regular contact among central bankers gave rise to 'a network of high-level officials who knew each other well and who cooperated in a number of efforts to manage the international monetary system during the 1960s' (Spero, 1980, p.146). This network was of invaluable assistance in ensuring the exchange of information and international cooperation needed to resolve the crisis. Of particular importance was the relationship that grew up between the Bank of England on the one hand and the US Federal Reserve and Federal Deposit Insurance Corporation (FDIC) on the other. As in so many of these cases, the relationship prospered in large part due to a strong personal connection - that made between Governor Richardson of the Bank of England and Governor Mitchell of the Federal Reserve. This axis of cooperation between New York and London, the United States and Britain, was one that was to prove pivotal in the future development of international regulatory cooperation.

The history of cooperation between the City of London and New York is one of tremendous interest to scholars of financial regulation for the two cities are rival financial centres. Let us not forget that it was London that picked up much of the business that left New York as a result of the regulatory developments of the 1960s (i.e. IET and VFCR). That the supervisory authorities in each centre should be so willing to cooperate in the resolution of international crises says much about both the enlightened self-interest of these two authorities and about the danger of the spread of financial uncertainty and instability.

However, moves toward international regulatory cooperation did not stop at ad hoc attempts to stem the crisis caused by Franklin National. Up to this point, the meetings of the central bank governors in Basel had been concerned, as noted above, only with monetary and economic issues. As Spero (1980, p.154) writes:

> The crisis of 1974 forced central bankers seriously to consider the problems raised by the internationalization of banking. The first joint effort of central bankers was their attempt to prevent the further erosion of confidence in international banks during the summer and autumn of 1974. The central bank governors sought to shore up confidence by convincing the world that they were ready and able to act as lenders of last resort in international banking.

At the scheduled monthly meeting of the BIS in July 1974, which was dominated by talk of the recent Herstatt crisis, current Franklin crisis, and ongoing instability in the Euromarkets, central bankers 'agreed in principle to provide emergency assistance to financially troubled banks wherever necessary to avert a crisis of confidence in the international banking system' but 'did not commit themselves to helping troubled institutions' (Spero, 1980, p.154).

This agreement was intentionally leaked to the press but was an insufficient measure in the attempt to bolster confidence in the markets. The lack of specific details in the communiqué was seen by the markets as indecision on the part of central bankers. Following the September meeting of the BIS, national authorities made an official announcement to the same effect, but again the lack of detail failed to impress the banking market that a true commitment to liquidity had been made. The markets perceived, quite rightly, that the political will necessary to create a true international lender of last resort was lacking. Something different was needed on the part of the central banks. In particular, public recognition was required that because of the events of 1974, 'national attitudes toward banking supervision and supervisory cooperation (had) changed abruptly' (Johnson and Adams, 1983, p.24).

Acknowledging that the revolutionary changes in the business of international finance had brought significant problems for national financial systems and hence national supervisory authorities, the central bank governors now sought to find a way to inspire confidence among market players in the ability of national authorities to provide a safe and stable international financial system. Therefore, in addition to their monthly meetings, in the fall of 1974 the central bank governors instituted a Standing Committee on Banking Regulations and Supervisory Practices within the BIS. This name would be simplified in 1989 to become the Basel Committee on Banking Supervision.

As in the handling of the Franklin crisis, the creation of the Basel Committee relied upon joint action by the US and Britain. Presumably because of London's status as the major centre for international financial activity, Governor Richardson of the Bank of England was the first to call for the creation of a standing committee to deal with international supervisory issues. The failure of international banks was an especially daunting prospect for the City, and thus for the Bank of England, and Richardson sought clearer rules on the assumption of regulatory responsibility for banks operating on foreign soil. Until this point, the main focus of the monthly meetings of the BIS had been monetary and economic policy; the events of 1974 demonstrated the need for detailed discussion and mutual understanding in the area of regulation and supervision.

The Richardson proposal of Fall 1974 was warmly received in both New York and Washington as international financial instability had already come to be seen as an issue of great importance in the Federal Reserve System. As Johnson and Adams (1983, p.25) point out, it was clear that 'the perceptions and techniques of banking regulation were not keeping pace with the integration and adaptations of the world's financial system. Supervisory techniques were primarily domestically oriented, and systems to oversee banks' international operations were not yet fully developed.'

In fact a Steering Committee on International Banking Regulation had recently been instituted in the Federal Reserve System under the chairmanship of Governor Mitchell. The support of the world's most important regulator made the passage of the Richardson proposal from theory to practice a rapid process.

## Make-up and Purpose of the Basel Committee

The Basel Committee on Banking Regulations and Supervisory Practices differs from the monthly meetings of the BIS in two main ways. First it is a standing committee, which allows for ongoing discussions and a permanent secretariat. The advantages of this facet lie in the Committee's ability to respond quickly to crises in the international banking system and in the benefits of regular contact between national regulatory officials. Second, the Committee is made up of officials from the G10 nations plus Luxembourg, Switzerland and Spain. Countries are represented by their central banks and by the leading bank regulatory and supervisory authorities where this function is not carried out by the central bank. For example, in the US the Federal Reserve plays both central bank and regulatory functions, with other governmental bodies sharing the regulatory burden. In Canada, however, the two functions are split between the Bank of Canada (the central bank) and the Office of the Superintendent of Financial Institutions (the banking system regulator).

Prior to the creation of the Basel Committee, there had existed no institutional mechanism by which the representatives of these agencies could maintain regular contact and communication. Although European Economic Community member states had begun cooperation in this field two years before through the *Groupe de Contact*, this association involved largely informal meetings between regulatory officials and had no institutional support. It did, however, provide a useful forum for exchange of views and information between European regulatory agencies. As mentioned above, before 1974 regulatory issues were not discussed even by those

BIS central banks bearing a regulatory function. The exchange of information and ideas between national regulators has been, and remains, a central goal of the Basel Committee.

The Committee officially operates through consensus, meaning that all members must sign on to any agreement. In reality, however, it might be fairer to say that concord rather than consensus is the guiding principle for negotiations. For, as will become apparent in the at several points in the analysis contained in this book, the history of the BCBS shows that the interests of its members are not always identical, nor is agreement always easy to find. Conflicts of interest, the use of power and even coercion have each played a key role in driving the Committee forward in its work.

The stated purpose of the Basel Committee has been to protect the health and stability of the international banking system. This it seeks to achieve in three main ways:

1.  by studying the international banking system, and developments in that system in the way of technology, innovation and national policies, and publishing papers on the Committee's findings;
2.  by maintaining surveillance of the international banking system and tracking problems as they develop;
3.  by negotiating agreements between member states to increase cooperation and harmonization between national regulators, as well as eliminate gaps in the supervision of international banking activities.

The first of these roles is made possible by the pooling of regulatory and supervisory expertise from the member states and by the existence of a professional and permanent secretariat, which is provided by the BIS. The free and ready exchange of information on national banking systems allows the Committee to build up a comprehensive picture of the international banking system. Publication of Committee research and deliberations provide a public good for banking regulators and supervisors throughout the system. The members' expertise and the existence of a permanent secretariat also facilitates the second role of the Committee, namely the surveillance of the system and the tracking of incipient problems.

The third role of the Committee is clearly more difficult and complex to carry out. International negotiations are rarely simple. The interests of domestic constituencies must be taken into account by each of the negotiating parties, often diverse interests between the parties must be accommodated, and the agreements must be accepted or ratified in each of the parties' home states. In the Basel Committee, however, these stringent requirements are made less exacting by the fact that agreements emanating from the Committee are not international treaties but merely agreements that have no legal force behind them. What's more, international banking regulation and supervision is an area that has attracted little public attention over the past sixty years and this lack of public interest makes the negotiating of international agreements significantly less tricky to achieve. Having said these things, the history of negotiations in the Committee shows that, while the Basel Committee's achievements have been considerable, attaining unanimous consent to a final document has sometimes been a long process. Part of the reason for this is the fact that unanimous consent is the only condition under which the Basel Committee can proceed. In practice this has meant that negotiated accords have had to sacrifice specificity in favour of agreement to broad principles.

It should be noted that an international lender of last resort function was rejected by the Basel Committee member states early on. This has limited the scope of both responsibilities and powers of the Committee, but it also made the Committee a more acceptable and accepted institution. To have adopted such a function would have been immensely problematic, as it would have meant either the duplication or replacement of existing LLR arrangements in member countries, and a level of supranational commitment that remains elusive today. An alternative scenario supposes that one Basel Committee member state act as the lender of last resort for the entire global banking system, in much the same way as Kindleberger (1986) described a stabilizer's duties. Little need be said about the dim prospects of such an offer from any of the states that possess major financial centres within their borders.

It is important to clarify the status and role of the Basel Committee. As an organ of the BIS, the Basel Committee reports to the governors of the central banks of the G10 countries, who in turn give their approval to major Committee initiatives. Because of the presence and participation of non-central bank banking authorities in the Committee, however, its reach and influence extend far beyond the circles of national central banks.

As with many international organisations, the Committee does not have any real supervisory control over national authorities. The conclusions drawn by the Committee do not carry any legal weight, nor was that ever the intention of the Committee's founders. Instead their vision of the organisation was for it to come up with broad supervisory standards, guidelines and recommendations that would be taken on by national authorities and applied in ways that were sensitive to national requirements. This means that the outcomes of Committee discussions and negotiations have by necessity been general and lacking in any great detail, although, as we shall see, the evolution of the Basel Committee has brought more and more detail as time has passed. This detail has come at a price as negotiations have become more and more controversial and disputed.

There are two other aspects of the Basel Committee's work that have grown out of its three main functions. First, the work of the Committee has served to spur national reform, even in the absence of negotiated agreements. By tracking developing problems in national banking systems that threaten to spread to the international level, by monitoring the health of the international system and by communicating concerns and information among its members, the Basel Committee has acted as a catalyst for change in national regulatory and supervisory practices.

The second additional aspect is that, by meeting on a regular basis, by sharing common concerns and goals, by spending time, both official and social, together, the national representatives who make up the Basel Committee have gone a long way towards developing a true international network for banking regulators. Moreover, this does not merely apply to members of the Committee. Regulators in non-member countries have been drawn into the Committee's work, accepting its agreements as standards for prudential supervision and regulation in their own banking systems. The Basel Committee now provides the yardstick for banking regulation standards across the globe, with developed and emerging markets alike looking to the committee for leadership in regulatory and supervisory issues.

The significance of this second point should not be missed. As private finance has become truly international over the past thirty years it has found ways to evade national regulatory and supervisory systems. The existence and work of the Basel Committee serve to rival that internationalism. This was not, of course, the motive behind the Committee's creation; rather, the original Richardson proposal emanated from a fear for London's financial stability in the aftermath of a major bank failure. However the Committee allows for a continuing learning process among regulators that, combined with an ever-increasing mutual trust, has vastly improved regulators' understanding and surveillance of the international banking marketplace. Indeed the Basel Committee has been examined from an epistemic community approach by Ethan Kapstein (1992), although the author himself recognizes that the applicability of such an approach to cooperation in banking regulation is as yet tenuous. As will be seen by the impressive list of Basel Committee achievements, international regulatory cooperation has benefited immensely from the Committee's work.

### The Significance of the Basel Committee

The formation of an international forum for the fostering of regulatory and supervisory cooperation in the form of the Basel Committee is undoubtedly the most important development in the regulation of international banking since the Bretton Woods system was created in 1944. The Committee embodies a realization on the part of national banking regulatory and supervisory authorities that, if private finance is to be allowed to continue to operate in a truly global manner, regulation and supervision must also become international in nature.

The end of the Bretton Woods system of organizing world finance is commonly taken to mark the beginning of an era in which the international market in financial services was left to national, rather than international, control. The formation of the Basel Committee on Banking Supervision in 1974, spurred by the crisis caused by the failure of Franklin National and Herstatt banks, however, marked the beginning of a concerted attempt on the part of authorities in the world's major national financial systems to meet the challenges posed by the internationalisation of private finance.

It is clear that the idea of an unfettered, unregulated international market in private finance suffered a severe blow with the banking crises of 1974. Though the general trend in the international political economy was towards freer markets and less state intervention, banking regulators across the G10 countries soon realized that purely national regulation and supervision was dangerously out of step with the increasingly international nature of the market in banking services. The purpose of the Committee and of its first major achievement were specifically to fill gaps in the international banking safety net by ensuring that no internationally operating bank escapes supervision. This realization occurred at the same time as a recognition that the old, 'gentleman's agreement' style of supervision, so prevalent in the UK banking system for example, was no longer an adequate defence against market failure.

The formation and work of the Basel Committee on Banking Supervision clearly demonstrates that the official rules governing the international market in banking services changed significantly after 1974. The first change was that regulation and supervision of banking was no longer merely a *national* concern. Though bearing no regulatory nor supervisory powers of its own, the Basel Committee has become a considerable force in the international banking system. Not only has the work of the Basel Committee brought about more consistent regulatory and supervisory standards across the G10 nations; its principles have been widely adopted in non-member states. The creation of broader regulatory and supervisory fora, such as the Offshore Banking Supervisors Group (to be discussed later in this book), improve the flow of information and regulatory techniques across the entire international banking system.

The mere existence of the Basel Committee points to an understanding, on the part of national regulators, of two elements integral to the behaviour of the market. The Committee's work is broadly focused on two main goals, namely the prevention of systemic crisis in the international banking market and the speedy resolution of such crises should they occur. The Committee was formed in response to a banking crisis that threatened the international bank system, a crisis that stemmed from instability, financial innovation and the internationalisation of banking. The recognition by regulators that the constant possibility of crisis is an integral characteristic of a truly global private financial marketplace, and the fact that they have attempted to develop methods of dealing with that possibility, demonstrates that regulatory authorities have learned much about the true nature of the international banking marketplace in the post-Bretton Woods world.

Both of these perceptions arose from a growing understanding that the business of private finance had changed fundamentally. Because the market in banking services was becoming truly global, problems in one national financial system could now be easily transferred to one, or many, other national systems. In much the way that Polanyi (1957) described the attempts by states to mediate the effects of the growth of market capitalism in the eighteenth and nineteenth centuries, national regulatory authorities became aware that a new approach to controlling the market must be adopted if financial, and then economic and social, crises were to be avoided.

Unlike the attempts by states to resist the growth of the market in former times and former economic systems, however, when the measures that society took to protect itself 'impaired the self-regulation of the market' (Polanyi, 1957, p.3), the cooperative attempts that the Basel member countries were to take in the 1970s, 80s, 90s and beyond sought to work with the grain of the market rather than against it. The role of regulation has become one of 'dampening the market's exuberance...to avoid excesses in both peaks and troughs of the economic cycle' (Wood, 1996, p.214). This in itself shows the primacy that the idea of the market had acquired across the G10 nations by this period. Nonetheless, the Committee has maintained a commitment to studying the market in banking services and has thus built up a body of knowledge about the workings of international finance, through the exchange of information and ideas among regulators, that greatly facilitates the tracking of, and finding of solutions to, problems in that market.

It would be of minimal interest (or utility) to remark that the make-up of authority in the international banking system has been changed by the creation of the Basel Committee. Clearly the institution represents a new locus for the exercise of authority over the market. However it is of more interest is to note that the creation and work of the Committee display the national sources of that authority in the international system. The founding of the Committee in 1974 was inspired by the concerns of the regulatory and supervisory authorities in the UK, but support from banking authorities in the United States greatly speeded international acceptance of the British proposal.

Johnson and Adams (1983, p.26) stress the importance of the human side of the Basel Committee's activities. 'The fostering of close, personal contacts between supervisors was to prove to be an important service of the Committee, since this permitted, *inter alia*, more rapid and effective cooperation when banking problems crossed national jurisdictions.' But the key point to consider here is that, through personal and official interaction since 1974, the representatives of banking authority have developed new institutional means of tempering the disruptive effects of the internationalisation of private finance.

Echoing this view, Spero (1980, p.164) has quoted George Blunden, chairman of the Committee from 1974-1977, who stated that within the BCBS there has evolved 'among ourselves such a degree of personal contact and trust that we can help to forestall troubles in the international system by working closely together'. However, while the ongoing contact between supervisors has been a key element in the *modus operandi* of the Committee, it has not always been smooth sailing. As will be shown in later chapters, conflict and tensions between regulatory authorities have been ever-present features in the Committee's negotiations.

It should be remembered that it was crises developing from the internationalisation of banking that spurred the founding of the Committee. The Herstatt/Franklin National crises demonstrated to regulatory authorities the possibility of a systemic disruption that would affect not merely banking business and the foreign exchange markets, but might bring about the interruption of international payments and a contraction in global liquidity and trade. What's more, this crisis can be seen to have been integrally linked to the instability of foreign exchange markets that followed the demise of the Bretton Woods system of organising world finance. The removal of international authority over financial markets had shown itself to have unacceptable consequences for the stability of the international banking system.

**Conclusion**

The Basel Committee should be seen as an attempt on the part of authority to match developments in the market, a market that had been freed by the gradual removal of controls over the international flow of private capital. To use Cohen's words (1986, p.303), the Basel Committee's purpose 'was to restore some of the authority of politics in its ongoing dialectic with markets. The jurisdiction of states, it was felt, must catch up with the domain of the market.' This concept, that public authorities are caught in a perpetual game of 'catch up' with the private sector is an important limitation on the ability of supervisors to maintain a strong grip on banking activities that threaten the overall stability of the market.

The creation of the Basel Committee was made necessary by the failings and the failure of Bretton Woods. As private banking became more international and escaped the restrictions imposed under the Bretton Woods system, national authorities increasingly found themselves unable to supervise banking activities. The creation of the BCBS marked an important first step towards filling the gap left by that failure. Though less powerful, less stringent and less catholic in its purpose and means, the Basel Committee has served as a substitute for the national control of finance as envisaged in the original Bretton Woods settlement.

# Chapter 3

# The Basel Concordat and the Consolidation of Banking Supervision

In its first few years of existence the Basel Committee made solid advances in enhancing regulatory cooperation among the banking authorities of its member countries. In addition to the less tangible elements of increased trust and friendship between national regulators (though these elements are, without doubt, of great importance), the Committee was able to codify that cooperation through numerous negotiated agreements.

Most important of these was the creation and revision of an agreement governing regulatory responsibility for banks operating on foreign soil. The Basel Concordat of December 1975 concerned the supervision of international banking groups and their foreign establishments and was aimed at filling the gaps created in the supervision of banking by the new international activities of private banks. These gaps had been made painfully clear during the crises of 1974 and national supervisory authorities recognised that individual efforts and ad hoc cooperation alone would not be enough to counter the challenges presented by the new realities of the international banking system.

## Background to the Concordat

The rapid internationalisation of banking, that had been underway since the 1960s, had clearly brought with it a range of new issues and challenges to banking supervisors. Bank failures in one country could now cause financial and economic problems in one or more others; for the first time since the 1930s financial contagion had become a real and present threat to the stability of the international system.

During the financial turmoil of 1974 ad hoc cooperation based in strong personal relations between central bank governors had been enough to avert a major international liquidity crisis. There was, however, a strong feeling among central bankers in the world's major financial powers that it was only a matter of time before international banking, if left untamed, would create a crisis that ad hoc cooperation would be unable to contain.

Policy-makers were now faced with the need to take measures to prevent a recurrence of such problems. The option of re-regulation through a return to post-war Bretton Woods-style capital controls was unfeasible due to the influence of banks and bankers in the political systems of the dominant financial powers, and because of the economic weight that international financial activity had come to hold in countries such as the UK and USA. Equally improbable was the second option, that of the creation of an international lender of last resort. While the International Monetary Fund existed to provide financing to governments facing balance of payments crises, the idea of an internationally mandated organisation that would use funds from, say US tax payers, to rescue French banks in crisis was quite unthinkable. Though the BIS stated that it was willing to play such a role, the markets quickly perceived that the political will necessary to make such an option work was missing. An alternative, less costly and less risky option was needed. The Basel Committee itself represented part of the answer. An institution with little real power, no autonomy, and no financial obligation, the BCBS seemed a poor substitute for real action. Nonetheless, the Committee provided a space for action and in time would become a significant institution, offering credible policy options to improve the international banking system.

Within this framework, what was needed was action to overcome the weaknesses of the international banking system caused by the disjuncture between existence of international markets and that of purely national supervisors. While a banking authority could oversee the operations of a bank within its national borders, the bank's overseas activities might escape supervision unless an international accord was reached to fully delineate supervisory responsibility.

What was clearly needed was an international agreement that would define which authorities were responsible for overseeing international banks, so that internationalised banking structures would not be left unsupervised. In addition, work was needed to ensure better quality information sharing between national authorities so that emerging problems in international banks could be swiftly addressed by all supervisors concerned. In essence an accord was needed that not only recognised, but more importantly provided a response to, the fact that banking structures had changed fundamentally and now posed severe problems for national authorities.

**The Concordat**

Thus the first issue to which the Basel Committee turned its attention after its creation was ensuring that all international banks and their activities received adequate oversight. A major issue in the new international banking system was responsibility for banks' foreign activities. Should the authorities in a bank's parent country also supervise that bank's operations internationally, or should the host country in which the bank is operating be held responsible? This conundrum, it was felt, left the system vulnerable as it was entirely possible for international banks to escape supervision.

Between 1974 and 1975 the Basel members negotiated an agreement that would specify supervisory responsibility for internationally active banks and create mechanisms to facilitate the sharing of information about the activities and status of such private actors. This had to be done in the context of internationalised finance, while at the same time recognising the sensitive nature of bank information. Many countries still have bank secrecy laws that limit the amount and nature of information that authorities can share with each other.

The result of the negotiations was the 1975 Basel Concordat. The Concordat outlines who is responsible for overseeing internationally active banks. Although the language of the Concordat seems to suggest that the parent country should generally be considered as the *ultimate* responsible supervisory authority, it recognises that the parent authority cannot be expected to oversee all the activities of international banks. The Concordat thus determines *joint responsibility* between parent and host countries for the supervision of a bank's international operation, the host country supervising the bank's foreign branch activities with the parent country supervising the liquidity of the bank's organization as a whole. Central to the Concordat was a spirit of cooperation to ensure that authorities would help each other in the task of closing supervisory gaps. The Basel Concordat of 1975 is short on details but it embodied a solid attempt by regulators to define regulatory and supervisory responsibilities and to reduce the scope for regulatory arbitrage by banks. For in the event that the host country authorities perceive that regulation and supervision of the banking organization by the parent country authority is inadequate, they may, of course, prohibit the establishment of a branch of that bank in the country. If the parent country regulators consider the supervisory system in the host country to be too lax, they have a responsibility to extend supervision to those foreign branches or even deter the banking organization from establishing branches in such countries.

There are five main areas of banking supervisory cooperation to which the Basel Concordat speaks. They are:

1. The supervision of foreign banking establishments should be the joint responsibility of host and parent banking authorities.
2. No foreign banking establishment should escape supervision.
3. The supervision of liquidity should be the primary responsibility of host country authorities.
4. The supervision of solvency of foreign branches should be primarily the responsibility of the parent country authorities.
5. The purposes of the Concordat and the Committee would be furthered by improved information flows between national authorities and by host countries allowing branch inspections by parent country authorities.

The codification of these guidelines into a document to which all Basel Committee members subscribe was an essential move towards formalising and institutionalising relations between banking supervisors, rather than just relying on the informal, friendly state of affairs that had marked their relations previously. The Basel Concordat represented the first step in a process leading towards the harmonization of banking supervision, a process that matches the internationalisation of the market in banking services. The Basel Concordat, according to Coulbeck (1984, p.81), puts pressure on banks that are not adequately regulated; the principles contained in the Concordat represent:

> an attempt to coordinate national regulations, and to provide for the fact that the quality of regulation varies between different financial systems. They effectively

exclude poorly-regulated parent banks and their authorities from the world banking scene.

The vague nature of the Concordat has been identified in some quarters to be a failing of the agreement. Indeed Kapstein (1989, p.330) urges that it be seen not as a regime for bank supervision, but more as a 'gentleman's agreement'. However the Concordat should be seen as a product of 'the politics of the possible', a phenomenon that guides all Basel Committee business. This is because voting in the Committee must be unanimous for an agreement to be passed and accords emanating from the Committee tend to be broad and general, rather than specific and detailed. Coulbeck (1984, p.82) claims that, despite the vague nature of the Concordat, in the late 1970s and early 1980s this 'approach has nevertheless been successful in averting crises in the markets'. What is equally important, however, is the intent of such agreements as the Concordat and the spirit of cooperation that they embody. By providing a forum for cooperation between national regulators, the Basel Committee has fostered the exchange of ideas and information; by providing guidelines for the supervision of international banking groups and their cross-border establishments, the Basel Concordat closed some of the widest gaps in the international supervisory net that were wrought by the internationalisation of banking.

At the same time, by attempting to institutionalise relations between banking authorities and to formalise the allocation of supervisory responsibility, the Concordat inevitably raised tensions between authorities when banks failed. Conflict would be unavoidable in situations where national authorities tried to protect national and particular interests at the expense of their international obligations, a problem highlighted in later years during the BCCI scandal (see below).

## The 1983 Revision

The Concordat was substantially modified in 1983, when the notion of 'consolidated supervision', accepted the year before as a guiding principle by Committee members, was incorporated into the document. The consolidation of banking supervision necessitates that an international banking group's overall business affairs be monitored, both in its home and foreign locations or, in the words of the 1983 revision itself:

> Banking supervisory authorities cannot be fully satisfied about the soundness of individual banks unless they can examine the totality of each bank's business worldwide through the technique of consolidation. (BCBS, 1983)

Calling for 'an appropriate allocation of responsibilities between parent and host authorities' the 1983 revision emphasised the need for 'contact and cooperation' between them. Indeed the report stated that 'effective cooperation between host and parent authorities is a central prerequisite for the supervision of banks' international operations'. It reiterated two basic principles to guide consolidated supervision:

1.   that no foreign banking establishment should escape supervision; and,
2.   that the supervision should be adequate.

The 1983 revision was seen as necessary because the Basel supervisors discovered the difficulties in the division of responsibilities between parent and host country supervisors. If the parent authority supervises a bank's activities in one country, and the host authority in another, it is entirely possible for each of them to miss potential risks that can only be seen when the totality of the bank's activities are examined. In particular, the BCBS was concerned about the limited capacity of some host authorities to conduct adequate supervision. As the report (BCBS, 1983) pointed out:

> While there should be a presumption that host authorities are in a position to fulfil their supervisory obligations adequately with respect to all foreign bank establishments operating in their territories, this may not always be the case.

The internationalisation of banking, of course, had brought G10 banks and their supervisors into contact with the authorities of non-G10 countries. Many of these, in particular in offshore banking centres, had proved themselves to be less than competent in their handling of the important tasks of supervising foreign banks. This is one of the main reasons why consolidated supervision had become so important. By placing extra emphasis on the capacities of the parent country banking authorities, the 1983 revision attempted to place supervisory responsibility firmly in the hands of authorities in the largest national financial systems.

> The principle of consolidated supervision is that parent banks and parent supervisory authorities monitor the risk exposure – including a perspective of concentrations of risk and of the quality of assets – of the banks or banking groups for which they are responsible, as well as the adequacy of their capital, on the basis of the totality of their business wherever conducted. This principle does not imply any lessening of host authorities' responsibilities for supervising foreign bank establishments that operate in their territories, although it is recognised that the full implementation of the consolidation principle may well lead to some extension of parental responsibility. (BCBS, 1983)

Consolidated supervision thus comes close to an extra-territorial extension of the capacities of supervisory authorities in the world's most important banking countries. It requires active and ongoing cooperation between authorities in Basel member and non-member countries. Relations with authorities in non-G10 countries was to become a priority for the Committee in the mid-1980s.

*Information flows and the Concordat*

The 1983 revision of the Concordat identified a key challenge in the implementation of consolidated supervision, namely the effective exchange of information between supervisory authorities. The mere existence of the BCBS had greatly helped mutual understanding and the exchange of pertinent information between the G10 banking authorities, but more formal standards were needed. A greater challenge was posed by the growing interaction between the G10 authorities and their counterparts in offshore banking centres, where adequate supervisory resources are rare, and sufficiently well-trained staff are at a premium. Furthermore, secrecy and cover from the gaze of other banking authorities are often seen as part of the competitive advantage of offshore banking centres, making it less likely that they will share information.

By the end of the decade it had become clear that the lack of adequate information flows posed a very real challenge to the effectiveness of the principles embodied in the Concordat. In order to strengthen access to information, and to formalise the process of consultation and cooperation between supervisors, in 1990 the BCBS emitted a supplement to the 1983 version of the Concordat. This supplement stemmed from collaboration with the Offshore Group of Banking Supervisors (OGBS) that had resulted in a paper discussed at the fourth International Conference of Banking Supervisors in October 1986. The consultative paper was circulated to supervisory authorities the following year for feedback and in 1990 the Committee published the supplement.

The expressed goal of the supplement was to 'extend and supplement the principles of the banking supervisors' Concordat of 1983 with some guidance of a more practical nature'. This guidance was intended to 'encourage more regular and structured collaboration between supervisors, with a view to improving the quality and completeness of the supervision of cross-border banking'. As such, the supplement focused on five key areas, setting forth a number of recommendations for supervisory collaboration in each:

1.  The authorisation procedure.
2.  The information needs of parent authorities.
3.  The information needs of host authorities.
4.  The removal of secrecy constraints.
5.  The importance of external auditing.

The 1990 supplement was an important step in the direction of formalising the nature of the Committee's work. By putting more 'meat' on the 'bones' of the Concordat, the BCBS was not only improving its contribution to closing the gaps in the international supervisory net, it was moving towards a qualitative change in its own modus operandi; whereas the earlier versions of the Concordat were vague and lacking in detail, the Committee now found reason to concentrate more on practical issues than merely abstract notions of regulation and supervision.

This aspect of the Committee's work not only contributed to the project of ensuring that internationally active banks do not escape supervision. Just as importantly, it pointed to the growing status of the BCBS as an organ of global governance. By extending its reach, the Committee was increasingly affecting the business of supervision outside the G10 and the rest of the developed world.

## BCCI and the Setting of Minimum Standards for International Banking Supervision

Unfortunately for the BCBS, and for the international banking system, the 1990 supplement came too late to stop a huge banking scandal from erupting in the summer of 1991. The same gaps in the international banking supervisory net that the Concordat had been intended to close allowed a multinational bank operating in 73 countries to engage in a variety of financial crimes such as money laundering, rogue trading, fraudulent record-keeping and evading bank ownership regulations. Very quickly the BCBS would be called upon to update and formalise even further its guidelines for banking supervisory collaboration.

### The Bank of Credit and Commerce International

In 1972 a Pakistani banker, Agha Hasan Abedi, set up the Bank of Credit and Commerce International (BCCI) with backing from Arab business interests. The bank was registered in Luxembourg but managed its business out of London and the Cayman Islands. In addition to these countries, BCCI conducted financial dealings in 70 other financial jurisdictions. It proved to be a perfect example of the challenges posed to national supervisory authorities by the international banking system in the post-Bretton Woods world.

The management structure of the bank was incredibly complex and served to confound banking regulators and supervisors across the world. The web-like design of the company was designed to frustrate investigation and oversight by national banking authorities. As a December 1992 report to the Committee on Foreign Relations of the United States Senate described:

> Unlike any ordinary bank, BCCI was from its earliest days made up of multiplying layers of entities, related to one another through an impenetrable series of holding companies, affiliates, subsidiaries, banks-within-banks, insider dealings and nominee relationships. By fracturing corporate structure, record keeping, regulatory review, and audits, the complex BCCI family of entities created by Abedi was able to evade ordinary legal restrictions on the movement of capital and goods as a matter of daily practice and routine.

Thus the bank was able to avoid close scrutiny as it was never under the sole jurisdiction of a single authority. Thanks to such evasive tactics, BCCI undertook the task of building a criminal financial empire in which it dealt with corrupt politicians, dictators and drug dealers. Money deposited in the bank by investors from many countries was used to fund criminal activities, to lend to the organisers of prostitution, terrorism and smuggling, and to bribe officials and politicians around the world.

Regulatory authorities in several countries became uneasy about the nature of BCCI's activities as early as 1983 but, due to the bank's complex structure, its control of key public officials and the lack of formalised mechanisms for international supervisory cooperation and information exchange, substantive action was only taken against the bank in 1988. The CIA had become involved in investigating the bank's activities in the mid-1980s due to its links to drugs, terrorism and money-laundering, but lack of communication between it and banking supervisory agencies in the US and elsewhere delayed intervention. More problematic for the BCBS and for the reputation of the Concordat, the Bank of England was apparently aware of a number of BCCI's criminal activities and withheld that information from its fellow authorities in the Committee.

In 1988 the US Customs Service arrested a number of high-ranking BCCI officials on the charge of money-laundering. In 1989 the Bank of England became aware of BCCI's connection to terrorism and money-laundering but, rather than close the bank, chose only to undertake additional supervision of the firm. Early in 1990 the Bank of England was informed by BCCI's accounting firm, Price Waterhouse, that the bank had losses amounting to billions of dollars which had been covered up through illegal accounting practices. Again the Bank of England chose not to seize control of the bank. This time the central bank entered into negotiations with BCCI, the government of Abu Dhabi (the home country of the bank's owners), and the bank's accountants to prevent the bank's collapse. The government of Abu Dhabi guaranteed the bank's losses while Price Waterhouse certified the bank's accounts. For its part, the Bank of England worked to prevent public knowledge of the bank's many problems.

In April 1990 the Bank of England permitted BCCI to move its headquarters, and thus its officials and records, from the UK to Abu Dhabi. In fact the bank was restructured as three separate entities, further complicating consolidated supervision of its activities. At the same time the British central bank decided to withhold important information on BCCI's US operations from its counterparts in the Federal Reserve when it was requested. These two actions together constituted a cover-up of the bank's illegal activities and implicated the Bank of England in the scandal.

On July 29 1990, only months after the publication of the 1990 Supplement to the Basel Concordat, the BCCI officials arrested in the US were convicted of money laundering. Over the next 12 months banking authorities around the world undertook a thorough investigation of the bank's operations. On July 5 1991, regulators in the Cayman Islands, France, Luxembourg, Spain, Switzerland, the UK and the US seized control of the branch offices of BCCI and the extent of the bank's criminal and fraudulent activities began to emerge (Adams and Frantz, 1993).

Investigators discovered that, although the bank's management and owners had been siphoning off funds for years, the bank itself had never made a profit during its entire 19 year life. By making unsecured loans to risky and often unsavoury individuals and corporations, the bank had lost billions of dollars, losses that were covered up through false accounting and the illegal use of monies placed in the bank by hundreds of thousands of small depositors. Losses from the bank amounted to between 10 and 17 billion dollars.

Legal action stemming from the BCCI affair continued throughout the subsequent decade, with law suits against the bank's owners and against the government of Abu Dhabi. Depositors were partially repaid their savings through various contributions made by BCCI, Abu Dhabi and the bank's Middle Eastern financiers. Indeed the effects of the scandal are still being felt today as, in March 2001, the liquidators of BCCI entered into legal action against the Bank of England for failing in its regulatory duties, asking for up to one billion pounds in compensation (Tait, 2003).

*The BCCI Scandal and the Concordat*

Clearly, a central and very important player in the Basel Committee, the Bank of England, had intentionally and willingly abrogated the spirit and letter of the Concordat. This was doubly troublesome for the Committee and the Concordat as the main challenges to the Concordat prior to the BCCI affair had been thought to come from interactions with non-BCBS members. Instead, in this the largest banking scandal in history, a founding member of the Committee, a central bank with a proud history of cooperation with fellow authorities in the US and other countries, had hidden pertinent information from its counterparts and allowed a scandal to develop while at the same time jeopardising the soundness of the international banking system and the savings of over a million depositors.

Political uproar concerning the scandal erupted in several countries, not least in the United States. There politicians called for a comprehensive explanation of how such a scandal could occur under the very noses of US regulators, and why the Bank of England had so obviously kept important information hidden from the Federal Reserve. A recurring theme of the US Senate report into the BCCI affair is the failure of US agencies to coordinate their actions; the most damaging issue in the development of the scandal, however, had been the lack of international supervisory cooperation and coordination. Nonetheless, the report did take pains to stress that:

> the rise and fall of BCCI is not an isolated phenomenon, but a recurrent problem that has grown along with the growth in the international financial community itself…the opportunities for fraud are huge, the rewards great, and the systems put in place to protect against them, far from adequate. (US Senate, 1992)

Moreover, the same report pointed out that the world had become vulnerable 'to international crime on a global scope that is beyond the current ability of governments to control'. To counter this, the Senate sub-committee in charge of the report called for the United States:

> to exercise far more leadership in helping develop a system for monitoring and regulating the movement of funds across international borders to replace the current, inadequate, patchwork system that BCCI, with all of its faults, so aptly took advantage of to defraud over one million depositors and thousands of creditors from countries all over the world. (US Senate, 1992)

Although efforts against international financial crime would develop on a number of fronts, the Basel Committee reacted quickly to the political storm by revising the principles and mechanisms of the Concordat. In July of 1992 the Committee took the notion of the Concordat one, highly significant, step further by formulating a set of minimum standards for cross-border banking supervision. The document, titled *Minimum Standards for the Supervision of International Banking*

*Groups and their Cross-Border Establishments*, made no explicit reference to the BCCI scandal, choosing instead to talk of 'recent developments'. It reviewed not only the Concordat of 1975 and 1983, but also the Supplement of 1990. The document recognised that:

> While the principles of the Concordat and its supplement are still viewed as being sound, members of the Committee now recognise that there needs to be a greater effort to ensure that these principles can be applied in practice. Accordingly certain of these principles have been reformulated as minimum standards, set out below, which G10 supervisory authorities expect each other to observe. (BCBS, 1992)

The importance of these standards was made clear by this last phrase. Not only were they minimum standards for supervision, they were given the quasi-status of prerequisites for membership in the supervisors' group. The phrase clearly reflected tension between the US and the UK over the failings of the Bank of England during the BCCI affair. Other sections of the document manifested these tensions, as the minimum standards referred only to the process of supervision and not to the practice of information flows between supervisors. Whether this was a consequence of a recognition of the difficulties faced by supervisors in overcoming secrecy and confidentiality requirements, or whether it marked a failure of the Committee to secure agreement between key participants in the face of the BCCI scandal is unclear, with the Committee merely stating that it had concluded:

> that the nature and extent of information-sharing possible amongst supervisory authorities must continue to be determined on a case-by-case basis and cannot, at this time, be usefully expressed in minimum standards. Nevertheless, consistent with the April 1990 Supplement, the Committee believes that supervisory authorities should undertake an affirmative commitment to cooperate, on a best-efforts basis, with supervisory authorities from other countries on all prudential matters pertaining to international banks, and, in particular, in respect of the investigation of documented allegations of fraud, criminal activity, or violations of bank laws. In addition, both the Committee and its members will continue their efforts to reduce impediments to the sharing of information among supervisory authorities. (BCBS, 1992)

With this final, very vague commitment to 'try harder next time' the Committee implicitly recognised its limited ability to influence members to share information and this significantly weakened the overall contribution of the 1992 report.

Nonetheless, as has been seen throughout its existence, the Committee was once again practicing the politics of the possible. Though unable to make concrete and formalised advances in the area of information flows, it was able to establish standards by which supervisory authorities could assess their relations with their counterparts in other member and non-member states and which, in theory, would contribute to the elimination of existing gaps in international supervision and to the furtherance of the principle of consolidated supervision.

According to the report, a central principle for all host authorities in deciding whether or not to allow a foreign bank to conduct business within its jurisdiction must be to 'determine whether that bank or banking group's home country supervisory authority has the necessary capabilities to meet these minimum standards'. This placed increased responsibility on host authorities to monitor supervisory developments and practices in other states and to adjust their treatment of foreign banks accordingly. What had now developed was a process of mutual verification.

The four minimum standards laid out by the report addressed the rights of both home and host country authorities and the prerequisites for authorising foreign bank establishments:

1.  All international banking groups and international banks should be supervised by a home country authority that capably performs consolidated supervision.
2.  The creation of a cross-border banking establishment should receive the prior consent of both the host country supervisory authority and the bank's and, if different, banking group's home country supervisory authority.
3.  Supervisory authorities should possess the right to gather information from the cross-border banking establishments of the banks or banking groups for which they are the home supervisor.
4.  If a host country authority determines that any one of the foregoing minimum standards is not met to its satisfaction, that authority could impose restrictive measures necessary to satisfy its prudential concerns consistent with these minimum standards, including the prohibition of the creation of banking establishments.

The report reflected the incredibly complex nature of international banking in the 1990s, as exemplified so perilously in the BCCI affair. Not only did supervisory authorities need to examine the activities of a particular bank, but also of its subsidiaries and branches in other countries, as well as those of its holding company. The BCCI scandal had made it clear that national authorities had once again fallen far behind the market in terms of their ability to grasp the big picture of banking activity.

Another area of the report foreshadowed an area of future concern and action for the BCBS. For, in discussing the implications of cross-border banking for supervision, it recognised that 'the business activities of major international banking groups increasingly cut across traditional supervisory categories'. Though not explicitly calling for it, this phrase brings to mind the need for increased coordination between supervisory authorities in banking and in other areas of financial activity. The Joint Forum, dealt with in the sixth chapter of this book, was an effort by the BCBS to address exactly this kind of issue in the international financial system.

## Managing the Reality of Cross-Border Banking Supervision

As might be expected, the mere setting of minimum standards by the Committee was not enough to resolve the problems facing international banking supervision. In the years after the 1992 report, the Committee examined the challenges of implementing the standards. In order to do so effectively, the BCBS decided to work closely with regional supervisors groups, in particular the Offshore Group of Banking Supervisors.

*Regional Supervisors' Groups and the BCBS*

During the late 1970s and early years of the following decade, the Basel Committee began to spread this cooperative spirit beyond membership of the BIS and OECD during this period. In 1979 the Committee organized an international conference for banking supervisory and regulatory authorities, held in the UK, an event that was repeated in 1981 and 1984, in the US and Italy respectively. Furthermore, and perhaps with more significance for the long-term development of international supervisory cooperation, the Committee sponsored the creation of an Offshore Group of Banking Supervisors in 1980. This group, which meets annually, has acquired a special importance in the governance of global banking as it affords the BCBS the opportunity to interact with and influence supervisory authorities from key non-G10 economies. The organization has accepted the principles of the Basel Concordat, which has ensured the extension of the agreements coverage to the most important offshore financial centres.

In addition, the Committee maintains close links with regional banking supervisory groups from North America, Latin American and the Caribbean, Africa, central and eastern Europe, central Asia and Transcaucasia, the Arab states, south Asia, South-East Asia and Australasia. Neither these, nor the Offshore Group, have been as active as the Basel Committee, yet the significance of their existence cannot be denied for, in collaboration with the Committee they have allowed for the creation of a truly global network of banking supervisors, with the BCBS acting as the hub.

*Implementing the Minimum Standards*

In June of 1996 a report on the challenges of implementing the standards proposed by the 1992 document was presented by a working group consisting of members of the BCBS and the OGBS at the Ninth International Conference of Banking Supervisors. The group had been set up in late 1994 to discover what impediments existed to the implementation of minimum standards in banking supervision and to recommend solutions to those impediments. In October of the same year the BCBS published the report as an official Committee document.

The timing of this new updating project coincided with the onset of new financial crises in the world economy, which were to shake up both the BIS and the BCBS and their position in global economic governance. These changes are discussed in greater detail in chapter six, but it should be noted here that Mexico's peso crisis and its pursuant banking crisis emphasised the necessity of the Committee collaborating with supervisors from offshore banking centres and from other developing economies.

Other issues of central importance during the mid-1990s were the continuing fight against money-laundering and international financial crime and, of course, the shock of the Barings bank crisis. In February 1995, headlines in newspapers around the globe told of how one, young banking trader named Nick Leeson had brought one of the world's oldest, most traditional banks to its financial knees. Barings, a 233 year old bank which had been named Europe's sixth great power in 1818 and had survived a huge 1890 default on loans to Argentina, collapsed on February 26th 1995 due to the actions of a 28-year-old rogue trader who had engaged in unauthorized derivatives dealings. In roughly two months, Leeson had exposed Barings to approximately $27 billion in futures contracts of various kinds, and the final tally of the bank's losses began at $1 billion.

Now the Barings collapse did not pose a threat to the integrity of the global banking and financial system. As *The Economist* (1995a, p.19) put it at the time, Barings, 'with £5.9 billion of assets at the end of 1993...is an international tiddler'. But the speed with which the bank's demise was brought about illustrated how turbulent the market in international finance can be, even for a bank with the tradition and history of Barings. The incident also made abundantly clear how fundamentally complex and varied the banking business had become, in terms of geography and the instruments involved.

By the middle of the decade it seemed as though every few months a new banking supervisory failure came to light, reflecting the inadequacies of the international supervisory net. Moreover, given the greatly increased levels of financial interdependence by the mid-1990s, the risk of financial contagion made banking supervisory failures a sensitive topic of international and domestic politics. The project of international financial reform that occurred in the latter part of the 1990s, discussed in more detail in chapter six, made the issue of cross-border banking even more pressing.

The report that came out of the BCBS-OGBS working group was titled *The Supervision of Cross-Border Banking* (BCBS, 1996) and recognised that significant obstacles continued to prevent the adequate implementation of minimum standards. It discovered two main categories of problems concerning the existence of obstacles to:

1. Information access.
2. Effective home and host supervision in three areas:
   a. lack of common standards to determine effective consolidated supervision
   b. lack of a mechanism to assess standards of supervision
   c. gaps in supervision represented by shell-branches, etc.

The report then went on to make a large number of recommendations for improving the supervision of cross-border banking. While it is unnecessary to outline all of these recommendations and conclusions here, it is worthwhile identifying the most important lines of argument.

First, a recurring interest in balancing the need for information exchange between supervisors with the interests of banking confidentiality and national bank secrecy laws can be detected. This task became especially complex in the face of negotiating with offshore banking supervisors whose governments had designed bank secrecy and confidentiality laws with the express purpose of attracting bank business. The 1996 report encourages host supervisors to press for reform to bank secrecy laws and to cooperate with home supervisors to the greatest extent possible, noting that in many cases information can be exchanged without violating confidentiality.

Second, the importance of allowing home country supervisors access to banks in host countries was emphasised. While information exchange between supervisory authorities can assist greatly in ensuring that banks do not escape effective supervision, consolidated supervision cannot effectively be managed without home supervisor access to the bank's operations in the host country.

Third, in order to improve the quality of host country supervision in offshore banking centres, the OGBS decided to condition membership in its organisation on the authority's agreement to independent assessment of its supervisory methods and standards. In fact the OGBS called for the Basel Committee secretariat to act as an independent observer in this process, a task which the BCBS declined to accept 'because of the moral hazard involved in appearing to give a 'seal of approval'' (BCBS, 1996).

The direct involvement by the Committee in the assessment of offshore banking supervision, and the refusal of the Committee to take on such a task, is a prime example of the internal culture of the BCBS. While occupying a central position in the governance of global banking, the Committee's members have consistently refused to authorise a drastic expansion in its responsibilities. While it could be argued that this is a lamentable lack of political will on the part of the Committee's members, it does reflect the concern of the BCBS to limit its functions rather than risk over-extending itself.

The final issue that merits attention here is the issue of remaining impediments to the international supervision of banking. In this area the report marks out 'shell branches', parallel-owned banks, and parent institutions incorporated in under-regulated financial centres for special attention. After the September 11th 2001 terrorist attacks on the United States, and the subsequent war on terrorism, the links between shell banks and terrorist financing propelled action by the Committee. These areas of investigation were to result in two reports, both published in January 2003 (BCBS 2003a; BCBS 2003b), that acknowledged the challenges posed by shell banks and parallel-owned banks for consolidated supervision and included a number of policy suggestions for supervisors. In general the Committee recommended the non-authorisation of shell banks and parallel-owned banks, but recognised the difficulties of closing existing institutions. To overcome this, the Committee suggested giving shell banks a period of less than a year to establish 'a meaningful mind and management' in the jurisdiction of the authority concerned, 'after which time their licences should be withdrawn if they have not complied'.

Although parallel-owned banks did not have the same connection with terrorist financing, it was clear to the Committee that they did pose a significant threat to effective consolidated supervision. For, although two banks owned by the same person or group may not be officially linked, they may increase concentration risk by providing each other with concessional financing, shifting low-risk assets between them and artificially generating capital. To counter the threats posed by parallel-owned banks, the BCBS emitted four guiding principles for supervisors:

1. Close cooperation between supervisors to gain access to information necessary for consolidated supervision.
2. The setting of a lead supervisor who would have access to foreign parallel-owned banks.
3. Imposing restructuring on the bank to facilitate more effective supervision.

4. Ring-fencing a parallel-owned bank to limit 'the exposure of the domestic bank to its related parallel banks and other members of the corporate group'.

## The Significance of the Concordat

Clearly the Concordat in its many incarnations has been an attempt by the G10 supervisors to match the internationalisation of banking by formalising the exchange of information and the responsibility for supervising international banks. By aiming to fill the gaps in the international supervisory net, the BCBS sought to ensure the soundness and stability of the international banking system without the creation of new regulations or restrictions on bank activity. Essentially the Concordat signified the extension of national supervisory methods to the international arena.

In addition to matching the internationalisation of banking, the Concordat has been highly responsive to other relevant developments in the banking industry, particularly those involving illegal behaviour by banks. It has also been modified to respond to its own weaknesses and as a consequence of the failures of BCBS members to act in the spirit of the agreement. This self renewal is an impressive element of the regime.

Notwithstanding the success of the Basel Concordat, its history does show another, less palatable though probably unavoidable, element of the regulation and supervision of banking. The Concordat was formulated and reformulated in response to crises (the 1974 banking failures and the BCCI scandal) that, though they could certainly recur, had already happened. Because of the speed of innovation in private international finance, banking authorities remain condemned to a largely responsive, reactive role. Regulation lags behind the market and generally deals only with established banking practices. Against the daunting speed of financial innovation, regulation has few defences.

This is not to say that these international agreements are without worth, for they have surely helped in preventing further crises in these areas. But it is for this reason that the renewed emphasis on supervision rather than regulation is so important. Supervision is an ongoing, interactive process that aims at keeping authorities abreast of market developments. The Concordat expands this goal from the national to the international arena.

## Conclusion

The evolution of the Basel Concordat has been a process in which the BCBS has, in a consciously limited way, attempted to fill gaps in the international banking supervisory net so that crises can be avoided. The process has been one of trial and error, of learning by the Committee and of reacting to new developments in the banking market. It has generated an atmosphere of cooperation and community amongst regulators, as well as a sense of common purpose.

However, it is also a process that has raised tensions, both between Committee members, and between the Committee and outside groups. Although banking supervision is a dry and seemingly apolitical topic for discussion, its sensitivity in financial circles, and in political ones during times of banking crises, has made negotiations and concessions difficult to reach. National methods and styles of supervision will only be harmonized if particular interests and the national interest are seen to be compatible with that process. As George Blunden has been quoted as saying (Reinicke 1998, p.105):

> The banking system of a country is central to the management and efficiency of its economy; its supervision will inevitably be a jealously guarded prerogative.

This sensitivity reminds us that in the Basel Committee, though consensus and unanimity are the official line, and the matters at hand seem esoteric, politics is never far from the surface. This can be taken one step further. Changes in banking regulatory and supervisory practices will have a profound and far-reaching impact on private financial actors. These actors will seek to protect and defend their interests by pressuring authorities to limit changes that affect profitability. National interest, and particular interests need to be reconciled to the games of negotiation and to the needs of maintaining the safety and soundness of the international banking system. The following two chapters of this book examine the most political, divisive and significant issue in the Committee's history.

# Chapter 4

# The Debt Crisis and the Basel Capital Accord of 1988

The Latin American Debt Crisis of the early 1980s demonstrated to national regulators that progress towards closing holes in the international supervisory net was insufficient if the international market in banking services was to be saved from itself. The Debt Crisis stemmed not from banks' evasion of supervision, but rather from banks' assumption of risk without adequately insuring themselves against the worst consequences thereof.

The crisis had brought the American and international banking systems to the brink of disaster. It was only through American leadership (however disputed and controversial that may have been) in the IMF that a working solution was (eventually) brought about. That history is well-documented but the domestic and international banking regulatory repercussions of the Debt Crisis, however, are less well-known.

The main purpose of this chapter is to show how the Basel Committee was able to react to an international financial crisis by generating new standards for capital adequacy in the hope that banks would become less vulnerable to similar situations in the future. But this chapter also demonstrates that this reaction would not have been possible without the exercise of power and leadership by key member states within the Committee. For, although the BCBS is sometimes characterised as a model example of inter-state cooperation, this tale shows that the factors of conflict and coercion, traditional elements in the study of international relations, have often played a key role in the development of Committee actions. Moreover, the story of the 1988 Accord demonstrates how US banks were able to pressure their regulators to internationalise standards that had inflicted a competitive disadvantage on them. In this sense the 1988 Accord must be seen as much as an effort to level the international playing field for American banks after the imposition of new national regulations in that country as an effort to correct the failings of the market. The tale of the Capital Accord, therefore, combines elements of domestic politics with considerations of international power.

The story of the 1988 Capital Adequacy Accord is of vital significance in this book as it marks a turning point in both the level of activity and the importance of the BCBS as an actor in the international banking system. This chapter argues that the Accord acted as a catalyst of cooperation within the Committee, moving it to take on new challenges, as well as an almost constant revision of that document. The Accord also dramatically raised the profile of the BCBS in both policy and academic arenas. Furthermore, the negotiation of the Accord highlighted the internal tensions and politics of the BCBS, and the impact that the domestic policy environment of the most powerful member, the US, has on the international coordination process. For these reasons this chapter is pivotal to the argument of this book.

## The Latin American Debt Crisis

While this is not the place to write a protracted and detailed history of the Debt Crisis, certain elements merit mention. First, it is worth noting that the crisis again showed the frailties of the post-Bretton Woods international financial system. What is interesting to note is that many of these weaknesses had previously been seen as strengths of that system. During the 1970s the traditional source of international credit, bilateral foreign aid, had not only been equalled but greatly surpassed by the loans coming from private financial actors. The innovation of the recycling of petrodollars following the OPEC oil price hike in 1973, seemingly accomplished so efficiently through the Euromarkets, linked the financial systems of all of the major economic powers and rendered them all vulnerable to the effects of the crisis. The level of interdependence was increased by another innovation of the post-Bretton Woods financial world, that of syndicated loans. Although collaboration between banks in lending practices had existed before the Second World War, this invention, designed to decrease the individual exposure of major banks and to allow smaller banks to participate in the windfall of profits envisioned to be had from developing country debt, in fact resulted in an expansion of the number of parties threatened by the crisis.

A second point is that the international response to the Debt Crisis primarily involved the IMF. The Fund was the lead negotiator with the debtor states and its seal of approval was essential if private banks were to come to the table. The crisis, we might argue, gave the Fund a new lease on life and a new function in the governance of the global economy. But this new role was one of crisis management, rather than crisis prevention. Its response to the Debt Crisis was to stabilise the situation and reduce the negative effects for the international system. This did not make the international system any safer, nor did it reduce the probabilities of similar crises occurring in the future. The job, therefore, of making the international banking system safer would have to be accomplished by another organ.

Thirdly, it must be noted that the Debt Crisis was of course also a looming credit crisis. For, although the effects of the crisis were mostly keenly felt by governments and citizens in the debtor countries, the crisis presented an enormous threat to the stability of the international banking and financial systems. The Latin American countries' inability to service their huge debts meant that creditor banks faced equally huge losses on their balance sheets, losses that would likely force them into bankruptcy or into the hands of a government bailout. Thus in the management of the crisis, the creditor governments in the advanced industrialised states felt impelled to intervene if their banks were not to be broken. The credit crunch that would have followed a large scale default by the debtor nations would have turned the economic recession of the early 1980s into a depression and would have greatly weakened the positions of the governments of the day. While not wishing to labour the point, it should also be remembered that the Debt Crisis coincided with the New Cold War under Ronald Reagan and a severe economic crisis would have greatly reduced his government's capacity to respond to the perceived Soviet strategic superiority.

The fourth point relevant for this chapter is that, although the Euromarkets and the innovation of syndicated loans had brought the involvement of banks from many different states, it was of course American banks that dominated lending to Latin American countries. US banks lent the most and also were the lead banks in most loan syndicates. As the world's most important banking system, this posed a challenge not only to the US but to the other leading financial powers, whose financial systems were highly interdependent with that of the US. Default by Latin American states would hurt every creditor state, but it would hit the US the hardest. If the US banking system fell into crisis, the consequences for other states could not be ignored. This position of American banks has been noted by many scholars of the Debt Crisis, and the consequences for American policy in the management of the crisis cannot be denied (Kahler, 1986). It also meant that the US would be the first to come up with a domestic policy response to the Debt Crisis.

### The US Domestic Regulatory Response

The atmosphere in Washington legislative and regulatory circles in 1983 was certainly conducive to a regulatory backlash of some degree. In addition to the problems of the Debt Crisis, during 1982 there were 34 insured bank failures and 8 bank mergers assisted by the Federal Deposit Insurance Corporation (FDIC, 1997). One Washington insider (quoted in Wood, 1996) described the prevailing attitude on the Capitol as focused on the belief that legislators and regulators:

> must do something about these bankers. These guys have created a big public problem and now they are asking the US government, and taxpayer, to provide more funds to the IMF. We don't want them to put us in this situation again.

Moreover, Kapstein (1991, p.10) points to a loss of public confidence in the American banking system after the traumas of the 1970s and early 1980s. This lack of public confidence influenced not only legislators, as Congress sought to appease the electorate by being seen to punish the banking industry, but regulators too. For the regulators felt pressure directly from Congress, as legislators demanded that the Federal Reserve and other banking authorities in the US perform their functions adequately and a feeling prevailed that regulators shared the blame for the Debt Crisis, at least in terms of its effects on US banks. For their part the regulatory authorities recognized the necessity of making the system safer and shoring up one of the foundations of the system, namely public confidence.

The outcome that emerged was the 1983 International Lending Supervision Act (ILSA). The response to the Debt Crisis had severely depleted the finances of the International Monetary Fund and much more money would clearly be needed if the crisis were not to turn into a major financial meltdown. As the largest contributor to the Fund, the consent of the US was absolutely necessary to authorizing the increase. Given the US Congress's traditionally sceptical attitude to international organisations, and its reluctance to commit taxpayer money to such endeavours, the legislative branch did not simply consent to US taxpayers' money being used to rescue the finances of foreign governments seen by many as profligate or corrupt. Before agreeing to an increase in IMF quotas, Congress demanded that regulators come up with a new regulatory program to prevent a similar need arising in the future. The heads of the Federal Reserve, OCC and FDIC produced a joint 'Program for Improved Supervision and Regulation of International Lending'. This program called for a five-pronged response to the problems incurred by, and underlying the contemporary crisis in American banking (US Congress, 1983):

1.  improving country risk evaluation and examination;
2.  greater disclosure of sovereign debt exposure;
3.  the creation of new, 'allocated transfer risk reserves', to protect against losses;
4.  enhancing international cooperation between banking regulators and at the IMF; and,
5.  a closer examination of the issue of capital adequacy, aimed at comparing bank capital with portfolio diversification.

This last point was not seen as directly linked to that preceding it, i.e. cooperation between national banking regulators. This linkage of issues was not achieved until US banks complained that as a unilateral measure, new capital adequacy demands would leave them with a competitive disadvantage against foreign banks.

At the same time as the onset of the Debt Crisis, another major competitive challenge for banks that had emerged by the early 1980s came from non-bank financial institutions, who were steadily eroding the business of many banks. The dis-intermediation of deposits not only meant that banks' deposit bases were shrinking, but also that banks had to compete against financial firms that did not have to meet capital adequacy requirements. Thus the impact of higher capital standards would hit US banks on both domestic and international levels, and made their protests about the ILSA that much more vociferous.

The link between the US bankers and the Basel Committee came in the person of Paul Volcker, Chair of the Board of Governors of the Federal Reserve, a post commonly recognised as the second most important job in Washington. When he was appointed to his position at the head of the most important regulatory body in the United States banking system, banks operating in the US found a valuable ally; Volcker was keenly pro-market and anti-interventionist. As Moffitt (1983, p.194) puts it, 'the bankers know him and understand him. He is one of them.'

Moffitt's evidence for this lies in the events of October 6th 1979 - the so-called 'Saturday Night Special'. Instead of disciplining the US banking industry for their speculative activities which were pushing inflation ever higher, Volcker chose to raise interest rates to an abnormally high level, which pushed the economy into deep recession. Rather than punish his own constituency, Volcker's decision to set monetary targets put the costs of adjustment onto the shoulders of the American and global economies in general, and of course helped to precipitate the Debt Crisis itself. With more than a hint of irony, Moffitt (p.204) notes:

The question arises as to why Volcker did not take any direct action to control the banks, which were fuelling the spiral of inflation and speculation. The answer is that the head of a central bank cannot be expected to take on his main constituents. He is there to protect their interests, not prosecute them.

This leaves little doubt about where Paul Volcker's allegiances lay. During the discussions over the ILSA, Volcker emerged as one of the keenest proponents of an international coordination of capital standards. If such a course of action was not pursued, he argued, US banks would be left at a terrible competitive disadvantage. Reinicke (1998, p.107) quotes Volcker:

> This is an area where it is important, to the degree possible, to have a common international approach....I would also note that—not as any kind of excuse, but as a fact—banks undoubtedly have felt under very heavy pressure internationally, and carrying more capital is a cost.

Though Volcker could not resist the Congress over the ILSA, he could make efforts to ensure that US banks did not suffer alone. Thus the 1983 International Lending Supervision Act called for closer international cooperation between banking supervisors and for a focus on bank capital in future US banking regulation. At the international level, the International Monetary Fund, the OECD, and the Basel Committee all recognized the threat that the Debt Crisis posed to the international financial system, and that concerted action was required to avert an even greater crisis, but there was little progress towards concrete actions to strengthen the foundations of that system. The US focus on bank capital was to prove a catalyst to international cooperation.

## The Importance of Bank Capital

The issue of bank capital had come to be seen as of growing importance in the early 1980s among banking economists, in particular the threat that low capital levels pose to individual banks and, in turn, the banking system as a whole (Maisel, 1981; Swary, 1980). This perception was confined not merely to the US but across the world's major financial centres. The problems of the debt crisis threw the issue of capital adequacy into high relief, as it became apparent that the risks that banks had taken in sovereign debt were dangerously unmatched by their capital reserves. It was clear that capital levels had to be strengthened if the perils of the Latin American Debt Crisis were to be avoided in the future.

Capital refers to the resources a bank is able to call upon to cover possible losses, such as might occur through loan defaults, and which it is required by regulators to maintain at a certain ratio to bank assets. Capital is important because it ultimately determines a bank's lending capacity. As Llewellyn (1989, p.42) points out, assets (such as loans):

are funded by deposits and capital but they cannot be expanded beyond the limit of the multiple of the minimum required capital-assets ratio. Thus the availability and cost of capital determines the maximum level of assets.

Capital requirements have traditionally differed between banking systems, and these differences provide competitive advantages for banks operating in systems with low capital requirements, a factor that was crucial to the development of the Basel negotiations.

Llewellyn (pp.42-43) outlines seven reasons why capital is required by banking institutions. He writes that capital is needed:

1. To absorb operating losses while enabling the bank to stay in business;
2. to support the basic infrastructure of the business on the grounds that it would not be appropriate for this to be financed by deposits;
3. to maintain public confidence by an indication that shareholders are prepared to make funds permanently available to support the business;
4. to enable the bank to absorb risks and sustain shocks while continuing to operate;
5. to enable assets to be written off;
6. to provide long-term funds to alleviate the hazards of maturity transformation;
7. to buy time to enable the institution to adjust to changing market conditions and patterns of business.

The debate on capital adequacy continued throughout the early 1980s and became one not about whether higher capital levels were required, but about how capital was to be measured. In the US, bank regulators enforced a 'static', or fixed, capital measurement system that set a certain level of capital for all on-balance sheet exposures, such as loans. This system failed to take account of off-balance sheet exposures, such as swaps, futures, note issuance facilities (NIFs) and letters of credit, a fact of which banks sought to take advantage by booking more and more of their liabilities off the balance sheet.

In Britain, however, the Bank of England had in 1980 introduced a risk-weighted capital measurement system that assessed assets both on and off the balance sheet, thus building up a clearer image of the bank's overall risk exposure. The 1984 Continental Illinois crisis provided the stimulus required to convert US regulators to the idea of risk-weighted capital-asset measurement. At the beginning of 1986, the Federal Reserve Board introduced new capital requirements that took risk-based measurement into account.

## The Basel Committee and Negotiations Over Capital Adequacy

The experience of the Debt Crisis was not the only factor that brought the issue of capital to the minds of regulators. Schuijer (1992, p.75) points out that the internationalisation of banking and the global trend towards banking deregulation 'confronted banks with greater risks or new types of risks' and regulators perceived 'a growing need of measures to strengthen the soundness, stability and integrity of the international banking system'.

This said, the Latin American Debt Crisis focused regulatory concern intensely on the issue of capital. Indeed, in June of 1982 the Basel Committee had issued a discussion paper that urged bank supervisors to examine their banks' capital levels and oppose any diminution in those levels. The main conclusions of this paper were that 'further erosion of capital ratio should, on prudential grounds, be resisted; and that, in the absence of common standards of capital adequacy, supervisors should not allow the capital resources of their major banks to deteriorate from their present level, whatever those levels may be' (BCBS, 1982). Thus, even prior to the ILSA of 1983, the issue of bank capital was seen as related to the Debt Crisis.

The 1982 *Report on International Developments in Banking Supervision* also called for work towards harmonizing national definitions of capital. It identified discrepancies between national regulatory structures as the main element in preventing a concerted effort on the part of the Basel supervisors to rectify the situation. Such discrepancies became even clearer over the next two years as the Committee studied the issue of capital in greater detail. In 1984 the Committee made its report to the member supervisory agencies and a consensus was reached that something should be done to improve banks' capital positions. However, progress on joint action soon stalled in the Committee as agreement could not be reached on the most suitable measurement of capital.

The impetus for joint action came from within the United States. The new regulations governing capital adequacy that were proposed by the Federal Reserve in January 1986 brought a vigorous response from US banks. As mentioned above, US regulators had employed a static or fixed capital to asset ratio until this point. Set at 5.5% (that is, banks were required to hold $5.50 in capital for every $100 of assets), the existing US capital standards neglected to take account of asset quality, unlike the systems put in place by some European regulators (such as Belgium, France and Britain). The new Federal Reserve Board proposal for risk-based capital reflected a change in regulatory thinking in the US for it brought in a capital measurement system that closely mirrored, and indeed was largely derived from, that in place in the United Kingdom.

Paul Volcker's loyalty to US banks has already been mentioned as a reason behind the Fed's pressure for an international accord. However, there is also evidence to suggest that by the mid-1980s he had come to the conclusion that the international regulatory competition in laxity had gone far enough (Kapstein, 1989, p.336). The interaction of market forces with deregulation had created the ideal circumstances for the development of a global banking crisis (Cohen, 1986, p.303). The ILSA gave the Federal Reserve a mandate to engage in international cooperative actions with other national regulators and Volcker seized upon this opportunity to foster international regulatory cooperation at the same time as he protected the interest of US banks.

Furthermore, the higher levels of capital held by US banks were soon to show their worth. In 1987 the Brazilian government stopped debt payments and threatened to default on its debt unless creditor banks were willing to renegotiate the total debt. By this point US banks had considerably higher capital levels than at the onset of the Debt Crisis in 1982 and were able to call the bluff of the Brazilians. Banks simply refused to re-negotiate but threatened to block Brazilian access to international loans. Within months Brazil had returned to debt payments. The episode was useful in two ways. First it demonstrated to banks that higher capital levels, although costly, greatly strengthened their bargaining position in times of crisis. Second, the episode proved to national regulators from other BCBS member countries that capital adequacy had become a central element of stability in the international financial system.

    For their part, the US banking industry maintained a high level of interest in the international negotiations through the following years. US banks had objected strongly to the unilateral raising of bank capital levels by the ILSA and complained to regulators now that the proposed risk-based capital measurements would further hinder their international competitiveness. Representatives of the banking industry argued that by operating with lower capital levels than US banks, foreign banks would be able to charge lower rates of interest on loans and still be able to meet the same profit margins as US banks. Clearly this would tip the competitive balance in the favour of foreign banks. Uppermost in US bankers' minds was the competitive advantage that the new regulation gave Japanese banks. Kapstein (1989, p.339) shows that the American Bankers Association (ABA) argued this point strongly in its comments paper to the Federal Reserve Board in May of 1986. In fact, a former advisor to Volcker stated that US banks were 'a pain in the ass' during the negotiations for the Accord, and that they kept a close eye on proceedings in the Committee (quoted in Wood, 1996).

    The other members of the Basel Committee were far from receptive to the idea of a harmonized capital standard. Japanese regulators claimed that the Japanese banking system maintained 'a high level of safety and soundness' that negated the need for them to impose new standards on their banks. German regulators argued that their 'universal banks' and the tradition of 'main banking' were so different from other Basel member countries' banking systems that a harmonized capital adequacy standard would be either too difficult to negotiate, or would fail to reflect the special situation of the German banking industry.[1]

## The US-UK Bilateral Accord

This left US regulators with two options: either maintain a unilateral risk-based capital standard or negotiate a narrower agreement outside the Committee. Pressure from US banks and Volcker's firmly-held loyalty to them ruled out the former option. The second choice, however, was far more appealing. A willing partner existed in the form of the Bank of England; negotiations would be made easier by the fact that the Fed's

---

[1] Universal bank is the term given to banks that embrace a wide range of financial activities in one organization, such as loans, insurance, pensions, etc. The main bank tradition is unique to the German system but exists in a similar form in Japan. Main banks are those financial institutions that are integrally linked to certain firms and industries, from whom they derive a large part of their business.

capital adequacy system was based on the Bank of England's. The existence of a single capital standard in the world's two most important international financial centres, New York and London, would put pressure on the remaining Basel member regulators to come to the negotiating table.

Volcker's suggestion of a bilateral accord was well-received by the then Governor of the Bank of England, Robin Leigh-Pemberton. In July 1986, Volcker announced to his General Counsel that the British were willing to talk about the issue and negotiations began in earnest. Although it was Volcker who originally explored the possibility of a joint US-UK accord on capital standards, neither he nor Leigh-Pemberton played an important role in the negotiations from this point on. Instead, the eventual agreement was largely shaped by the personal relationship between William Taylor, Head of Supervision at the Federal Reserve, and Brian Quinn, Executive Director of the Bank of England responsible for Banking Supervision. In addition, on the US side the Comptroller of the Currency and the FDIC were involved in the bilateral talks.

Kapstein (1992) notes that the UK was keen to negotiate a joint accord with the US in order to balance the EC negotiations on harmonizing capital adequacy standards that were proceeding at the same time. This, however, is only one reason why the Bank of England was so cooperative. As was noted in the rationale behind the creation of the Basel Committee in 1974, London's position as an international banking centre makes the Bank of England particularly sensitive to problems affecting the international financial system as a whole. Any crisis that threatens that system will be felt strongly in The City. Moreover, British banks were almost as keen as US banks to see a levelling of the international banking playing field that saw Japanese banks required to operate with capital ratios equivalent to those in Britain. A less easily demonstrated reason behind the ease of negotiations between the US and UK regulators is the long tradition of cooperation between the two banking systems.

A joint accord was soon reached by the US and UK, titled 'Agreed proposal of the United States federal banking supervisory authorities and the Bank of England on primary capital and capital adequacy assessment', which set common standards for bank capital assessment. The accord set out two main categories or classes of bank capital. 'Base primary capital', which counted fully towards meeting capital adequacy ratios, was defined to consist of common stock, capital surpluses, retained earnings, minority interests in consolidated subsidiaries, general reserves and hidden reserves. 'Limited primary capital', which was permitted to make up no more than half of total base capital, was determined to include perpetual preferred stock and qualified subordinated debt, including perpetual debt (Bardos, 1987/88, pp.27/28). The fact that the two sets of regulators' starting positions were close to one another greatly speeded the conclusion of an agreement.

Though hailed as a 'landmark in financial regulation' by the *Financial Times*, this accord had no legal status, and was put forward merely as a consultative paper. US banks were less than impressed with the bilateral accord; in their comment papers on the proposal, one regulatory official recalls that banks indicated that the accord was all very well, 'but this is not our competition' (quoted in Wood, 1996).

American banks may well have missed the point of the bilateral accord, however. Its purpose seems to have been to act as a stimulus to the other Basel member countries to come to the negotiating table to draw up a broader accord. While regulatory officials in both London and Washington claim that the two countries would have gone ahead with a bilateral agreement in the absence of broader acceptance (Wood, 1996), the unspoken threat of market closure and hence exclusion from the world's two most important international banking centres clearly acted as a catalyst.

Indeed, regulators from the two countries immediately set about trying to secure wider agreement among the Basel member countries on the issue of bank capital. Brian Quinn acted as envoy to European regulators, while Gerald Corrigan, president of the Federal Reserve Bank of New York, journeyed to Tokyo to persuade Japanese officials of the importance of a wider accord. In addition to these talks, British and American representatives at Basel demanded discussion of the issue of capital adequacy. This discussion revealed that other (particularly European) Basel members were less than happy with the bilateral approach taken by the US and UK, and that they would not agree to a broader accord on the terms laid out in the bilateral proposal.

While discussions continued in Basel, the Japanese officials were anxious to reach some kind of agreement with the US and UK Though Japanese officials insisted publicly that their regulations were sufficient to guarantee safety and soundness in the national banking system, Volcker's former General Counsel has suggested that Japanese officials didn't want to be left out of such an accord (Wood, 1996). Japanese regulators were aware that international expansion by Japanese banks had left them dangerously exposed, and the highly-leveraged nature of Japanese lending allowed little room for error, a point of particular poignancy since the Asian financial and economic crises of the late 1990s. The impression that new, stricter capital standards were being imposed from outside, through an international agreement, would help them fend off criticism from Japanese banks and implement the standards more easily. Moreover, higher capital requirements were not expected to impose any hardship on Japanese banks as the bullish Tokyo stock market of the late 1980s would allow Japanese banks to build up capital reserves cheaply. The accuracy of this expectation was hotly debated during the following decade as Japan's banking system went into deep crisis.

This said, there were hints that the bilateral accord represented an implicit threat to banks from countries other than the United States and Britain. Brian Quinn's comments shortly after the bilateral accord was signed are telling: 'If I were a Japanese bank or a Japanese supervisor, I would be a little worried' (Duffy, 1987, p.2). It may be that US and British officials underestimated the willingness of Japanese officials to come to an agreement on an issue that they already perceived to be a potential problem in the Japanese banking system.

The trilateral discussions were much tougher than those between the US and UK alone, with Bank of Japan and Ministry of Finance officials arguing for a different valuation of base capital than that laid out in the bilateral accord. In particular, the Japanese delegation wanted 'hidden reserves' such as corporate equity held by banks, a practice far more common in the Japanese than in the US or UK banking systems, to be marked at its market rather than book value. This concern reflected the bullish nature of the Japanese economy at the time. American and British regulators were reluctant to allow this form of capital to be counted as base capital as their banks were prevented from doing so by national accounting rules. It is said that the British negotiators were particularly tough on the Japanese during this process, threatening the future access of Japanese banks to London's international banking market, the world's most important centre for the Euromarkets (Wood, 1996). Largely due to the British obstinacy, the eventual trilateral agreement only allowed banks to count 45% of the gains on corporate equity towards base capital.

By September of 1987 the three nations' regulators had agreed on an accord that was acceptable to all groupings concerned. The conclusion of this trilateral agreement was the final push needed to get the remaining parties at Basel to move forward on a multilateral capital accord and negotiations began in earnest at Basel shortly afterwards. It would be fair to say that though the bilateral and trilateral accords had the desired effect of hastening a broader agreement, there was some bad feeling about the implicit threat involved. Dr Mark Lusser, Vice Chairman of the governing board of the Swiss National Bank (quoted in Norton, 1989) hinted at this when he noted that:

> Countries not prepared to join an agreement among this group of three countries could easily be put under pressure. It would be sufficient to bar their banks from using the three financial centres or to subject them to special treatment there. If they wish to remain competitive internationally, the large banks that operate worldwide can no longer be absent from these centres today. They would quickly encourage their governments to cooperate internationally…In the light of the urgency of the problem, the pressure originating from the agreement…is acceptable

The use of such coercive action however, does raise questions about the ability of the Committee at the time to reach effective agreement on issues of cooperation relating to its mandate. It must not be forgotten that the primary purpose of the BCBS was and is to protect the health and stability of the international banking system. In the mid-1980s a majority of the member countries of the Committee seemed unwilling to take any major steps to bring this about. While the actions of the US and UK to force cooperation had a successful outcome, Lusser (Norton, 1989) questioned the viability of repeating this experiment:

> However, should the example set a precedent and the strategy of the two powers be extended to other fields of harmonizing banking supervision - as a substitute, so to speak, for internationally negotiated compromises - then the willingness to cooperate internationally could suffer damage in the long run. In view of the problems that need to be solved, this would be a harmful development.

Despite the ill-feeling, by the end of 1987 a multilateral accord had been reached between the Basel Committee members. In December of that year the proposal was presented to the banking industries in each of the member countries, each of which gave their comments to the national regulators. These comments succeeded in bringing about a few major changes to the final draft of the accord which was signed in July 1988, under the title 'International Convergence of Capital Measurement and Capital Standards'.

## The 1988 Capital Accord

If one considers the difficulties of negotiating a multilateral agreement, the content of the Accord is impressive in its detail. It was by far the most specific agreement concluded by Basel member countries to this point, although it paled in comparison to the agreements that followed in the Nineties. Its level of detail indicates a considerable convergence of views on the importance of this issue, especially if we consider the prior disputes. The Committee appears to have been successful in satisfying the concerns of supervisors from all member countries and the final document differs significantly from both the bilateral and trilateral agreements that preceded it.

The Accord calls for international banks in member countries to observe a minimum standard ratio of capital to risk-weighted assets of 8 percent by the end of financial year 1992. An interim minimum standard of 7.25 percent was set to be observed by the end of financial year 1990 (see below). The 8 percent mark signified a substantial increase in many countries' capital adequacy standards, in particular in Japan and Germany.

The report announced in its opening line that it presented 'the outcome of the Committee's work over several years to secure international convergence of supervisory regulations governing the capital adequacy of international banks'. Furthermore, in keeping with the broader international goals of the Committee, the report stated that it was 'being circulated to supervisory authorities worldwide with a view to encouraging the adoption of this framework in countries outside the G10 in respect of banks conducting significant international business' (BCBS, 1988, p.1).

Two main objectives are identified by the Accord and the second is indicative of the reasoning behind the political manoeuvring described in an earlier section. First the Committee noted the by now traditional concern with strengthening the soundness and stability of the international banking system. The second objective identified in the Accord, however, made explicit reference to the desire to 'diminishing an existing source of competitive inequality among international banks'. While this does not seem to be an earth-shattering announcement, we must remember that the Committee was set up with one, limited goal in mind, namely protecting the health and stability of the international banking system. This was to be achieved by three methods:

1. studying the system;
2. surveillance of the system;
3. negotiating agreements to increase cooperation and harmonization and to eliminate gaps in the supervision of international banking activities.

While the 1988 Basel Accord is a fine example of the success of each of these three methods, and was obviously intended to protect the health and stability of the system, the supplementary concern over competitiveness and levelling the playing field marks a clear extension of the mandate of the Committee.

In its introduction the Accord also notes that national discretion would be necessary in the implementation of the new capital adequacy standards. This opened the door to criticism of the agreement as some commentators remarked on the potential lack of rigidity and uniformity in implementation. In fact, the Accord resulted in an impressive level of harmonisation once implemented, and not only across the BCBS member countries, but throughout the world. One significant difference, however, emerged in the type of banks to which the capital adequacy standards were applied. Some national authorities, such as those in the US and UK insisted that all banks abide by the capital standards emerging from Basel. Other nations' authorities, such as those in Japan, applied these standards only to banks that operate internationally. In later years, the question of scope was to re-emerge as a point of dispute between the major Basel members.

A third point worthy of attention in the agreement's introduction is its reference to the changing nature of the international banking industry and the implications for capital adequacy. Recognising that 'ownership structures and the position of banks within financial conglomerate groups are undergoing significant change' the Committee called for consolidated application to banks and promised to monitor developments in this area to 'ensure that ownership structures should not be such as to weaken the capital position of the bank or to expose it to risks stemming from other parts of the group' (BCBS, 1988, p.3). This sensitivity to the rapid and fundamental changes taking place in banking foreshadows the creation of the Joint Forum in the 1990s and the Committee's concerns over financial conglomerates.

There are three main elements to the 1988 Basel Accord on Capital Adequacy. Seeking to not only define capital but also the particular types of assets and risk against which capital should be set, and the time scale for implementing the measures, the Accord examines:

1.  The constituents of capital – how capital is to be defined.
2.  The risk weights – how banks assets are to be measured.
3.  Target standard ratio – how much capital banks should reserve.

*1. Defining Capital*

Deciding which elements of a bank's holdings could be included in the measurement of its capital was an issue of central importance and the Accord contains a two-tiered definition. The Accord requires banks to divide their capital into:

> *TIER 1*, or core capital: The accord considers that the key element of capital on which the main emphasis should be placed is *equity capital* (defined as issued and fully paid ordinary shares/common stock and non-cumulative perpetual preferred stock, but excluding cumulative preferred stock) and *disclosed reserves*. This key element of capital is the only element common to all countries' banking systems. This emphasis on equity capital and disclosed reserves reflects the importance the Committee attaches to securing a progressive enhancement in the quality, as well as the level, of the total capital resources maintained by major banks. At least fifty percent of a bank's capital base must consist of Tier 1 capital.

*TIER* 2, or supplementary capital: this element is defined to be capital of lower quality which can nonetheless be counted towards the total capital base. Several elements may be included in this second tier, elements which may differ across different countries: *undisclosed reserves* which have been phased through the profit and loss account and which are accepted by the bank's supervisory authorities; *revaluation reserves*, that is assets which have been re-valued to reflect their current, or market, value; *general provisions/general loan loss reserves*, that is, funds put aside against the possibility of future, unspecified, losses; *hybrid debt capital instruments*, which may vary in type between countries, but which have close similarities in kind to equity; *subordinated term debt*, which may make up secondary capital to a maximum level equivalent to fifty percent of core capital.

The agreement was aimed at pushing banks to maximise their holdings of Tier 1 capital as an element more stable, more reliable and less likely to erode than Tier 2 elements.

*Measuring Risk*

Rather than treating all bank assets equally, the parties to the Accord determined that:

a weighted risk ratio in which capital is related to different categories of asset or off-balance-sheet exposure, weighted according to broad categories of relative risk, is the preferred method for assessing the capital adequacy of banks.

Each item making up a bank's total exposure, therefore, is weighted according to a predetermined relative risk of counter-party failure. The Accord creates five such risk weights - 0, 10, 20, 50, and 100 percent depending upon the perceived risk level inherent in particular types of assets.

The Accord assumed that the major kind of risk for banks is credit, or counter-party, risk, further recognising that country transfer risk is an element of credit risk. However, it recognises the existence of other kinds of risk, mentioning investment, interest rate, exchange rate and concentration risk, but leaves the weighting of these risks to individual countries, stating that 'no standardisation has been attempted in the treatment of these other kinds of risk in the framework at the present stage'.

**Transitional Arrangements**

The Accord, while demanding that the 'arrangements in this document will be implemented at the national level at the earliest possible opportunity', gave member states four and a half years in which to implement the capital adequacy levels stipulated. That meant that members had until the end of 1992 to change

*Governing Global Banking*

**Table 4.1:**     **Basel Accord on Capital Adequacy**
                   **Risk weights by category of on-balance-sheet asset**

| | |
|---|---|
| 0% | Cash; Claims on central governments and central banks denominated in national currency and funded in that currency; Other claims on OECD central governments and central banks; Claims collateralised by cash of OECD central-government securities or guaranteed by OECD central governments |
| 0, 10, 20, or 50% | Claims on domestic public-sector entities, excluding central government, and loans guaranteed by such entities |
| 20% | Claims on multilateral development banks (IBRD, IADB, AsBD, AfDB, EIB) and claims guaranteed by, or collateralised by securities issued by such banks; Claims on banks incorporated in the OECD and loans guaranteed by OECD incorporated banks; Claims on banks incorporated in countries outside the OECD with a residual maturity of up to one year and loans with a residual maturity of up to one year guaranteed by banks incorporated in countries outside the OECD; Claims on non-domestic OECD public-sector entities, excluding central government, and loans guaranteed by such entities; cash items in process of collection |
| 50% | Loans fully secured by mortgage on residential property that is or will be occupied by the borrower or that is rented |
| 100% | Claims on the private sector; Claims on banks incorporated outside the OECD with a residual maturity of over one year; Claims on central governments outside the OECD (unless denominated in national currency – and funded in that currency – see above); Claims on commercial companies owned by the public sector; Premises, plant and equipment and other fixed assets; Real estate and other investments (including non-consolidated investment participations in other companies); Capital instruments issued by other banks (unless deducted from capital); all other assets |

*Source:* Adapted from Basel Committee on Banking Supervision, *International Convergence of Capital Management and Capital Standards*, July 1988

domestic regulations and force compliance by international banks. However, a mid-term date of end-1990 was set by which international banks were expected to meet a suggested capital-assets ratio of 7.25%. Though this standard was not formal or obligatory, the Accord made it clear that internationally active banks in all states would be expected to meet it.

In the interim, the Accord set out a number of measures to be implemented by national authorities. While they do not merit extended attention here, they do point to a concern on the part of some members of the Committee that others might lag in the implementation and thus demand a longer transition period. Japan, in particular, was identified by analysts as having a long way to go to meet the Accord's demands.

Despite the specific nature of these interim arrangements, the agreement recognised that the regulatory and supervisory differences between member countries would mean differences in interpretation and implementation:

Each country will decide the way in which the supervisory authorities will introduce and apply these recommendations in the light of their different legal structures and existing supervisory arrangements.

While clearly an important concession, it is important to note that this sentence, tacked on as it is to the end of the document, should probably only be seen as an attempt to safeguard the Committee against the charge that it had interfered too deeply in the internal affairs of national banking authorities.

## The Significance of the Accord

By concluding the 1988 Accord on the International Convergence of Capital Measurement and Capital Standards, the Basel Committee took another important step forward in seeking solutions to the problems posed by the internationalisation of private finance. The Accord aimed at removing a great number of the discrepancies in capital requirements across the G10 nations, both levelling the international playing field and, more importantly, ensuring that most internationally operating banks carry a level of capital deemed safe and sound by most national regulators.

The traditional view in finance and IPE circles is that the Accord represented a concerted effort on the part of national regulators to rectify a looming problem in the international financial system. By harmonizing capital standards for internationally operating banks, the Basel Committee succeeded in greatly reducing the prospect of an international banking crisis stemming from loan defaults and consequent loss of bank customer confidence. It is this element on international cooperation that has been emphasised by Kapstein in his various studies of the 1988 Accord (1989, 1991, 1992). Correcting market failure, for Kapstein, must be seen as a driving force in the achievements of the Committee.

The idea of the market, then, after triumphing in the elimination of the Bretton Woods system of organizing international finance, did not for long hold the undisputed loyalty of regulators. When problems emerged in an international financial system regulated only by national authorities (and they did not take very long to occur), policy-makers recognized the need for some method of matching the internationalism of private finance. The 1988 Accord, in particular, is commonly recognized by regulatory authorities as an attempt to satisfy a clear and present need for an international regulatory standard.

But just as importantly as this, the creation of the Basel Committee had required leadership on the part of two major financial powers - the United States and United Kingdom. The decisions and actions taken by regulatory authorities in these two states have been key in altering the international banking marketplace, both prior to 1974 and after, but the 1988 Accord on Capital Adequacy highlights the importance of the US in particular in the international banking system even more clearly. The Latin American Debt Crisis hit US banks harder than their counterparts in other countries and when policy-makers in the US demanded stricter capital requirements from internationally operating US banks, these institutions demanded that such standards be internationalised. This points to the continuing centrality of American financial institutions in the international system.

However, the United States was unable to procure immediate acceptance of a regulatory agenda on the part of its fellow Basel members. Instead, US authorities found themselves in a position where they had to build a gradual coalition, using diplomacy, the hint of a threat of de facto market closure, and most importantly the support of supervisory authorities in another state. The support of the Bank of England was critical in the final success of the Basel capital negotiations. By embracing the world's two most important financial centres, London and New York, the bilateral accord between the UK and US forced the issue of capital adequacy on to the Basel agenda.

The importance of this supporter-ship is perhaps best seen by comparing the success of the 1988 Accord to an earlier attempt by the US to regulate the Euromarkets. In 1979 the then chair of the Federal Reserve, William Miller attempted to build an international consensus on the need for reserve requirements for Eurocurrency deposits. Though supported at first by authorities in West Germany, the US proposal failed to secure broader agreement on the part of other G10 nations, and soon lost even Bundesbank support. The agreement was effectively killed off by opposition from the Bank of England and the Swiss National Bank (Dale, 1984, p.28; Helleiner, 1994), both of whom recognised that international regulation of the Euromarkets would jeopardise the highly profitable business being carried out in their jurisdictions.

The exercise of authority in the international banking system, then, relied upon the leadership of the United States but also required support from other states if it was to succeed. While the Basel Committee provides a forum where that support may be procured, it is by no means assured. In the case of the 1988 Accord, the United States was forced to work outside the Committee before it could obtain cooperation within. Simmons has emphasised the element of power in her study of the harmonization of international capital market regulation, stressing that the US and UK are 'the prime centers in which foreign financial institutions conduct business' (2001, p. 593). The US, she states, must be seen as 'hegemonic' in international finance 'in the sense that it is costlier to alter its preferred regulatory innovation than to try to change the policies of the rest of the world' (2001, p. 595). In the case of the Basel Capital Accord, the possibility of either unilateral action or market closure by these two states, must be seen as a credible threat that pushed other states to comply with US/UK preferences.

The tactics used by the United States point to a feature of hegemonic leadership in the late-1980s. The failure of the US to gain universal acceptance in the Committee of its preferred capital adequacy framework forced it to work first bilaterally, and then to rely on British supportership to coerce other states to accept. This seems to contradict notions of a concert system (Kirton, 1995) while supporting the idea of the US working with one or maybe two other powers (Putnam and Bayne, 1984). Again, David Lake's ideas (1983) of hegemons and supporters seem appropriate.

The element of international competition and the importance of domestic politics must also be identified in the Accord. For not only were US regulators attempting to protect their banks from the effects of the ILSA, an additional motive was to raise the capital levels of banks in other countries that were significantly below those in the US. When viewed in the light of the dramatic rise in the influence and power of Japanese banks operating internationally, the Basel Capital Accord provided a useful way for US regulators to reduce one of the causes of Japanese bank competitiveness. This is also why the Bank of England proved such a willing ally.

Nabors and Oatley's study of the 1988 Accord discards Kapstein's view of the Capital Accord as an attempt to respond to market failure in favour of an argument that stresses the ways in which 'domestic politics create incentives to propose international redistributive institutions' (1998, p.36). Their conclusions are that the US regulatory authorities did not seek to contribute to international financial stability but rather to gaining important competitive advantages for their banks.

A significant final observation is that the Accord shows us once again the dilemma faced by authorities in the international banking system. Disturbingly, even if their intention is to further the cause of stability, safety and soundness in international banking, they must wait for a crisis to flare up before steps are taken to prevent its occurrence. This reactive approach to the regulation and supervision of international banking means that they are permanently at least one step behind the market.

## Conclusion

In the 1980s the Basel Committee relied upon the twin factors of leadership and supporter-ship in its creation and policy coordination achievements. Through the Concordat and the 1988 Accord on Capital Adequacy, the Committee has significantly reduced the scope for regulatory arbitrage by private banks, and has closed some of the larger gaps in the international banking safety net by ensuring that no internationally operating bank should escape supervision. Through the fostering of personal contacts and the exchange of information and views, Basel Committee members have been able to 'observe and reduce the weaknesses within their own systems as well as to take advantage of the strengths of other systems' (Johnson and Adams, 1983, p.29). Furthermore, by sponsoring the formation of other international supervisory groups, the Committee has ensured a broader exchange of supervisory information and views. Finally, the Committee's own ongoing research into the workings of the international banking system has been of particular importance in disseminating data and analysing trends in that system.

The 1988 Accord on the International Convergence of Capital Measurement and Capital Standards marked a watershed for the Committee. By achieving the negotiation of a detailed agreement on one issue of concern, the Committee proved that it had evolved into a force in the international banking system. The next chapter analyses the effects of the Accord on the international market in banking services, on national regulatory authorities and on the Committee itself.

# Chapter 5

# Evaluating the 1988 Accord: Market and Authority Reactions

## Introduction

The 1988 Basel Accord on the International Convergence of Capital Measurement and Capital Standards was the clearest indication to date that regulatory and supervisory authorities recognised the need for international standards in banking regulation. The Accord went a long way toward harmonizing capital standards for internationally operating banks across the international financial system and reduced the scope for regulatory arbitrage. Furthermore it laid the groundwork for the Committee to expand into other areas of international supervisory concern.

The central purpose of this chapter is to evaluate the impact of this, the Committee's most important work to date and to thus determine the standing of the Committee as an organ of global financial governance. Moreover, by studying the impact of the Accord, it is hoped that an idea may be obtained of how the work of the Basel Committee affects the ever-changing dynamic between public authority and the market.

This chapter has three, more specific goals. First it seeks to evaluate the Accord by examining its impact on the private side of the international banking system, namely the international market in banking services. The effects on the market are examined by studying how the Basel Capital Accord has affected the banking industry in both its structure and practices, looking at industry consolidation and the differential effects on different national banking systems.

Second, the chapter examines the impact of the Accord on the authorities regulating that market. Looking at banking regulation and supervision in key national banking systems, the chapter argues that national and regional (European Union) supervision and regulation were noticeably affected by the success of the 1988 Accord.

The third specific goal is to try to evaluate the impact of the Accord on the Committee itself, in terms of its output and its international reputation. In the years following the Accord the Committee increased its output significantly and rapidly came to be seen as a vital actor in the international financial system and in the business of setting rules and standards for that system. Within a relatively short space of time the BCBS had become established as a leading organisation in establishing norms and rules for banks in the entire international system, not merely in the member countries of the Committee.

A key point that should be made here is that the impact of the Accord was both positive and negative, and may even be seen to be perverse in some cases. Certainly the simplicity of the Accord, with the benefit of hindsight, has come to be seen as both a strength and a weakness. Either way, the extent of the impact of the Accord should not be underestimated and deserves closer attention.

## Evaluating the Impact of the 1988 Accord

The impact of the 1988 Accord should be viewed in a way that takes into consideration the twin elements of international political economy, that is markets and the authorities that govern them. Therefore a satisfactory evaluation of the impact of the 1988 Capital Accord must be undertaken on three levels. First it should address the impact of the Accord on the industry of banking, examining the effects on stability, competition, and industry structure. Second it must be analysed in terms of its impact on the business of supervision in the key banking centres, to understand how the authorities in these centres embraced and continued the work of the Committee. Third, it is vital that we examine the impact that the Accord had on both the work and the reputation of the Committee itself.

It is always problematical to establish cause and effect in these situations. How do we know, for example, that the industry would not have undergone the changes it experienced without the influence of the Accord? And how can we be sure that supervisory authorities would not have embraced such reforms anyway in the absence of international agreement? This chapter posits that the changes described here can best be explained, although not exclusively, by reference to the 1988 Accord on Capital Adequacy.

The story told in this chapter will be continued in chapter seven. For the true impact and importance of the 1988 Accord was only seen in full when the BCBS member states came to negotiate a new version of the agreement. During the international debate over a replacement capital framework that began in the second half of the 1990s actors from public and private arenas paid testament to the importance of the 1988 Accord through the intensity with which they engaged each other.

## Impact on the Market in International Banking Services

The reception given the 1988 Accord by the banking industry was both positive and negative. Naturally enough, internationally operating banks praised the Accord not for the way it helped regulatory agencies match the internationalism of finance, nor for the perceived contribution to international financial stability, but for the competitive benefits they perceived as emanating from the Accord. It was seen by market players as a move that greatly reduced regulatory discrepancies among the world's major banking centres, thus creating a more level playing field for international banking. Furthermore, banks saw great advantage in the boost to banks' customer confidence inspired by increased capital levels. As noted in a previous chapter, confidence is the bedrock on which a stable banking system is built, and the 1988 Accord was seen as strengthening confidence in individual institutions and the system as a whole.

On the other hand, banks were quick to complain that the Accord was not the great leveller it seemed at first glance. These complaints focused on two areas of the application of the Accord. First, the Accord only applied to banks and not to non-bank financial institutions, such as securities firms. This issue was to prove particularly irksome to banks as non-bank financial institutions had come to be a major rival to banks in the supply of capital to the economies of G10 nations. As mentioned earlier, banks in the advanced industrialised economies had been hit by competition at both the deposit and borrowing side of the equation. By the mid-80s depositors (particularly large depositors) could obtain a far higher rate of return on their money by handing over their deposits to an investment or fund manager. At the same time, large corporate borrowers could now bypass banks and obtain funds directly from the capital market through the use of bonds, notes and commercial paper. This pincer-like movement on banks' business left them with fewer depositors and lower quality, higher risk borrowers. The Basel Capital Accord further aggravated the banks' problems by foisting upon them a new regulatory demand that did not apply to non-bank financial firms. Some economists, putting an improbably high-level of faith in the market, have claimed that this regulatory inequality could actually work in favour of banks. They claim that depositors would be drawn to the extra security given banks by the new capital requirements and choose quality over high rates of return for their money. While this is an interesting theoretical conjecture, it is rare that the market follows rules such as this. Evidence of the impact of the Accord on bank competitiveness can be seen in the headlong rush towards consolidation in the banking industry through mergers and acquisitions that was seen throughout the 1990s.

The second aspect of the Basel Accord that worried the banking industry was the uneven effects that the Accord would have across the world's major financial centres. As noted in the previous chapter, the Accord allows for a certain degree of discretion by national authorities in the application of the Accord's guidelines. This meant that while Japanese authorities initially applied the guidelines only to internationally operating banks, those in the US and the UK chose to apply them to all banks. However, more important than this were the market conditions prevailing in the various national financial systems. Japanese banks complained that the Accord was more burdensome for them as their capital levels required most improvement. Furthermore, Japanese banking regulations until 1993 outlawed the securitization of bank assets (*Economist*, 1994b, p.85), one method of raising capital ratios that became increasingly popular among US banks. For their part, US banks complained that the Accord favoured Japanese banks as they had access to cheaper, more readily available sources of capital through their business linkages and the booming Tokyo stock market. This assertion was challenged in a study conducted by Kester and Luehrman (1992) in the *Harvard Business Review*, which argued that Japanese capital was in fact much more expensive than it first appeared.

From 1988 to 1992 the verity of these concerns was tested. However, the added ingredient of a deep recession across the industrialised economies somewhat altered the banking equation. The recession hit banks across the G10 through the poor performance of loans and bad debts. Borrowing activity switched from so-called 'voluntary credit' to 'distress borrowing', which greatly raised the level of risk involved with lending. The steep decline in property prices after 1988 in the UK and US and after 1990 in Japan inflicted huge losses on banks. Japanese banks were doubly hit by the property crash. A large part of their overseas expansion had focused on lending to property developers abroad, and the earlier crash in the US and UK served to weaken their asset sheet before their losses on Japanese real estate (*Economist*, 1992b, p.104). Later in the decade Japanese banks would of course be hit hard again by the Asian crisis. The sum of these problems made it more difficult for banks to focus on capital improvement at a time when profits were threatened.

But Japanese banks were also hit by the recession in another way, one that was directly related to the 1988 Basel Capital Accord. As the recession hit Japan, the Tokyo stock market experienced a contraction that made the raising of bank capital more difficult for Japanese banks. As the market value of corporate equity declined, banks were forced to readjust the structure of their capital bases to reflect the lower value of these stocks. Though this phenomenon also affected banks from other countries, Japanese banks' reliance on equity-based capital meant that they were hit harder than their contemporaries abroad (BIS, 1991, p.116).

However, Wagster's 1996 study of the impact of the Accord on international banks argues that the impact on Japanese banks was in fact less than it first appeared. Studying the wealth effects of international bank shareholders in a variety of countries he established that Japanese bank shareholders benefited from the imposition of the new Basel standards.

More importantly, although the Basel Accord can be seen to have hindered bank profitability over the period from 1988 to 1992, there is also a case to be made that the higher capital levels demanded by the Accord made banking systems safer and may have prevented bank failures. By raising bank capital ratios, the Accord helped to maintain confidence in banking systems beset by a myriad of problems. In the case of the Japanese banks, a November 1991 article in *The Economist* (1991d) quoted one financial analyst who projected that the bad debts accumulated by Japanese banks would hit their profits but would not wipe out their now much improved capital levels. Of course the Japanese banking crisis proved to be much larger than first imagined. However, as the article explained, the newly raised capital ratios helped prevent the failure of one City of London bank from loan losses and certainly helped maintain consumer confidence in the system.

Indeed, a 1994 study conducted through the Group of Thirty which examined the impact of the Accord on the international banking industries of Japan and the United States argued that the value of the Accord is to be seen not in its achievements in levelling the international playing field, but rather in its contribution to the safety of the international banking system. Citing discrepancies in public subsidies, accounting rules, legal regimes and enforcement procedures, the report underplayed the impact of the Accord on competitive inequalities. On the contrary, the report claimed in conclusion, the value of the 1988 Capital Accord 'should, instead, be determined by its contribution to increasing the safety and soundness of international banks' (Scott and Iwahara, 1994, p.69). It is interesting to note that the debate over the Accord's impact had shifted so much by this point that it was considered necessary to re-affirm the original goal of systemic stability.

Completely eliminating competitive inequalities between national banking systems, however, was never a stated goal of the 1988 Accord, and would be an impossible target at which to aim. Brian Quinn (1992, pp.303-304), then Executive Director of the Bank of England responsible for Banking Supervision put it best when he wrote:

> ...supervisors should be seeking to establish a reasonable equivalence of regulation between the various financial institutions and across financial markets. I say 'equivalence' and not 'equality' or 'harmonization', because I believe that those objectives are a chimera, unachievable in anything like the time we have to decide the policy issues...It is not realistic to expect that legal, fiscal, and accounting frameworks will be harmonized along with the regulatory framework, just for banks or financial institutions. Broad equivalence of regulatory frameworks is therefore an appropriate target, and one for which the BIS (Bank for International Settlements) Capital Convergence Standards aimed.

The Basel Accord also seems to have contributed to significant changes in industry structure in the banking sector, reflecting the ongoing dialectic between authority and the market. Increasing levels of competition in financial services markets have pushed several banks into mergers that leave them more profitable and better capitalised. Though this process had begun by the end of the 1980s, the emphasis on the quality of capital, rather than merely size of assets, increased the move towards larger and fewer banks (Llewellyn, 1989, p.46). Furthermore, the fact that non-bank financial institutions were exempt from the Basel guidelines added to the competitive pressures already felt by banks. This issue continued to be a point of contention in the discussions over the Basel Capital Accord for several years and pushed many banks to consider mergers with non-bank financial institutions, not covered by Basel rules. By merging, banks were able to consolidate capital and take advantage, at least in principle, of economies of scale. This change in the structure of the banking industry, the emergence of fewer but larger banks, would play a key role in shaping the preferences of the US in the Basel II negotiations (see chapter seven).

The 1988 Accord also contributed to changes in the business practices of the banking industry. By focusing on capital-asset ratios, the Basel Accord removed the rationale, so prevalent throughout the 1970s and 1980s, for banks to aim at asset growth. The size of banks throughout this period had been measured by the total amount of assets on their balance sheets. By the beginning of the 1990s a more usual measure applied to banks was the amount of capital at their disposal. Because the size of a bank's assets were now more tightly restricted by capital ratios, banks began to move increasingly towards fee-based financial instruments and away from the traditional banking business of financial intermediation, that is, the lending of funds deposited with the bank. This move had already begun because of the growth of the twin factors of direct capital market access by corporate borrowers and the availability of higher rates of interest for depositors through investment funds. However, the added incentive of higher capital-asset ratios provoked many Japanese banks, after March 1990 (*Economist*, 1991f, pp.108-111), to attempt to sell off loans on their portfolio to reduce total asset size and thus boost capital-asset ratios.

Furthermore, instead of looking to asset growth as a main business strategy, banks have turned to strategies based on the highest rate of return on assets (Llewellyn, 1992, p.22). This is a fundamental shift in the business of banking.

The trend towards off-balance-sheet activities, exacerbated by the provisions of the Basel Capital Accord, again demonstrates the interaction between authority and the market in banking services. Just as American banks circumvented US interest rate and lending restrictions in the 1960s by moving offshore, so banks in the late 1980s and early 1990s have reacted to competitive and regulatory pressures by shifting a large proportion of their business away from traditional instruments and towards those not reflected on the balance sheet. It can be argued that the focus on capital ratios was one of the main reasons behind the boom in banks' derivative-based activities in the 1990s. To some degree these new instruments have implied the assumption of greater risks for banks, thus requiring additional attention from regulatory and supervisory authorities, something that will be addressed in the following section.

Another area of criticism of the 1988 Accord is that it led to significant distortions in the market in bank lending. The area of country transfer risk was to become one of the most controversial elements of the Capital Adequacy Accord. In these risk-weightings (see Table 4.1) there is an obvious bias towards OECD states. At the time of signing the Accord this seemed to make a certain degree of sense as the OECD was made up of the world's most successful, advanced and stable economies. The Accord itself argues that these states make up a 'defined grouping of countries considered to be of high credit standing'. The justification for this bias is made by rejecting only one other form of measuring country transfer risk, the overly simplistic distinction between loans to domestic institutions and those to foreign institutions. The logic behind the rejection of this other option, clearly a 'straw man', is laid out in the Accord as follows:

1.   a simple domestic/foreign split ignores the wide variation in transfer risk between countries;
2.   a domestic/foreign split ignores the global integration of financial markets and would deter banks from holding foreign government securities as liquid cover against Euro-currency liabilities;
3.   the European Community members wanted to treat all claims on banks, central governments and the official sector within the EC countries in the same way.

The question arises as to why the Committee did not spend more time putting together a more credible treatment of the issue of country transfer risk. Was it merely to speed the process forward that the issue was addressed in such a cursory manner? Or was it rather that the BCBS member countries, also all members of the OECD, wanted to grant each other advantages within the Accord that would help to encourage banking business between them at the expense of less credit-worthy states?

Since the signing of the Accord two things have happened that have altered the underlying logic and made it seem even less satisfactory. First, countries such as Turkey and Mexico have become full members of the OECD, granting loans to their governments, public-sector entities and banks a lower risk weighting than previously granted. Secondly, new instabilities have emerged in certain OECD countries that were previously viewed as being highly stable. The financial and economic woes of Japan, for example, have exposed fundamental weaknesses in that country's banking and real-estate sectors. Both these new realities were to form part of the logic behind a drastic reworking of the Basel Capital Accord in the 1990s.

A further problem with the risk-weightings concerned the preference shown for OECD banks over other private firms. Claims on banks incorporated in the OECD received a 20% risk weighting whereas all private sector claims, both in and outside the OECD, received a full 100% risk-weighting. It thus made more sense for a bank to lend to a bank in Mexico, one that perhaps posed a high risk of default, than to lend to IBM or General Motors. In this case, and that mentioned immediately above, the Accord could be said to have provided an incentive for banks to take on riskier loans. This peculiarity was to receive considerable attention during the negotiations towards a second Basel Accord (see chapter seven).

In answer to the question posed earlier, however, it appears far more likely that the omission of a more sophisticated approach to country risk reflected the needs of political expediency and the desire on the part of the US and UK to avoid lengthy negotiations over matters of detail. The dictates of national competitiveness, while always an important consideration in international economic negotiations, can be seen to have been limited in this case to concerns over Japanese bank competitiveness and the desire to create a level playing field.

There remains one area of significance concerning the impact of the Basel Accord on the international market in banking services that deserves mention. The recession that hit the global economy at the end of the 1980s and early 1990s, it has already been noted, made the boosting of some banks' capital ratios more difficult as the market value of corporate equity, on the whole, declined. However, the new capital ratios had another connection with the recession. Evidence has been brought forward that the need to comply with higher capital ratios was one factor restraining bank lending during the recession. Although other determinants should be taken into account, such as the obvious decline in loan demand during a recession, the need to boost capital and limit growth in, or even shed, assets during this period played a role in creating a 'credit crunch' (Peek and Rosengreen, 1993). This was clearly not a goal of the Basel Accord, and again shows how the interaction of authority with the market often has unintended consequences. Questions of procyclicality would become a central theme for debate in the negotiations towards a reformed capital accord in the 1990s.

A 1999 working paper produced by the Basel Committee (Jackson et al, 1999) analyzed the impact of the Capital Accord in a number of areas, looking at capital ratios, the ways in which banks adjusted their capital ratios after the Accord, risk-taking, capital arbitrage, credit crunches and competitiveness. The study found that 'the average ratio of capital to risk-weighted assets of major banks in the G10 rose from 9.3% in 1988 to 11.2% in 1996'. Furthermore, banks were more likely to cut back lending to meet capital requirements rather than increasing overall capital levels and that capital arbitrage had increased during the 1990s. Its studies on credit crunches, risk-taking and competitiveness were inconclusive. The fact that banks were becoming more likely to engage in capital arbitrage was seen by the Committee as a major challenge to the effectiveness of the Accord and would eventually lead it to negotiate a successor agreement.


## Impact on the Business of Banking Supervision

Though there has been an obvious impact on the international market in banking services, the consequences of the 1988 Basel Accord for banking regulation at the national level have been far more interesting. For the Accord has served as a catalyst for regulatory and supervisory authorities, both national and regional, in ways that went far beyond the mere implementation of the Accord's capital guidelines. This aspect of the Accord's impact in the international banking system confirms that the contribution made by the Basel Committee to increasing the safety and soundness of that system consists of more than just the creation and execution of regulations. The Committee stands out as an example of international cooperation and hence of the possibility of redressing the balance between the market and authority.

On a more abstract level, but one that has serious policy implications, the Accord introduced a new concept into the business of supervision, that of using market discipline to assist authorities in their work. By establishing a common standard for measuring safety and soundness of a bank, one that could easily be used by market players to evaluate individual banks, the Accord found a way to harness the power of the market to the goal of market stability. This concept has since grown in popularity and has become a quasi-mantra for most financial supervisors.

Indeed the Basel Committee itself has recognized that the nature of the 1988 Capital Accord and the importance of consumer confidence are such that the enforcement of its provisions is greatly aided by the discipline of the market. Kapstein (1991, p.30) notes that the Committee's 1990 Annual Report claims:

> Banks have found a distinct advantage in being able to satisfy the rating agencies and the market generally that their capital was adequate in terms of the final Basel standard.

The notion of authority using the market as a tool was still a novelty at the end of the 1980s and it highlights the extent of market understanding reached by regulatory and supervisory authorities.

The implementation of the Basel guidelines was completed in all member countries ahead of the deadline set by the Accord. British authorities showed particular zeal, demanding that their banks meet the Basel standards by December of 1989 (Bank of England, 1988). One issue that has been raised concerning implementation, however, is that of the differences between national regulatory and supervisory systems. Of particular importance to banks in the US is the perception that Japanese banks are less strictly supervised than themselves. In fact, Japanese bank capital levels are measured by supervisory authorities only twice a year, whereas their US counterparts receive quarterly evaluations as well as one randomly timed check every year (Scott and Iwahara, 1994, p.55). This of course allows much greater scope for evasion of capital requirements on the part of Japanese banks.

No single nation's banking industry has been affected more deeply by the Basel Accord than that of Japan and this has been reflected in changes in the regulatory system there. The previous section of this chapter outlined the changes to industry structure and practice. In addition, though, due to the low pre-Basel Accord capital levels of Japanese banks and the depth of the recession in Japan, regulators have been pressured into allowing banks to engage in alternative business practices to boost profits and capital levels. In March 1990, the Ministry of Finance brought in legislation that allows banks to sell commercial loans under certain conditions. This move was clearly aimed at helping banks reduce the size of their assets to ease their capital ratio worries. Furthermore, banks lobbied regulatory authorities heavily for a change that would allow them to get involved in the securities business, again to reduce the size of their assets, a change which finally came into effect in July 1993 (*Economist*, 1993). Though US banks have complained that the lower cost of capital in Japan has made it easier for banks there to comply with the Basel Accord, there can be little doubt that the quest for higher capital ratios could not have come at a more uncomfortable time for them.

Equally, if not more, important in determining the long-term shape of the international banking system has been the impact of the Basel Accord on regulatory and supervisory authorities in the US. Of particular significance is the continuing focus on capital in US regulatory circles and a move towards greater legalism in regulation and supervision that culminated in the Federal Deposit Insurance Corporation Improvement Act (FDICIA) of 1991. FDICIA's main goals, in addition to re-capitalising the FDIC after the Savings and Loans disaster of the 1980s, consisted of:

1.  a new code of safety and soundness standards covering management and financial practices;
2.  bringing into effect new capital rules that exceed Basel requirements; and,
3.  introducing an element of 'automaticity' into banking supervision, called Prompt Corrective Action (PCA).

The last of these goals marks a distinct shift in the character of US supervision away from discretionary powers and flexibility on the part of banking authorities. In their place FDICIA imposes a grading system that supervisors must observe in examining banks.

Five categories are outlined by the Act: well-capitalised (10%), adequately capitalised (8%), under-capitalised (6%), significantly under-capitalised (4%), and critically under-capitalised (2%). The Basel standard of 8% is considered 'adequately-capitalised' under FDICIA, although Tier 1 capital should make up three quarters of that total. At each grade of capitalization, there is a specified course of action to be taken by bank supervisors. PCA still allows for considerable flexibility on the part of supervisors, although less than was available before. Should a bank slip down a grade it would be prohibited from acquiring new assets without either approval from regulators or the payment of a dividend to shareholders. Should a bank reach the bottom two grades, it would be required to issue stock to re-capitalise or merge with another bank, or undergo a change in management structure (*Economist*, 1991a).

As part of the same legislative package, Congress passed the Foreign Bank Supervision Enforcement Act (FBSEA) that made the supervision of foreign banks operating on US soil significantly stricter. Most important of the new rules are that every foreign bank will be supervised by both the Federal Reserve and by either the OCC or a state banking authority. Though the FBSEA was inspired by the scandal surrounding the Bank of Credit and Commerce International (BCCI), it was a clear sign of the mood in Washington concerning the banking industry at the beginning of the 1990s (*Economist*, 1992a). The feeling against bankers prevailing at this time can be compared to that in Washington a decade earlier, when the problems of the Debt Crisis first began to emerge and the 1983 ILSA was passed in Congress (*Economist*, 1991e).

The 1988 Basel Accord can also be seen to have had a catalytic effect on banking regulation in the EU, which increasingly sets standards for banking supervision and regulation across Europe. This is of particular importance when one considers that, located in the UK, the City of London is covered by EU regulations. On December 15th, 1989, a little more than 17 months after the Basel Accord was signed, the countries of the European Union (then European Community) adopted the Second Council Directive on the Coordination of Laws, Regulations and Administrative Provisions Relating to the Taking-up and Pursuit of the Business of Credit Institutions and Amending Directive 77/780/EEC, more commonly known as the Second Banking Directive. The main goal of the Directive was to speed the creation of a truly single market in banking services in the EU. This shows the continuing trend towards more open markets. But the Second Banking Directive was also aimed at harmonizing banking supervision and regulation across the Union. The Directive's regulations concerning home state responsibility and 'passporting' closely mirror the principles contained in the 1983 Basel Concordat. Also included in this piece of legislation, though, were two directives that dealt with bank capital that were clearly influenced by the decisions made in Basel in 1988. The Own Funds (Directive 89/299/EEC) and Solvency Ratio (Directive 89/647/EEC) Directives defined and determined the quantity of qualifying capital required by banks operating in the member countries of the EU. The second of these Directives set the minimum amount of capital for banks operating in the EU at five million ECUs, rather than a specific percentage of total bank assets. This aspect of the Second Banking Directive was obviously more onerous for smaller than for the major banks.

More important, however, than both of these directives was the negotiation of a Capital Adequacy Directive (Directive 93/6/EEC), which would not be passed into European law until March of 1993. The standards put in place by the Capital Adequacy Directive are similar to those of the Basel Accord, setting a general 8% capital-asset ratio, but are more detailed, and include provisions made for netting and specific risks, including foreign exchange and settlement risks. Though this Directive took four years to negotiate and be passed into European law, its roots in the work of the Basel Committee are clear. It should be remembered that seven EU members were then also represented on the Basel Committee and there is an undoubted cross-over of opinion between regulatory and supervisory representatives on the two groupings.

## Impact on the Basel Committee

But what of the ramifications of the 1988 Accord on the Basel Committee itself? Though significant and welcome, the work of the Committee during its first fifteen years of existence can hardly be said to have proceeded at a break-neck pace. The three major agreements in that period made important contributions to the safety and stability of the international banking system, but it seemed as though the Committee achieved little of substance in between the negotiation of these accords. The Capital Accord, however, appears to have acted as a strong stimulus to the Committee and its output has been impressive since 1988.

The 1988 Accord, it can be argued, acted as a potent catalyst in the work of the BCBS. Even if we merely examine the publication list of the Committee issued on the official web-site, we can see that in the fourteen years prior to the Capital Accord (1974-1988) the list includes only three publications. Now that does not include the Concordat, which has been revised many times and thus appears under later publication dates. But in the fourteen years following the Accord the number and frequency of publications increased dramatically. From July 1988 to July 2004 the Committee published a total of one hundred and six documents, and this does not include its publications through the Joint Forum.

But it is not only the number of publications or agreements produced by the Committee that is illustrative of the impact of the 1988 Accord on the Committee. The sheer number of diverse topics that the BCBS has addressed in the period since the Accord illustrates how the success of the agreement spurred the Committee onwards and encouraged it to fulfil its potential as an organ of international financial governance. In addition, Committee expanded its target audience, from the member countries of the Committee to all countries in the international financial system, including the developing world. As will be shown in chapter six, the Committee was to evolve into a central organ of governance during the 1990s. It not only worked continuously to update and improve the Accord, but it sought to address new areas of supervisory activity and, perhaps most importantly, began to coordinate its work with a number of other international financials institutions (IFIs). When financial crisis hit the system in the middle of the decade, the Committee became a central player in the dominant states' response.

In contrast we should look at the international response to the Debt Crisis of the 1980s. Although the Basel Committee was eventually to play a role in international efforts to avoid a repeat of the crisis, its involvement in the process of crisis management was not an automatic assumption. As was shown in chapter 4, it took significant efforts on the parts of the US and UK to secure such involvement. But when the Mexican and Asian crises hit in the 1990s, states and the other organs of international economic governance, in particular the G7, automatically turned to the BCBS to develop standards to improve the safety and soundness of the international banking system. Moreover, they called on the Committee to coordinate efforts with other organs of financial governance to develop common rules and guidelines for establishing supervisory responsibility.

**The Significance of the Impact**

This chapter has argued that the Basel Accord of 1988 has had a twin impact on the international banking system, first in its effects on the international banking industry, and second as a catalyst for regulatory reform. The new focus on capital has had effects on the industry in terms of structure, practice and competition. As for the representatives of authority in the international banking system, the Basel Accord can be seen as both reflective of, and a stimulus to, a trend amongst regulators to match the growing internationalism of banking with international cooperation and policy coordination.

The Basel Accord is indicative of the strength of the hold that the idea of the market has over regulatory and supervisory authorities. The focus on capital can be seen as a response to a perception that the market was unable to provide sufficient safety and soundness to the international banking system without help from banking authorities. This is not to say that regulators sought the submission of markets in the period following the Basel Accord. Instead, the new wave of supervisory vigour (and rigour) has largely taken the form of an attempt to change regulations and supervisory practices so that they bring stability and safety without stifling the market. To quote the Executive Director of the Bank of England responsible for supervision, the feeling among regulatory and supervisory authorities is that 'supervision should go with the grain of the market rather than against it' (Quinn, 1992).

This belief amongst banking authorities that the role of regulation and supervision is to provide stability while encouraging market efficiency can be seen in the twin goals of the Basel Accord. For the intent of the Accord was to first 'strengthen the soundness and stability of the international banking system' and, secondly, that the Accord would work towards 'diminishing an existing source of competitive inequality among international banks' (BCBS, 1988, p.2).

Banking industry practice has been going through a period of transition for the past twenty years and the Basel Accord has served to stimulate and quicken the rate of change. The need to set aside increased levels of capital for on-balance-sheet assets such as loans has encouraged banks to turn away from the traditional business of financial intermediation towards new fee-based instruments such derivatives. This shows once again that the market reacts to new regulation by seeking out areas that are as yet unrestrained by the dictates of authority.

Furthermore, the need to increase capital levels has forced many banks to look to the securitization of assets. This has meant a change in bank balance sheets, but more importantly a change in the way banks do their business. Banks' trade in securities in the period after the 1988 Basel Accord received a boost (which in turn led to regulatory reform in Japan) and, more importantly, a shift in business strategy from asset growth to an approach based on the highest *rate* of return on assets.

The impact of the 1988 Accord on Capital Adequacy can also be evaluated with reference to the organisation of the international market in banking services. Three major effects can be determined. First, the Accord aimed at 'diminishing an existing source of competitive inequality' arising from different capital requirements in national banking systems. Though the degree to which this goal has been achieved is in question, regulators in all participating countries surveyed in a United States

General Accounting Office study 'generally agree that the Basel framework is a step toward reducing competitive inequality, or levelling the playing field, among banks from different countries' (GAO, p.23).

This strengthening of competition in the international market for banking services has resulted in a second effect on the structural organisation of that market. Higher capital-asset ratios and increased competition have hastened the already present trend towards mergers between banks. Mergers have, of course, meant fewer and larger banks: a contraction in the number of market players without a correspondent contraction in the size of the market itself. It is often assumed that bigger means safer and better in banking. It can also mean that problems more readily visible in smaller financial institutions go unnoticed by supervisors in larger financial conglomerates.

One last aspect of the structural transformation of the international market in banking services is that the market itself has changed. Because of banks' adoption of new financial practices, and the removal of regulatory 'fire-walls' between different types of financial institution, the market is rapidly being transformed into an international financial, rather than merely banking, market. Increasingly, securities firms are competing in the same markets as banks; banks in the same markets as insurance firms. These changes continue to the present.

A review of the history of banking regulation in advanced financial markets suggests that regulation receives its largest impetus from political reactions to financial crises and it was a crisis that inspired the negotiation of the 1988 Capital Adequacy Accord. However, though the round of regulatory and supervisory reform that followed the Basel Accord was inspired by a crisis, that regulation and supervision focused on crisis prevention rather than mere crisis management (Kapstein, 1989, pp.330-331). Regulatory and supervisory responses are thus not merely about shutting the stable door after the horse has bolted (*Economist*, 1992c). The Basel Committee's work in 1988 demonstrated that supervision can be purposive and can make a valuable contribution to systemic safety and soundness.

In the previous chapter it was noted that leadership from the United States and support exhibited by the United Kingdom were crucial in achieving international cooperation on the issue of capital adequacy. That cooperative success has clearly spawned further attempts at the coordination of national regulatory and supervisory stances. The Basel Committee appears to have acquired a degree of momentum that is carrying it forward and has given it a central place in the regulation of international banking. This is not to say that momentum is enough to ensure the future success of the Committee's work. As the rest of this book shows, politics continues to drive and complicate the development of the harmonisation of international banking rules.

The work of the Basel Committee has also acted as a stimulus to banking regulation in another multinational body, the European Union. The EU's banking legislation has clearly taken its lead from the work of the Committee but it differs from that emanating from Basel in one major aspect. EU banking legislation is precisely that - legislation. It becomes law in EU member countries, unlike Basel agreements which are mere recommendations. These recommendations naturally have some force behind them as international denunciation would follow an abrogation of a Basel agreement. However, the fact that the Basel Committee has acted as a catalyst to

EU banking legislation that bears the status of European law is a testament to the importance of the Committee.

## Conclusion

The Basel Accord on the Convergence of Capital Measurement and Capital Standards had a significant impact on the international banking system at both the market and regulatory levels. It reflected, and affected, the strength of the hold of the idea of the market over policy-makers; it contributed to far-reaching changes in the economic organisation of the banking market; and it helped bring about a shift in the structure of the international banking industry. Furthermore, the Basel Accord has been influential in bringing about regulatory and supervisory changes in national banking systems and its success has brought a sense of momentum to the Committee itself.

In these ways, therefore, the signing of the Accord can be seen as a pivotal moment in the history of the Basel Committee. Before the Accord the Committee had achieved very little in concrete terms, beyond the development of mutual understanding and very general agreements on cooperation. The Capital Accord carried the Committee firmly into the territory of policy and the setting of minimum standards. It also put a document on the table that could be revised, re-thought, and re-worked over time.

But the success and impact of the Accord also raised the profile of the Committee and made it more obviously political than it had been before. One of the major themes of this book is that, behind the technicalities and abstractions of the Basel Committee, lie a number of hard political realities that, as much as anything else in the realm of banking, drive and shape the Committee's work. Chapter seven gives us more evidence of this and of the importance of national and particular interests in determining outcomes in the Committee, but for now this book turns to the broader activities of the BCBS in the 1990s concerning the governance of international banking.

# Chapter 6

# The Basel Committee in the 1990s: Governing Global Banking

## Introduction

The decade of the 1990s was to prove the most eventful in the Committee's history as it pushed the organisation to the fore of global governance issues and into the broader consciousness of policy-makers. Not only the success of the 1988 capital Accord, but more importantly the major financial crises of the 1990s and the subsequent search for a new international financial architecture (IFA) gave a strong impetus to the BCBS as it consolidated its earlier achievements.

In some senses this involvement was a logical follow-on from the Committee's prior work, and certainly echoed the style and approach of what had been done in the 1970s and 1980s. In much of its response to the troubles of the global financial system during the 1990s the BCBS maintained an elevated, procedural position, focusing on the techniques of banking supervision. By steering clear of politics as much as possible and by dealing with macro-level issues rather than attempts at micro-management (unlike its later efforts in Basel II), the Committee was able to establish itself as a respected organ of financial governance without falling prey to the problems of clashing national and particular interests. In a sense this was easy to do; on the one hand the Committee was asked to develop general principles about which there could be little dispute, while on the other it worked alongside other regulatory bodies to formulate a framework for cooperation in financial supervision.

This chapter examines the work of the Committee throughout the 1990s in dealing with the changing face of banking through the Joint Forum, and in facing the challenges of repeated financial crisis in the international system through its collaborative work with the G7 and IMF. These two areas of exertion, along with the revision of the Basel Accord (to be described and analysed in chapter seven), defined the Committee's existence throughout the 1990s, and showed the growing strengths of the Committee in responding to changes in the international financial system, but also the emerging limitations of the BCBS and its frequent inability to move beyond mere prescription. By sticking to general principles rather than policy oriented specifics, the Committee's work in these areas has been comparatively unaffected by political wrangling, but it has also limited the effectiveness of the end-product.

## The Basel Committee and Crisis Prevention

The 1990s will always be remembered as a decade of great turmoil in the international financial system, as crisis after crisis hit national economies and indeed entire regions. Crises in Mexico, Asia, Russia and Brazil, alongside a prolonged period of financial depression and scandal in Japan, haunted the system and threatened to interrupt the flow of credit around the globe. Yet a global meltdown of finance was avoided and the most powerful states in the system began a process of piecemeal reform of the arrangements governing international finance.

The Basel Committee played an important role in this process, responding to calls from the G7 to formulate basic standards of banking supervision that could be applicable to all countries in the system and methods for their application. Furthermore, the Committee has worked towards building confidence in the system and assisting developing countries through its participation in the newly-created Financial Stability Institute.

## Banking Crises and International Financial Turmoil

The 1990s posed a number of challenges to the organs of global economic governance. Although the United States experienced a prolonged period of economic growth, and Europe continued its project of integration (with a few considerable hiccups), the rest of the global economy did not fare so well. Chronic recession in Japan, beginning in the early 1990s, continued to defy the attempts of the Japanese government to jump-start economic recovery. Africa remained mired in incurable economic and political underdevelopment and appeared to have few opportunities to escape from its status as the basket-case of the world economy. But perhaps most worrying for the governing bodies of global finance, the other basic feature of the international economy between 1990 and 2000 was the frequency and severity of international financial crises. Latin America, Asia, and Russia all experienced costly periods of capital flight and deep economic and financial turmoil.

The onset of the Mexican peso crisis in December 1994 marked the beginning of a new period of deep instability in the international financial system. The combination of a growing balance of trade deficit and political instability brought about an abrupt fall in the value of the peso and a flood of capital out of the country. The crisis needed $50 billion in emergency credit from international organizations and bilateral aid.

Michel Camdessus, then managing director of the IMF, announced that the peso crisis was the 'first financial crisis of the 21$^{st}$ century', stressing that it represented a new kind of threat to the stability of the international system. Like many others, Camdessus had noted the speed with which capital had fled from Mexico, a function of the nation's over-dependence on portfolio investment. But, despite this novelty, the Mexican crisis had one aspect that was very much in common with other financial crises of the twentieth, and indeed previous, centuries. For in addition to problems in its balance of payments position, the

Mexican economy was undermined by a deep crisis in its banking system. This crisis not only contributed to the onset of the peso's devaluation, it also aggravated the impact of the devaluation on the Mexican economy and society.

Mexican banks had been re-privatised in 1991 after a decade of nationalisation that had followed the debt crisis in 1982. In that time an entire generation of bankers had been lost to the Mexican financial system and banking supervision had become lax and unaccustomed to the demands of the market. On privatisation in 1991, the banks were sold to groups with little or no experience in banking. Instead, the typical profile of a Mexican bank owner in the early 1990s was someone with a background in industry. Banks were sold for exaggerated amounts, at dramatically more than their book value. This meant desperate efforts to recuperate the purchase price through huge credit expansion and an absence of necessary risk management methods and mechanisms.

When the peso crisis hit and interest rates hit over 100% in some cases, Mexican banks themselves fell into crisis. Borrowers found themselves unable to service their debts and thus defaulted. As banks became burdened with bad debts, credit to the economy dried up, and most banks needed huge injections of government capital through a bank rescue scheme to save them. The banking crisis would eventually cost the country over 15% of GDP.

But the Mexican crisis was just one of a string of banking crises to hit developing countries since the early 1980s. No region of the developing world was left untouched; banking crises hit Asia, Africa and Europe, as well as Latin America. Indeed, a number of scholars have shown that banking crises became increasingly frequent and severe through the last two decades of the twentieth century (Lindgren, Garcia & Saal, 1996; Sundararajan & Balino, 1991).

Banking crises in developing countries are costly in a number of ways. Firstly, of course, for the local economy in which they take place, absorbing huge percentages of the gross domestic product that could be more effectively used for other purposes, thus negatively impacting on national economic development. Banking crises do not only absorb precious government resources in the form of bailouts. In most developing economies banks are overwhelmingly the largest players in the financial system and the largest providers of credit. A banking crisis interrupts the flow of liquidity in the national economy, causes a credit crunch and can handicap economic development for years afterwards. The case of Mexico is relevant here: by 2002 bank lending had still not returned to its pre-crisis levels, stunting the growth of small- and medium-sized business and holding back the development of the national property market.

Secondly, banking crises in developing states are costly for national governments and political stability. In many cases of banking crisis in the developing world, the crisis has been followed by a period of political instability or change of government. While, if we look at countries such as Mexico, in the long term this can be a force for positive change, the effects on the national economy can be highly disruptive in the short- to medium-term.

A third cost of banking crises can be perceived on the regional level, as the phenomenon of contagion can spread financial problems from one country to its neighbours, particularly if, as in the case of the MERCOSUR economies, they have achieved a significant level of commercial interdependence.

Last, we must consider the costs of developing country banking crises for the developed states. Although individually there are only a small number of LDCs of real economic importance for the global economy in terms of GDP (see Garten, 1998), as a group they now account for approximately 50% of world economic activity (according to some calculations and adjusted for purchasing power parity). LDCs are now significant importers and exporters, large recipients of capital, and sources of human migratory flows that can destabilise the political and economic situations of neighbouring states. Of more relevance for this study, certain developing economy financial systems have become highly integrated into the network of global finance. Thus the effects of financial instability in these states can have an immediate and long-term impact on the economies of the more developed states.

In the case of Mexico the threat of negative spill-overs was felt most keenly, of course, in the United States. The long-term project of the North American Free Trade Agreement (NAFTA) had brought huge American investment in the Mexican economy and a financial meltdown threatened the immediate interests of US investors, producers and consumers. In the case of the Asian crisis from 1996 onwards, Japanese banks saw their investments and interests in Asia severely weakened or destroyed, further aggravating the problems already afflicting the Japanese financial system and national economy.

A sense arose among national economic policy-makers in the G10 states that the international financial system was no longer functioning in a way that contributed to economic welfare at the global and, more importantly from their perspective, national levels. Finance seemed out of control. A growing feeling that the system needed restructuring had begun in the early 1990s with the crisis in the European Exchange Rate Mechanism (ERM). Now, in the mid-90s, financial fragility in the developed world threatened to damage global economic prosperity.

## International Response: Reform of the International Financial Architecture

The reform of the international financial architecture (IFA), was to become a favourite topic for the G7/8 over the next few years (Kaiser, Kirton, Daniels, 2000) and for academic investigation and postulation (Akyuz, 2002; Kenen, 2001; Armijo, 2002; Eichengreen, 1999). A broad-based examination of the structure of the international financial system began that would have produce uneven results.

The G7, meeting in Halifax, Nova Scotia in the summer of 1995, called for reform of the international financial architecture and considered a number of different options. Reform of the international financial institutions, greater levels of transparency and disclosure, and the possibility of an internationally-applied Tobin Tax all featured in their discussions.

In its meeting the following year in Lyon, the G7 called directly on the Basel Committee to formulate principles of supervision that could be applied to the banking systems of the developing world. The final communiqué of the G7 heads of government called for banking authorities to work towards 'the adoption of strong prudential standards in emerging economies'. The same year, the G7 finance ministers' report called on both the Basel committee and IOSCO to contribute to the process of international financial architecture reform in five key areas (G7, 1996):

1.  Cross-sector supervisory cooperation through the Joint Forum in general and, more specifically, the issue of lead regulators.
2.  The strengthening of prudential standards in emerging markets.
3.  Encouraging transparency in the private sector.
4.  Improving standards of reporting and disclosure in the area of derivatives trading.
5.  Enhancing cooperation and information sharing arrangements among securities exchanges.

While the first area will be addressed later in this chapter, the second is of direct relevance here. The finance ministers recognised the unique position of the BCBS and IOSCO to formulate basic standards of supervision for developing country financial systems and asked them to:

> strengthen prudential standards in, and supervisory cooperation with, emerging markets. Effective prudential regulation and supervision must cover all important financial marketplaces, particularly those which are experiencing high growth rates and/or substantial capital flows.

The report went on to acknowledge the two organisations' work already accomplished in this area before stressing the urgency of achieving better financial supervision in LDCs if future crises were to be avoided:

> Because emerging markets are growing in significance, these Committees, and other appropriate fora should be encouraged to strengthen their outreach to and cooperation with emerging market supervisors in order to promote high prudential standards. The International Financial Institutions should give more attention to promoting effective regulatory and supervisory structures in emerging markets.

The Basel Committee itself had already come to the realisation that what had been achieved, though significant, still left a huge gap in the world of banking supervision and regulation. While the progress made in improving capital adequacy had been impressive, and had done much to improve the soundness and stability of banking systems in the G10 states, an eight percent capital requirement meant little in financial systems marked by deep political and economic instability. The Committee realised that, with the exception of its work in the regional supervisors' groups, it had essentially ignored the question of banking supervision in LDCs.

Part of this failing was due to the Committee's concentration on issues of capital adequacy and an unspoken assumption that higher capital levels meant greater stability for international banking as a whole. Banking in emerging markets, however, has always been a fundamentally different affair to its counterpart in the developed world. Accounting practices, weaknesses in the legal system, political interference, and overall instability in both economic and political systems pose a wide variety of challenges to banks and supervisors alike.

Given all of these intervening factors, the quality of banking supervision in LDCs is uneven and often below par. Many LDC authorities lack the resources, training and expertise necessary to maintain proper and adequate oversight of the banking system. As has been discussed in chapter three, until the mid-1990s, the Committee had only examined the issue of information exchange with supervisory groups from LDCs. Now the urgent need for basic supervisory assistance from Basel became clear.

**The Need for Universal Basic Supervisory Standards**

Unlike many of the issues contained in the rhetoric surrounding the reform of the IFA, the importance of focusing on financial reform in developing states and of including their interests in the international debate (Wood, 2000; Porter & Wood, 2002) did receive some attention from the IFIs. This importance was stressed by a number of scholars of the international financial system. Barry Eichengreen's contribution to the debate over the reform of the IFA (1999) offered a package of practical, workable measures that the world's leading nations could implement to improve the soundness of the international financial system. Interestingly, Eichengreen's package of measures begins with two areas for crisis prevention, international financial standards and bank risk assessment and risk management. His thoughts on preventing future crises therefore are firmly centred on the formulation of international regulatory and supervisory standards that can restrain risky financial behaviour.

Morris Goldstein (1997), in a now famous study of banking crises and the need for an International Banking Standard (IBS), compiled a near-exhaustive list of the causes of banking crises in developing economies. He noted predominantly the domestic factors that contribute to developing country crises, all of which serve to show the increased proclivity of LDCs to financial sector problems:

1.  Higher economic volatility, creating relatively high credit and market risk.
2.  Excessive lending by LDC banks during economic booms.
3.  Poorly organized financial liberalisation.
4.  Government involvement in the banking sector and connected lending.
5.  Weak accounting, discounting, and legal systems.
6.  Problems of moral hazard and regulatory forbearance.
7.  Poor quality of credit review processes and credit information systems.
8.  Exchange rate regimes that complicate crisis prevention and management.

Goldstein noted that it was not only developing countries that had been afflicted by banking crises in recent memory for industrialised states had also been guilty of creating the conditions for financial fragility that led to banking disasters, with Japan being only the most recent example. But Goldstein chose to focus on the problems of LDCs because, 'there is no precedent for the wave of severe banking crises that have enveloped developing countries over the past 15 years' (1997, p.59) and there is a growing amount of evidence that suggests that developed countries are affected more and more by problems originating in these economies.

Goldstein's answer to the problem of banking crises in developing states was to formulate an international banking standard. His call for an IBS that would reduce the frequency and severity of (but not eliminate) banking crises, included wholesale reform of not only banking regulations and supervision, but also accounting rules and the legal framework within which banking takes place. He thus suggested that countries, not regulatory authorities, become signatories to an IBS in order that the necessary cross-jurisdictional reforms take place. His international standard consisted of eight separate but connected factors:

1.  Public disclosure.
2.  Accounting and legal framework.
3.  Internal controls.
4.  Government involvement.
5.  Connected lending.
6.  Bank capital.
7.  An incentive compatible safety net and resisting pressures for regulatory forbearance.
8.  Consolidated supervision and cooperation among host- and home-country supervisors.

Goldstein's determination that the considerable achievements attained thus far by the Basel Committee alone and in its work with other fora needed to be supplemented by new international efforts to prevent future crises highlighted the comprehensive nature of financial reform that was needed in the international system. It also laid bare the inadequacy of the overall international response to the challenges facing the system.

**Formulating the Core Principles**

The Basel Committee wasted no time in formulating a response to the crisis in the international financial system and was one of the first international financial institutions to make a tangible contribution to the process of IFA reform. In 1997 the Committee emitted a document that claimed to 'provide a comprehensive blueprint for an effective supervisory system'. Its *Core Principles for Effective Banking Supervision* (1997) was published in April of that year, the product of a working group that brought together national supervisory authorities from the Basel members and representatives from Chile, China, Czech Republic, Hong Kong, Mexico, Russia and Thailand (eight other LDCs were also involved in the discussions at a less formal level). Furthermore, the principles included in the document were immediately endorsed by the Basel Committee's eleven regional supervisors groups. This was the first time that LDCs had been so deeply involved in the formulation of international standards for banking, or indeed for any area of finance. The principles, formulated as a sort of 'recipe' for banking system soundness, reflected the diverse challenges facing supervisors in LDCs as well as developed country banking systems.

Twenty-five principles were included in the document, grouped into seven distinct areas. They covered every aspect that the Committee deemed necessary 'for a supervisory system to be effective' (BCBS, 1997, p.2):

1. Preconditions for effective banking supervision.
2. Licensing and structure.
3. Prudential regulations and requirements.
4. Methods of ongoing banking supervision.
5. Information requirements.
6. Formal powers of supervisors.
7. Cross-border banking.

The principles were set out as minimum requirements and the Committee stressed that 'in many cases may need to be supplemented by other measures designed to address particular conditions and risks in the financial systems of individual countries'. Moreover, the Committee noted that the successful implementation of the core principles would require 'substantive changes in the legislative framework' in many countries (BCBS, 1997, p.3).

By drawing together basic standards and principles in a number of such diverse areas of banking supervision, the Basel Committee was essentially summarising much of its work to date and bringing together a body of expertise that, at least in theory, provided a valuable tool for banking authorities around the world. The innovation was to consolidate the principles in one document and to do so with an eye to their impact on developing country banking systems. Although the Committee was keen to stress that the principles were for application equally in developed as in developing countries, the timing of the publication, the involvement of LDC supervisory authorities in its creation and the immediate endorsement by the regional supervisory groups made its target audience quite clear.

In announcing the Core Principles, the Committee urged authorities around the world to endorse them as soon as possible and to speed implementation. Furthermore it suggested that the IMF and World Bank 'use the principles in assisting individual countries to strengthen their supervisory arrangements in connection with work aimed at promoting overall macroeconomic and financial stability' (BCBS, 1997, p.2). This opened the way for the two Bretton Woods organisations to insist on endorsement and implementation of the principles as a condition of loans.

The principles were issued for consultation and officially approved in September of the same year. Although the principles revisited favourite Basel themes such as capital adequacy, their emphasis was clearly on the need for autonomy and resources for banking authorities. Without adequate resourcing and independence, supervisors would remain powerless to ensure that stricter regulations were actually enforced. The principles stress operational independence, adequate resources, clearly defined authority and responsibilities and access to bank information through on-site inspections. Echoing the problems felt in most LDC supervisory authorities, Juan Antonio Niño, head of the Panamanian Bankers' Association, was quoted by the *Financial Times* at the time:

> Capital is not really the problem, the problem is the quality of supervision...The budget has to increase. We have to have professionals as well paid as the professionals at Coopers and Lybrand or Price Waterhouse. (Graham, 1997)

In addition to the publication of the Core Principles, the Basel Committee also released a compendium of existing BCBS recommendations, guidelines and standards, bringing together all of the Committee's work in one place for the first time. The Compendium was divided into three volumes, looking at basic supervisory issues, advanced supervisory methods, and international supervisory issues respectively. This work has been repeatedly updated since April 1997.

What the Committee did not do at this time was to offer concrete proposals for implementation and assessment of compliance. This was to follow in October 1999 when the Committee published the *Core Principles Methodology*, a series of guidelines designed to facilitate the implementation of the Core Principles through self-assessment, assessment by outside actors (such as the IMF and World Bank) and peer reviews. The methodology not only explained how supervisors could carry out an assessment of the supervisory system, but also gave a detailed examination of each of the twenty-five principles and the criteria necessary for compliance. It enumerated 'essential criteria' and 'additional criteria' for each principle, and insisted that the former must be met 'without any significant deficiencies'.

In the interim period the idea of the core principles had been warmly received and widely endorsed in the international financial community. At the annual meeting of the World Bank and IMF in Hong Kong in October 1997 the two Bretton Woods institutions had given their blessing and then incorporated the principles into country evaluations. The Group of 22 made explicit reference to the Core Principles in its report on the international financial architecture issued in October of 1998. The same month the International Conference of Banking Supervisors gave its endorsement to the principles. The Basel Committee itself was later to call the principles 'the most important global standard for prudential regulation and supervision' (BCBS, 1999b).

## The Financial Stability Institute

While the formulation and publication of core principles of banking supervision and guidelines for their implementation were undoubtedly an important contribution to the process of improving stability in the international financial system, the Basel Committee recognised that it needed to make a more direct and long-term effort to help developing country supervisors in their work. In March 1998 the Committee, in conjunction with the BIS, announced the creation of a Financial Stability Institute (FSI). The stated purpose of the FSI at its creation was to 'improve the effectiveness with which training is planned, co-ordinated and delivered' (BCBS, 1998) in all countries, though with an obvious emphasis on LDCs; the FSI later expanded on this by outlining four key objectives for itself:

1.  To promote sound supervisory standards and practices globally, and to support full implementation of these standards in all countries.
2.  To provide supervisors with the latest information on market products, practices and techniques to help them adapt to rapid innovations in the financial sector.
3.  To help supervisors develop solutions to their multiple challenges by sharing experiences in focused seminars and regional workshops.
4.  To assist supervisors in employing the practices and tools that will allow them to meet everyday demands and tackle more ambitious goals.

In the period since the FSI began work in 1999, it has organised seminars and workshops and has helped to distribute information to supervisors through its quarterly newsletter, *FSI World*. In addition it has published a couple of occasional papers examining the changing structure of the financial industry. Though the immediate benefits of the FSI's efforts are hard to see, it offers the prospect of a credible long-term role in enhancing the effectiveness of banking supervision in developing country markets.

**The Financial Stability Forum**

The Basel Committee has also been involved in the work of the Financial Stability Forum (FSF), a grouping of financial authorities created in February 1999 to further the causes of information exchange and international cooperation in finance. The chair of the BCBS attends the biannual meetings of the FSF, alongside counterparts from other international financial institutions, the central bank deputies, Treasury deputies and heads of supervision from the G7 nations, and the central bank governors of Australia, Hong Kong, the Netherlands and Singapore. The FSF has served as a mechanism to coordinate the actions of different national authorities and IFIs, and to provide oversight of the ongoing process of IFA reform. The Basel Committee's work make up a large portion of the FSF's bi-annual reports on progress in securing sound financial systems (see, for example, FSF, 2003) and this has served to highlight the high level of BCBS activity when compared with other bodies such as IOSCO or the International Association of Insurance Supervisors (IAIS).

### The Basel Committee and Transparency

The Core Principles themselves were to a certain degree overtaken by the financial implosion that took place in Asia during 1997. Clearly banking problems there had contributed greatly to the crises, especially in countries such as Thailand and South Korea. But one issue above all others emerged in the aftermath of the Asian financial crises, that of transparency, and the Basel Committee was once more called on to formulate a standards-based response for the international banking system.

The issue of transparency became a central concern for the IFIs and for the G7/8 after the Asian crises. The 1998 meeting of the G7 finance ministers in Birmingham in May of that year identified it as the number one issue in its report *Strengthening the Architecture of the Global Financial System* (G7, 1998), and called on the IFIs to increase openness in their operations, and those of their members. The BCBS set up a sub-group on bank transparency that examined the impact of information availability on market discipline and on improving the effectiveness of banking supervision. Its report, issued in September 1998, stressed the importance of the disclosure of 'timely information' in a number of areas:

1. financial performance;
2. financial position (including capital, solvency and liquidity);
3. risk management strategies and practices;
4. risk exposures (including credit risk, market risk, liquidity risk and operational, legal and other risks);
5. accounting practices;
6. basic business, management and corporate governance information.

The report placed special emphasis on the benefits to be had from market discipline, reflecting once again the Committee's growing adherence to the philosophy of working with the market in the business of banking supervision. The report also noted that improving bank transparency was a necessary element in ensuring the success of the Core Principles, to allow sufficient amounts of quality information to flow to supervisors.

The report on bank transparency was the first in a series of efforts made by the Basel Committee, alone and in conjunction with IOSCO and IAIS, to formulate standards and guidelines for transparency and disclosure in international banking. Over the next few years the Committee continued to examine the issue of transparency, emphasising bank disclosure, looking at trading and derivatives disclosures (1998, 1999, 2002), best practices for credit risk disclosure (1999, 2000), and sound practices for loan accounting and disclosure (1999).

### Industry Consolidation and the Changing Face of Banking in the 1990s

As banks struggled to compete against new competitors in the late twentieth century, a consolidation process began in which banks grew bigger and sought to benefit from economies of scale. In addition to mere expansion, however, they took on new activities and merged with firms from other areas of finance. This, along with the twin phenomena of the internationalisation of financial markets and the deregulation of domestic financial markets combined during the late 1980s and early 1990s to push financial actors to form new corporate groupings which provided a complete range of financial services.

Three kinds of merger and acquisition (M&A) have been seen in the international financial system since the early 1990s. The first, where two firms in the same sector merge is largely undertaken in an effort to cut costs and benefit from economies of scale. Thus when two banks from the same country merge and later cut staff and branches, the new entity should (though not always) be more efficient. The second kind of M&A concerns two firms from the same sector merging across national boundaries. Though this kind of M&A is still relatively uncommon in Europe, it has been observed increasingly frequently in the case of financial firms (especially banks) from developed countries buying up the operations of counterparts in developing economies. This form of internationalisation of finance continues the process begun back in the 1950s and 1960s of international expansion.

The third kind of M&A occurs when a firm in one sector of finance, say a bank, merges with a firm from a distinct sector, say insurance. This kind of M&A, often involving internationally active firms, means that the conglomerate would be able to offer its clients a complete financial services package and avoid the problem of disintermediation of deposits that had afflicted banks since the 1980s.

Integrating insurance and securities activities as well as traditional banking services into a single entity, sometimes called Universal Banking, meant that by the early 1990s the landscape of international banking and of finance in general had been fundamentally altered by the emergence of cross-sector financial conglomerates. These new behemoths of international finance posed an entirely new set of challenges for national supervisors, and increased the risk of contagion from one area of finance to another.

These entities had long existed in Germany and Italy, where the terms *Allfinanz* and *Bancassurance* are part of the financial lexicon. However it was the spread of financial mergers throughout the banking systems of the US and UK that transformed the competitive backdrop against which international financial activity took place. Not only were the new corporations huge, dwarfing the previous giants of the marketplace, but they could offer a complete range of financial products and services to their clients, as well as access to enormous financial resources.

In the second half of the 1990s 'merger mania' was rife in financial circles for a number of reasons. In the US the booming stock market propelled shareholders to seek gains that could be made from such deals, and managers and CEOs to make cost-cutting efforts to increase shareholder value. In Japan the financial crisis pushed the banking system to disaster and then forced an enormous consolidation in which four gargantuan players have survived. In Europe the creation of the Euro had pushed many banks to cut costs by merging and to look at potential foreign partners. The 2000 purchase of Credit Commercial de France by

HSBC for 11 billion Euros marked what some saw as the beginning of large-scale financial consolidation in Europe.

Interestingly, the move towards financial mergers was hastened by the 1988 Capital Accord. The smoothing out of the competitive playing field among banks had meant that non-bank financial actors had gained a competitive advantage over them. For, while banks were required to put aside capital equal to eight percent of their assets (risk-weighted), not all non-bank financial actors were subject to the same regulatory demands concerning capital adequacy. This meant increased pressure on banks and a need for them to branch out into new activities.

The Group of Ten's *Report on Consolidation in the Financial Sector*, published in January of 2001, demonstrated that the '1990s saw dramatic change in the financial services industries of the 13 countries examined' and 'M&A activity contributed to a decreased number of banks and increased competition in the banking industries of most of the countries included in this study' (G10, 2001, p.59). It showed that during the decade of the 1990s, in the 13 countries covered by the study (the G10 plus Spain and Australia), 'there were more than 7,300 deals in which a financial firm in one (country) was acquired by another financial firm' with a total value of approximately $1.6 trillion US (G10, 2001, p.33). As the decade came to a close, this activity was picking up in speed. During the last three years of the 1990s, 'there were nearly 900 transactions annually involving the acquisition of a financial company' (p.34). The size and pace of the consolidation process impelled supervisors to seek closer collaboration with their counterparts in other sectors of finance.

## Collaborating with Supervisory Groups from Other Sectors

Immediately following the successful conclusion of the 1988 Capital Adequacy Accord, the Committee had begun to examine the growing competitive inequalities emerging between banks and non-bank financial institutions which the Basel Accord had aggravated. In 1989, talks began with the International Organisation of Securities Commissions (IOSCO), focusing on capital requirements for investment activities undertaken by banks and securities firms. The negotiations that followed were far from smooth and involved a good deal of compromise between the two bodies (*Economist*, 1991c). The aim of the discussions was an agreement between Basel and IOSCO that would follow the example of the Basel Accord by setting minimum standards applying to at least all internationally active banks and securities firms, with national supervisors having the discretion to impose higher capital requirements and to apply them to all institutions.

Porter's 1993 study of the Basel Committee and IOSCO highlighted many of the differences in the organisation and impact of the two institutions, and the fact that IOSCO remains a much more loosely configured organ of governance. The same can be said to be true of the IAIS and this has reduced the impact and effectiveness of the coordination efforts between the three bodies. Nonetheless, the attempts to harmonize standards among the three sectors of international financial markets demonstrates a willingness on the part of national authorities to try to level the playing field to some extent.

Common standards were sought for banks' and securities firms' positions in traded debt instruments and equities and related derivative instruments. The need for such standards stemmed not just from the perceived unequal treatment given banks and securities firms but also because banks had turned increasingly to non-traditional financial instruments in recent years to boost profits.

IOSCO had begun to discuss common minimum standards for securities firms at its first meeting in July of 1987 and on January 29th, 1992 in Geneva, the two organisations came to a preliminary consensus on such capital requirements and details followed in the summer of that year in the form of consultative papers. This consensus is credited with speeding the acceptance of the EU's Capital Adequacy Directive, which again shows the catalytic effect of the Committee's work (Quinn, 1992). Unfortunately, despite such broad agreement between the two bodies, IOSCO was unable to come to an agreement among its members on suitable minimum standards for capital, and a final accord was not then signed with Basel.

In 1993 the Committee, along with IOSCO and the IAIS came together to form the Tripartite Group of Bank, Securities and Insurance Regulators (Tripartite Group). This temporary grouping was created at the initiative of the Basel Committee to try to formulate supervisory standards for financial conglomerates. It spent the next two years identifying areas of concern for financial authorities stemming from the emergence of these new actors in the international financial system.

In early 1994, work began in the Committee on harmonizing different approaches to risk assessment for financial conglomerates (*Economist*, 1994). In order to undertake such a task, the necessity for extensive consultation with supervisory authorities in other areas of financial activity became apparent. Only by examining the distinct and diverse challenges facing supervisors in each area of financial activity could the Committee begin to understand the bigger picture of risk assessment at the level of financial conglomerates.

On July 27th 1994, the Basel Committee and IOSCO issued a joint press statement and each issued documents providing guidance on the sound risk management of derivatives activities. The press statement ended with a commitment to 'further consultations in the area of derivatives and other topics of common interest' between the two organizations.

A year later in July 1995 the Tripartite Group published a report that identified several challenges posed by financial conglomerates for supervisors. The goal of the report was to examine the 'problems which financial conglomerates pose for supervisors and to consider ways in which these problems might be overcome'. Identifying financial conglomerates as 'any group of companies under common control whose exclusive or predominant activities consist of providing significant services in at least two different financial sectors (banking, securities, insurance)' the report looked at diverse issues arising from their existence.

The three main areas identified by the report as issues for supervisory attention were:

1.  capital adequacy – the need for a group-wide perspective of capital and how to achieve such a perspective;
2.  cooperation between supervisors responsible for different entities within a conglomerate and the need for them to exchange prudential information;
3.  the complex structures of financial conglomerates that often impede supervisory attention.

In addition to these areas of concern the group addressed the issues of contagion, large group-level exposures, shareholder and management tests, gaining access to information in non-regulated entities within a conglomerate, supervisory arbitrage, and the problems posed by mixed (i.e. financial and non-financial) conglomerates.

The major area of focus for the report of the Tripartite Group was, naturally enough, capital adequacy in financial conglomerates. The group attempted to draw up principles for the supervision of capital adequacy so that a complete picture of the capital levels of conglomerates as a whole would be possible. The group's members agreed that in this area, a 'desired group-wide perspective can be achieved' by one of two methods. The group's final report (BCBS, 1995a) identifies them as:

1.  *Consolidated supervision* - This supervisory approach focuses on the parent or holding company, although individual entities may (and the Tripartite Group advocates that they should) continue to be supervised on a solo basis according to the capital requirements of their respective regulators). In order to determine whether the group as a whole has adequate capital, the assets and liabilities of individual companies are consolidated; capital requirements are applied to the consolidated entity at the parent company level; and the result is compared with the parent's (or group's) capital.
2.  *Solo-Plus Supervision* - This supervisory approach focuses on individual group entities. Individual entities are supervised on a solo basis according to the capital requirements of their respective regulators. The solo supervision of individual entities is complemented by a general qualitative assessment of the group as a whole and, usually, by a quantitative group-wide assessment of the adequacy of capital. There are several ways in which this quantitative assessment can be carried out.

To some extent these principles echo the early work of the Basel Committee on the Concordat, namely that no bank escapes supervision, and of the capital Accord, to ensure adequate capitalisation of banks, but they update that work for the changing face of international finance and apply it to financial conglomerates. The basic idea was clearly that risk be evaluated at the level of the conglomerate, not merely at the level of its individual units. To carry this work forward the report also made a number of important recommendations to the three parent organizations and concluded that:

> In order to take work forward in what each regards as an important area, the Basle Committee, IOSCO and the IAIS have agreed to the establishment of a joint forum to develop practical working arrangements between the different supervisors of financial conglomerates for consideration by the three groups and their individual member authorities. The new group will be expected to propose improvements in cooperation and information exchanges between supervisors, and work towards developing the principles on which the future supervision of financial conglomerates would be based. The group will consist of a limited number of

nominees from each of the three supervisory disciplines and will work under the present Chairmanship of the Tripartite Group, Mr. Tom de Swaan, Executive Director of de Nederlandsche Bank N.V. (BCBS, 1995b)

## The Joint Forum

Thus a new body was created in the system of international financial governance in 1996. The Joint Forum on Financial Conglomerates brought together representatives from the increasingly linked worlds of banking, securities and insurance supervision to discuss issues of mutual interest and concern in the supervision of cross-sector financial groupings. Its original mandate was fourfold (BCBS, 2001b):

1.  to facilitate the exchange of information between the three groups;
2.  to examine the impact of corporate and legal structures on effective consolidated supervision;
3.  to examine the possibility of establishing criteria to identify a 'lead regulator' or 'convenor';
4.  to develop principles for the future supervision of financial conglomerates.

The Joint Forum immediately set to work to develop institutional mechanisms by which regulators in the three areas could cooperate effectively in the supervision of conglomerates. Meeting three times a year, the group's goal was not to establish minimum standards or to harmonize regulations. Instead it was to find ways to help the individual parent organizations to effectively oversee the operations of financial conglomerates. The Joint Forum has worked on a number of issues:

1.  Capital adequacy;
2.  Supervisory principles for the oversight of financial conglomerates;
3.  Information sharing and mutual understanding among supervisory authorities.

### *The Joint Forum and Capital Adequacy*

The first area, capital adequacy, featured as an important component in the Joint Forum's early work, serving as a continuation of the Basel Committee's work since 1988. However, unlike the minimum standards set by the Basel Committee's Capital Accord, the Joint Forum chose to focus its attention on supervisory techniques to measure capital and to assess adequacy on a group-wide basis in financial conglomerates. Because the group decided to focus on supervisory techniques rather than determining minimum levels of capital adequacy, the proposals that emerged were less controversial than the Basel Committee's solo work had been.

The Joint Forum's main interest was to prevent financial conglomerates from using the complex structure of the conglomerate in ways that would weaken their capital position. For example, the conglomerate as a whole might employ double- or multiple-gearing of their capital, meaning the use of the same capital reserves to cover multiple risks in the different areas of the conglomerate. In the words of the Joint Forum,

> Double gearing occurs whenever one entity holds regulatory capital issued by another entity within the same group and the issuer is allowed to count the capital in its own balance sheet. In that situation, external capital of the group is geared up twice; first by the parent, and then a second time by the dependant. Multiple gearing occurs when the dependant in the previous instance itself downstreams regulatory capital to a third-tier entity, and the parent's externally generated capital is geared up a third time. (BCBS, 2001, p.13)

Because of both the complex structure of many financial conglomerates and the presence of separate supervisory authorities for each function within the conglomerate (banking, insurance and securities), it is possible for a group to use the same capital simultaneously to cover risks in distinct parts of the conglomerate, say in both banking and insurance. Unless supervisors could guarantee that conglomerates did not double- or multiple-gear their capital, capital adequacy ratios would be meaningless. In addition to weakening the overall capital position of the conglomerate, double- or multiple-gearing 'can permit difficulties in one entity to be transmitted more quickly to other entities within the group', thus raising 'prudential concern' on the part of supervisory authorities (BCBS, 2001, p.14).

A similar problem emerged from the practice by some conglomerates of issuing debt at the level of the parent company and then downstreaming the resulting funds as equity to dependants. This places extra strains on the capital position of the conglomerate as whole and produces situations in which excessive leverage can jeopardise the stability of the group.

The other areas of the capital adequacy principles developed by the Joint Forum concerned the activities of other entities within a conglomerate that remain unregulated by any of the three major supervisory authorities. A financial conglomerate, for example, may include entities engaged in activities such as leasing or reinsurance that bear a resemblance to the activities of regulated entities within the group but which are not covered by any regulatory authority. The Joint Forum's report recognised that such activities could place strains on the overall capital position of the conglomerate and called for authorities to consider demanding 'proxy capital' from the regulated entities to cover risks incurred by the unregulated entities.

The partial ownership by conglomerates of regulated entities was also considered an area for concern by the Joint Forum, in particular where the conglomerate holds a substantial but not controlling interest. The Joint Forum was particularly concerned about participations of between 20% and 50% where the conglomerate as a whole might be threatened with contagion without having control over the entity.

Central to all of these tasks was, of course, ensuring sufficient cooperation and information exchange between regulators in different areas. But the Joint

Forum also developed a number of supervisory measurement techniques that could be used to fully consolidate the assessment of capital on a group-wide basis:

1.  Building block prudential approach.
2.  Risk-based aggregation.
3.  Risk-based deduction.
4.  Fall-back treatment for double-gearing.

Each of these techniques were seen as viable methods for evaluating group-wide capital, depending on the availability of information and the preferences of the supervisory authorities involved. The Joint Forum later issued a supplement to the capital adequacy principles paper in which it gave numerical illustrative examples of the situations described in the original paper and comments on the suitability of capital structures.

*The Joint Forum and the Oversight of Financial Conglomerates*

In addition to its work in the area of capital adequacy, the Joint forum also sought to develop a number of principles that would assist supervisors in their efforts to supervise conglomerates on a consolidated basis and to facilitate cooperation and consultation between them. This set of principles was essential to meeting the challenge presented to regulatory authorities by the existence of financial conglomerates and reached further than mere questions of capital adequacy. First the Joint Forum published a set of 'Fit and Proper Principles' to ensure the sound and proper management of conglomerates. Their goals were:

1.  To ensure that supervisors of entities within a financial conglomerate are able to exercise their responsibilities to assess whether those entities are soundly and prudently managed and directed and whether key shareholders are not a source of weakness to those entities.
2.  To promote arrangements to facilitate consultation between supervisors and the exchange of information on individuals and regulated entities, on a case-by-case basis, when requested by other supervisors, to achieve the objective set out above.

The paper proposed applying tests to managers and directors of entities within financial conglomerates if they also exert significant influence on the activities of regulated entities within the same conglomerate. This principle sought to extend the reach of supervisors outside of their immediate area of oversight, by looking more closely at ownership and management structures within conglomerates.

In later papers the Joint Forum addressed the issues of intra-group transactions and exposures and risk concentration, formulating supervisory principles to assist supervisors in their treatment of these areas of risk.

*The Joint Forum and Supervisory Cooperation*

Following the lead of the Basel Committee, the Joint Forum recognised that one of the biggest challenges facing supervisors in their oversight of financial conglomerates was securing mutual cooperation and adequate information sharing. To achieve this, the Forum formulated a general framework and a set of guiding principles for information sharing, and then issued a paper that sought to address the question of identifying coordinators in crisis and non-crisis situations who could act as lead supervisors among the various authorities. The completion of this final task received strong backing from the G7 finance ministers in May 1998, who also called for swift implementation of the principles it contained.

Of all the work thus far undertaken by the Joint Forum, that carried out in the area of coordination and information is perhaps the most significant in the long-term and holds the most potential benefit for the safety and soundness of national and international financial systems. For, by determining a framework and principles to guide their collaboration, the Forum has been able to begin to match the growing tendency in international finance towards cross-sector financial firms.

If we focus exclusively on the principles for information sharing, we can see how they marked a significant step forward in reducing the obstacles supervisors face in accessing data on activities not under their immediate supervisory sway, and in increasing mutual understanding among them. The Forum gave explicit credit to earlier work by all three parent organisations (Basel, IOSCO and IAIS) as a basis for their work on inter-sectoral cooperation.

1. Sufficient information should be available to each supervisor, reflecting the legal and regulatory regime and the supervisor's objectives and approaches, to effectively supervise the regulated entities residing within the conglomerate.
2. Supervisors should be proactive in raising material issues and concerns with other supervisors. Supervisors should respond in a timely and satisfactory manner when such issues and concerns are raised with them.
3. Supervisors should communicate emerging issues and developments of a material and potentially adverse nature, including supervisory actions and potential supervisory actions, to the primary supervisor in a timely manner.
4. The primary supervisor should share with other relevant supervisors information affecting the regulated entity for which the latter have responsibility, including supervisory actions and potential supervisory actions, except in unusual circumstance when supervisory considerations dictate otherwise.
5. Supervisors should purposefully take measures to establish and maintain contact with other supervisors and to establish a climate of cooperation and trust amongst themselves.

While all of this is still at a highly abstract level and reflected the 'Ten Key Principles on Information Sharing' published by the G7 Finance Ministers in May

1998, the foundations have been laid whereby supervisors in the three areas can fruitfully work together to provide adequate oversight of financial conglomerates.

In December 1999 the Joint Forum broadened its mandate to include not only the theme of financial conglomerates, but also issues of common interest to the three parent committees. To further this goal, the Forum set up a number of working groups in March 2000. In November 2001 two of these working groups published their reports. The first dealt with a cross-sectoral comparison of core principles for supervision (BCBS, 2001c). Since the creation by the BCBS of a set of Core Principles for Effective Banking Supervision in 1997 (see above), and the subsequent emission of Insurance Supervisory Principles (1997) and Objectives and Principles of Securities Regulation (1998) by the IAIS and IOSCO respectively, there had been an interest in the Joint Forum for supervisors to acquaint themselves better with each other's core principles and to evaluate the potential for tension or conflict between them.

The second working group to report in November of 2001 examined the area of risk management practices and regulatory capital across the three sectors. The report stressed the importance of sophisticated, but most importantly of effective risk assessment and management practices in financial firms across the three sectors, and urged supervisors to demand that firms engage in such practices. It concluded that as changes in risk management practices gather pace, some convergence between the three sectors would emerge, and supervisors would 'need to re-evaluate their sectoral regimes for capital and provisions to ensure that they provide an appropriate means of evaluating the capital held by firms in relation to their activities' (BCBS, 2001d, p.71).

By 2002 the expanded mandate of the Joint Forum embraced risk assessment, management issues, internal controls, audit functions, corporate governance, outsourcing and common core principles for the three areas. More specifically, the Forum has set up working groups to investigate the areas of:

1. Risk-aggregation.
2. Operational risk management.
3. Credit risk management.
4. Disclosure of financial risks.
5. Cross-sectoral implications of extreme exogenous shocks.

These areas of study and cooperation, along with the already established focus on financial conglomerates, guarantee that the forum will have an extended life-span and will continue to influence the development of regulatory and supervisory coordination between banking, insurance and securities authorities. What remains to be seen is if the Joint Forum can establish itself as the pre-eminent organ of governance for the international financial system as a whole.

## Other Contributions to the Governance of International Banking

In addition to its work on reforming the international financial architecture and meeting the challenges of change in the structure of international finance, the Basel Committee also took a number of steps during the late 1990s and the early years of the new century to respond to specific problems that arose in the system of international banking. In January 1999 the Committee responded to the near-collapse of Long Term Capital Management (LTCM) the previous September by calling for new methods of monitoring bank lending to hedge funds and to other highly leveraged institutions (HLIs). Though the total collapse of LTCM had been avoided through close collaboration between the Federal Reserve and a number of top US banks, it had threatened to bring about a national and international financial meltdown if the firm had been unable to meet its obligations. This, as much as the international financial crises in Mexico, Asia, Russia and Brazil earlier in the decade, posed a serious threat to global financial stability. The Committee put forward a number of recommendations in its report (BCBS, 1999a) stressing information gathering, due diligence and credit analysis. Without calling for official controls on bank interactions with HLIs, the BCBS did emphasise the need for limits on total exposure and accurate measurement of that exposure. A year later the Committee issued a report (BCBS, 2000) commenting on the implementation of the sound practices suggested in its January 1999 paper, and noted that overall bank exposure to HLIs had fallen significantly.

An issue that attracted Basel's attention early in the new century was that of money-laundering. A topic that had been on the G7's agenda for several years, in April 2001 the Committee issued a consultative paper that was issued in official form in October of the same year. Seeking to build on the work of the Financial Action Task Force (FATF) the Basel Committee noted the various risks for banks associated with money-laundering, be they reputational, operational, legal or concentration risks. The Committee called on banks to put in place Know Your Customer (KYC) rules to guarantee customer due diligence.

Finally, as part of the international response to the September 11th 2001 terrorist attacks against the United States, on 14 December 2001 the BCBS held a meeting of Supervisors and Legal Experts of G10 Central Banks and Supervisory Authorities. In April 2002 the Committee released a report that committed the organisation to further work on limiting the potential for banks to channel funds to terrorist groups.

## The Significance of the Core Principles and Joint Forum

The mere fact that the Basel Committee was called upon to formulate a response to the growing turmoil in international finance in the mid- to late-90s tells us much about the elevated stature to which the organisation had risen. It was by now seen as an integral organ of global financial governance and a central player in the effort to stabilise the international financial architecture.

But the nature of the Basel Committee's responses to the emerging challenges in the international financial system tells us much more about the significance of the institution. In meeting the need for basic standards of banking supervision, the BCBS worked closely with supervisory authorities from LDCs to formulate guidelines that reflected the realities of banking in emerging markets. The Core Principles noted the need for legislative reform in many cases as well as changes in other areas of economic governance if stability was to be assured. The standards became a valuable tool for the World Bank and IMF in their evaluations of member country banking systems, and were widely endorsed by banks and regulatory authorities. Moreover, the Committee responded rapidly to the turmoil afflicting the international financial system, being among the first of the IFIs to formulate a policy-oriented response. It avoided political debates and the problems of micro-management, thus steering clear of controversy. The Committee has also focused on the internationally-favoured theme of transparency and disclosure, topics entirely in keeping with its interest in market-oriented regulation and market discipline.

Nonetheless these guidelines remained vague and general and, although the Committee made efforts to facilitate their implementation, there was little done to ensure that national supervisory authorities complied with both the spirit and the letter of the principles. And, despite the inclusion of LDC authorities in the formulation of the Core Principles, the Committee has done little to incorporate them into the more substantive areas of decision-making in the BCBS. As they stand, the Core Principles represent a gesture of good intention from the Committee without the punitive force to back it up. The focus on transparency and disclosure did produce important guidelines for supervisors on the importance of access to information, on best practices and on the possibilities for assistance from market-discipline, but has not culminated in basic minimum standards for information disclosure, nor the necessary corrective action necessary to ensure it. All in all, the Basel Committee's contribution to the reform of the IFA is reflective of the attitude of the dominant economies. Indeed, it is sad to say that the Committee has achieved more than any other IFI in the process.

Similar criticisms could be levelled at the Basel Committee's efforts in the Joint Forum, the second element discussed in this chapter. It is fair to say that the attempt to formulate common perspectives and responses to the challenges of financial conglomerates has thus far dealt almost exclusively in fact-finding and the emission of general statements regarding supervisory methods and cooperation.

However, as finance has innovated to produce these huge and complex conglomerates, so have authorities at the level of the international system. The institutional innovation of the Joint Forum has laid the foundations for ongoing cooperation and coordination among the world's leading supervisory groups. Already the Joint Forum has developed common approaches between insurance, securities and banking supervisors in the areas of supervisory principles, information sharing and, most importantly, capital adequacy. In this last area, the Joint Forum was able to provide solid guidance for supervisors in the three sectors so that they could overcome the problem of double- and multiple-gearing. More recently the Joint Forum has moved beyond the issue of conglomerates to look at other areas of cross-sectoral interest and will continue to build on this in the future.

## Conclusion

Basel's efforts as an organ of global financial governance throughout the 1990s and into the early years of the 21$^{st}$ century demonstrate the elevated status to which the organisation has risen over the past two decades. Called on by the G7/8 to formulate a response to the turbulence of the mid- to late-90s, the Committee came up with basic standards for effective banking supervision and a methodology for ensuring the proper implementation of these guidelines. In response to fundamental changes in the structure of the banking industry and the emergence of cross-sectoral financial conglomerates, the BCBS cooperated with other international financial institutions to develop common perspectives and common approaches.

But the results of its efforts were mixed. On the one hand the creation of the Joint Forum has made ongoing cross-sectoral cooperation and coordination possible among supervisors and marks a willingness on the part of the Committee to match innovation in the market. On the other hand, in the area of IFA reform, though responding rapidly and with due consultation with LDC authorities, the Committee's Core Principles lacked teeth and stand only as a guideline for effective supervision. The conclusions of its work on transparency and disclosure have outlined 'best practices' and 'sound practices' but have failed to establish common minimum standards among authorities for access to information.

The Committee's efforts to move beyond its traditional focus on supervisory cooperation and capital adequacy, therefore, have not been without problems. The BCBS has been able to participate in the efforts to reform the International Financial Architecture through institutional innovation and has attempted to match developments in the market with new cooperative arrangements. However, as of 2004, the Committee seems to have been unable to deepen its work in areas other than supervisory information sharing and capital adequacy. In other areas the BCBS appears to have found it difficult to move beyond the emission of declarations of intent. On the one hand this reflects the lack of meaningful progress in reform efforts at the international level in general, and the failure of the G7 to propose truly innovative responses to the crises of the 1990s. But it may also reflect a reluctance on the part of BCBS members to engage in highly political debates that might jeopardise the progress of negotiations in areas of central concern to the Committee. For controversy and political entanglement have indeed marked the Committee's attempts to update its capital adequacy regime, and it is to this that the next chapter turns.

## Chapter 7

# Updating the Capital Accord: The Road to Basel II

## Introduction

The impact of the 1988 Capital Accord was undeniable. It soon became widely accepted that the Accord had fundamentally changed the landscape of global banking and that the Committee had established itself as one of the leading organs of global financial governance. But the Accord itself, like the group that created it, was far from perfect and a number of actors called for improvements to the capital regime.

This chapter examines the work undertaken by the Committee to update and modify the Accord and the debates surrounding that work. Since its inception the Accord has been a controversial and contested achievement in international banking supervision and work on improving and updating it began almost as soon as it was issued. Throughout the 1990s the Committee worked alongside banks and banking experts to devise methods of improving the efficacy and efficiency of the Capital Accord.

The chapter once again shows the central role played by politics in determining outcomes in the Committee's work. Both national and particular interests have been influential in shaping the reform process and the final policy result. Conflicts between the interests of key members of the Committee as well as between different visions of banking and its supervision play a central role in the story of this chapter.

However, the tale told during this period also raises serious questions about the ways in which the Committee carries out its work, particularly with reference to its autonomy from the industry that it is supposed to be supervising. During the updating and reform process the BCBS has been forced to back down on a number of issues where big banks have refused to accept the Committee's proposals. Thus regulatory capture again features as an issue in this chapter.

The determination of the BCBS to create a new version of the Capital Accord has resulted in several years of work, many thousands of pages in discussion briefs, and countless consultations with regulators and the private sector. Just as with the original 1988 Accord, the final outcome is seen as controversial and contested. Just as with the original Accord, conflict and power have been key elements in deciding that outcome.

## Updating the Accord: The Road to Basel II

Almost as soon as the capital accord of 1988 had been signed, a discourse began between regulatory authorities and the banking industry over the strengths and weaknesses of the agreement. It became clear early on that the broad brushstrokes given by the Accord to the definitions of capital and their respective risk-weightings would not go unchallenged by those most affected.

### Early Amendments

The Committee responded by engaging in a dialogue with banks concerning possible improvements to the Accord. The principal complaint in the period immediately following the signing of the capital accord was the lack of precision given in the definitions of capital. In November 1991, a year before the end of the transition period, the Committee issued an amendment to the Accord. This 'Amendment of the Basel capital accord in respect of the inclusion of general provisions/general loan-loss reserves in capital' improved the definition of general provisions

> so as to ensure greater consistency in the extent to which unidentified provisions are included in capital and in the extent to which elements designed to provide against identified deterioration in the role of particular assets are excluded. (BCBS, 1991)

The amendment also removed the limits imposed by the original accord on the amount of general provisions to be included in Tier 2 capital. The 1988 accord had determined that, by the end of the transition period, general provisions or general loan loss reserves should only be allowed to count for up to 1.25% (2% in exceptional cases) of total risk assets in Tier 2 capital. The original accord had included the phrase 'in the event that agreement is not reached on the refined definition of unencumbered resources eligible for inclusion in supplementary capital', and so the amendment of 1991 usefully tidied up a loose end. The final date for implementation of the amendment was set for end-1993.

Two further amendments were to emerge in 1994. First, the Committee responded to complaints from the banking industry in several countries by changing its rules to make the use of netting easier by banks for capital adequacy. In financial services netting refers to the grouping together of all obligations in multiple contracts between two parties. By thus consolidating the total of the financial obligations, it gives a better idea of the total value of a bilateral relationship. This amendment to the Accord was a concession to banks as it facilitated the determination of capital levels and made more elements eligible for use in that capital. This amendment was finalised in April 1995 with the conclusion of Committee work on off-balance-sheet items (BCBS, 1995).

The second amendment in 1994 was more important to the overall impact and contribution to stability of the Accord. As noted in the previous chapter, in the early 1990s three less-developed countries became members of the OECD, Mexico, South Korea and Turkey. In the eyes of many, this greatly weakened the risk weights set by the Accord as loans to all OECD country governments and their banks had been granted preferential treatment. The new amendment stated that a country would be disqualified 'from inclusion in this group if it has rescheduled its sovereign external debt within the previous five years' (BCBS, 1994). By this measure the less developed members of the OECD were put on notice that bad management of the nation's finances would be punished by making it more expensive for banks to lend to their economies. This amendment was to become particularly important in light of the crises in Mexico, South Korea and Turkey.

In January 1996 the Accord was further modified to incorporate sensitivity to market-risk in the risk-weightings and thus apply a capital charge to market risk. This was the outcome of several years debate between the Committee, national regulatory bodies and banks over the issue of allowing banks to use their own internal risk-assessment models to evaluate market risk and adjust bank capital accordingly. The January 1996 amendment offered banks the option of either using a standardised approach to the question of market-risk, or using their own internal models to carry out the same task. This was to prove a major departure for the Committee and a major issue of debate that would continue into the new millennium.

At the heart of the issue lay a number of questions about banking and banking regulation. They were each to prove pivotal in determining the evolution of the Basel Accord over the next few years:

1.  Does regulation necessarily impede bank efficiency?
2.  Can banks be trusted to effectively measure risk and can they be relied upon to set aside sufficient capital against such risk?
3.  What is the best way to structure the relationship between regulators and the regulated?

The first of these questions had become relevant in the discussions over the Basel Accord because many in the banking industry were arguing by the mid-1990s that the capital accord was pushing banks away from higher quality lenders and towards more risky ones because of the standardised risk-weightings. A loan to a bank in an OECD country, it should be remembered, received a risk-weighting of 20% while a loan to a blue chip corporation was weighted at 100%. Banks argued that this approach to setting capital was not only clumsy, but it also encouraged banks to lend money to borrowers who were not necessarily of the highest quality, and punished them for loans to some high-quality, low-risk clients.

The second question concerned the age-old scepticism amongst regulators as to whether the market is able and willing to provide adequately for its own stability, or whether the drive for profits will inevitably push market actors to take risks that propel the market towards crisis. Recognising the regulators' responsibility to promote the stability and soundness of the banking system, could they realistically depend on banks to act in ways that provide that stability without intervention?

Third we encounter the controversial question of regulatory capture. Clearly close consultation with market actors is essential if authorities are to create efficient, effective and acceptable regulations. But how much input should these market actors be allowed into the policy process? To what extent should regulators abdicate their privilege to control the market, and instead seek to work with it? These two sub-questions are crucial if we are to understand the dynamics of the evolution of the Committee and the capital accord.

For several years banks had been calling for the Committee to allow them to use internal modelling to calculate the total level of risk to which individual banks were exposed, and subsequently to set capital levels accordingly. The Committee resisted through the first half of the decade, but eventually capitulated in 1996 by accepting that banks, on the approval of national regulators and after extensive back-testing, should be allowed to use such modelling to calculate capital. Those banks that did not qualify to use internal models should use the Committee's approved standardised approach to calculate necessary capital. However, the Committee insisted that capital levels calculated through the use of internal modelling needed to be multiplied three times, as a precaution against bank abuse of the system. These new rules would come into effect at the end of 1997.

Of course the January 1996 amendment did not mean the abdication of regulatory and supervisory responsibility on the part of national regulators. For banks to qualify to be able to use their own internal models, regulators would have to ensure that they met a number of qualitative and quantitative standards. Qualifying banks would have to 'demonstrate that they have the appropriate management sophistication and controls' and regulators must 'ensure that their own staff possess the necessary technical skills to evaluate the use of models by the banks in their charge' (*Financial Times*, 1998a).

Throughout 1996 banks demanded that this 'times three' element in the amendment be withdrawn. Banks argued that, if the models used by banks were accurate in their assessment of risk, then there was no need to multiply capital by a factor of three. The Committee agreed to investigate the impact of the two methods and in December 1996 issued a press release on the subject. The Committee recognised that 'the internal models approach will generally produce a lower capital charge than the standardised approach' but admitted that this was because 'the internal models approach appropriately recognises the benefits of risk diversification strategies'. However, despite this, the Committee confirmed 'that the quantitative parameters, including the multiplication factor of three times the outcome of the value-at-risk calculations, will be retained' (BCBS, 1996c).

This was, of course, a huge disappointment for banks who had been pressuring to be granted more flexibility in the use of internal modelling. The London Investment Banking Association deemed the 'times three' factor 'punitive' (Graham, 1996), and throughout the industry banks protested that the amendment remained far too conservative. In addition, banks had to contend with the announcement that the Committee continued to prohibit the use of internal modelling to determine capital levels for specific risk, that is the risk that a specific security might not perform as expected.

Banks, however, refused to surrender the point and continued to pressure regulatory authorities and the Committee to make further amendments to the Accord. The continual pressure from banks was a key factor in bringing about a replacement for the 1998 Accord, and a *Financial Times* headline at the time tells its own story: 'Harassed regulators try to draw the line' (1998c). During the upcoming negotiations for a revised capital accord, the question of internal modelling would become a central area of bargaining and controversy as banks would push regulators to accept the superiority of internal modelling over external standards.

April 1998 saw the emission of another amendment to the Accord. In this the Committee reduced the risk-weighting for bank claims on regulated securities firms to 20% from its original 100% weighting. This was a significant advantage to banks who had become involved in lending to the rapidly growing securities industry in the mid- to late-1990s. It also further demonstrated the increasing links between the several worlds of finance, and the growing dependence, one on the other.

*Breaking the Camel's Back*

Due to all of these amendments the 1988 capital adequacy accord now looked dramatically different to its original version. Regulators had consistently bowed to bank pressure to allow more and more items to be counted as bank capital and this seriously weakened the Accord. But the final straw was to come in 1998 over the issue of tax-deductible preference shares.

For several years banks in a number of countries had been pressing for regulators to allow them to issue perpetual preference shares that could then count towards regulatory capital. The big attraction of these shares was that they raised money and the banks' interest payments on them would be tax-deductible. Banks felt that they had found a near perfect solution as it looked like debt to tax authorities and equity to regulators and an international debate began as to whether these financial instruments, which came to be known as 'hybrid securities' were indeed equity or in fact debt. In October 1996 the US Federal Reserve gave its approval to bank holding companies to issue perpetual preference shares, the proceeds of which could be passed down to banks to be used as regulatory capital. Counting as Tier 1 capital, the funds raised were of special importance to banks. Although regulators placed no official limits on the use of such funds as a percentage of capital, the most important rating agencies let it be known that 'if it were to go over 20% of the total tier-one capital, a bank's rating could well be in for a downgrade, so 20% became a de facto limit' (Currie, 1998, p.48).

The American regulators' capitulation to their banks forced competitive pressures on Japanese and European banks and thus on their regulators, who in turn looked for ways to coordinate their approaches through the Basel Committee. A dispute between German and US regulators over the issue delayed an announcement until October 1998. This turned out to be rather vague and general in nature, although it did set a limit of 15% on the use of what the Committee called Special Purpose Vehicle (SPV)[1] issues for capital adequacy purposes. The BCBS left it up to national

---

[1] An SPV refers to a private business organisation created for a limited period of time to serve as the temporary legal owner of assets being transferred. The SPV is used to purchase assets from the originating company, securitizes them, and then makes them available to

authorities to determine implementation of the amendment to the Accord. Thus a decidedly sub-par solution was found. To many it looked as though capital standards had been seriously weakened, and it remained an issue likely to cause conflict and controversy between regulators. As the *Financial Times* (1998d) put it, this was a 'dangerous game' to play.

Further amendments to the Accord had been foreseen in 1998 and a consultative paper was emitted, again concerning the use of netting. However, this and other prospective changes to the Accord were swept away by the announcement in June of 1999 that the Committee would introduce a new capital adequacy framework to replace the 1988 Accord.

## Basel II: Opening Up the Worm Can

The Committee's decision to revise the Accord of 1988 served both as a commendation and a criticism of the existing capital adequacy framework. On one hand the Committee was recognising that the Accord had been proved useful in guaranteeing minimum levels of capital adequacy in banks. The minimum standards, it should be remembered, had been designed for application to internationally active banks in the BCBS member states. In fact the Accord had exceeded in original mandate in two main ways. First, the standards had been applied to all banks, regardless of whether they were internationally active or not. Second, the standards had become almost universally accepted and applied across the globe, extending the influence of the Committee to both developed and developing states.

This simple and rather simplistic Accord, therefore, had helped to establish the Basel Committee on Banking Supervision as a source of authority and governance in the global banking and financial systems. Not only was the prestige of the Committee enhanced, but so was its ability to set norms and standards for the international banking system as a whole.

But the Accord was far from perfect, despite the extensive amendments described above and it continued to receive criticism from both the industry and national regulators. Banks consistently complained that the Accord threatened their efficiency, profitability and competitiveness, with the Institute of International Finance (IIF) calling for the Committee to fundamentally alter the formula for calculating risk-weighted capital. The IIF argued that the Accord was flawed and that it encouraged more, rather than less risk-taking by banks (*Financial Times*, 1998b). Regulators recognised that there had been a process of slackening in the interpretation and application of the capital standards. In efforts to reduce the regulatory burden on their national banks, regulators had increasingly allowed them to count more and more items as Tier 1 capital, and had gradually lowered the risk weighting applicable to several on-balance-sheet and off-balance-sheet items. Again the issue of private actor influence over the regulatory process and of regulatory capture must be raised,

---

investors. This serves to protect investors from bankruptcy risk in the originating company. SPVs are generally thinly capitalised entities.

as well as the importance of constant revision of both market developments and the regulatory environment by public authorities.

All of this meant that, by July 1998, bank capital levels had actually begun to shrink. In a survey conducted by *The Banker* magazine, the top 1000 banks saw their Tier 1 capital adequacy ratio shrink to 4.48 per cent of total assets, its lowest level since 1992 (*Financial Times*, 1998e). Clearly the time had come for a far-reaching examination of the fundamentals of capital adequacy and the pre-requisites for a safe, stable and sound international banking system.

A study of the Capital Accord (Jones, 2000) by a researcher at the Federal Reserve in Washington, DC supported evidence produced earlier by a Committee working group (Jackson et al, 1999) that banks were engaging in regulatory capital arbitrage (RCA) in order to get around the letter and spirit of the Accord. This confirmed that banks' effective risk-based capital requirements were in fact much lower than the required nominal 8% total risk-based capital standard. The paper outlined a number of RCA methods used by US banks, highlighting securitization and other financial innovations. The paper concluded (p.51) that

> Regulatory capital standards seem destined to become increasingly distorted by financial innovations and improved methods of RCA – at least for those large, sophisticated banks having the resources to exploit such opportunities.

In September of 1998 an international meeting of experts in banking supervision openly called for the reworking of the 1988 Accord, described by one as 'useless for regulators and costly for banks' (*Financial Times*, 1998f). The newly-appointed (since June 1998) chair of the Basel Committee, William McDonough (also governor of the New York Federal Reserve Bank), accepted the need for such a revision, and the next day, the 23$^{rd}$ of September 1998, the Committee officially began a review of the Accord, led by Claes Norgren, director-general of the Swedish Financial Supervisory Authority.

Within months controversy had emerged in the review process. Banks became aware that Basel, although it intended to make the rules for capital more flexible and free up funds for productive use by banks, also intended to include a new type of risk in the new capital adequacy framework. Operational risk, that is the risk that something will severely disrupt bank operations and 'can cover everything from hurricane damage to staff fraud or sickness' (Graham, 1999a), would be covered under the new framework by banks putting aside a set amount of capital. Banks responded by arguing that, although operational risk certainly could not be ignored, it would be better dealt with internally by banks themselves, rather than by a standardised and fixed percentage imposed from outside.

This complaint from banks, however, paled into insignificance beside a row that was soon to develop between regulators in the US and their counterparts in Germany. The Committee had announced that its proposals for a new capital adequacy framework would be released on the 9$^{th}$ of April 1999 for comment by regulators and the banking industry. Just as they had squabbled over the issue of hybrid securities, American and German authorities now fell into an argument over the question of external ratings. In the early stages of the revision of the capital adequacy framework in 1999, the United States was actively pushing for a reduction in the risk-weighting (currently 100%) for bank loans to private sector companies that had obtained investment-grade ratings by external agencies. Since all large corporations in the US are subject to scrutiny by these agencies, this seemed like a perfectly reasonable suggestion. However Germany lacks the same ratings structure as the US and only 175 companies there have external ratings (Graham, 1999b). This would thus potentially and probably give US banks a considerable advantage over German banks as they would not have to put aside as much capital on their loans to large corporations.

Another controversy that emerged at this time concerned the issue of commercial mortgages. Termed 'a big diplomatic punch-up' by the magazine *Euromoney* (Walker, 1999) the debate centred on German regulatory rulings that allowed their banks to hold commercial mortgages at a 50% risk-weighting, in contrast to the rest of the Committee member states where only residential mortgages receive such a weighting. The German regulator, *Bundesaufsichtsamt für das Kreditwesen* or *BaKred*, claimed that the US was 'reneging on an agreement to allow special treatment for these loans' (Graham, 1999c) and argued that they deserved special treatment due to their historically low default rate. In addition, German mortgage banks issuing *Pfandbriefe*, a special kind of bond, were only required to give them a 10% risk-weighting when calculating their capital, which gave them a huge advantage over the bonds issued by other countries' banks.

During the negotiations in early 1999 the US complained that these peculiarities of the German regulatory system gave German banks an unfair competitive advantage. The US, UK and Italian authorities pushed Basel for a ruling that would even out this disparity in the implementation of the 1988 Accord, while French and Spanish authorities speculated that they would allow their banks to issue the national equivalent of *Pfandbriefe* (*Economist*, 1999a).

The dispute broke into the public eye only days before the April 9th deadline. At this point German authorities still maintained that they had obtained a special dispensation for commercial mortgages. However, the penultimate draft of the proposed revision lacked any mention of such an allowance. According to Shirreff (1999), Hans Tietmeyer, president of the Bundesbank, telephoned McDonough in a fury, demanding to know what had happened, and it required the moderating influence of Howard Davies of the UK's FSA to get the combatants back to the negotiating table.

This dispute took two more months to settle so the consultative package for a new Basel capital accord did not in fact emerge until June 1999. The new accord was a revelation, and dramatically distinct to the original attempt. Rather than limit itself to the issue of capital standards, the new consultative package adopted a more comprehensive approach to the question of banking safety and soundness in general. For the Committee decided to incorporate diverse methods in an attempt to strengthen regulatory approaches and combine new banking methods and technologies into the process. The June 1999 document thus outlined a 'new capital adequacy framework to replace the 1988 Accord' and it set a number of supervisory objectives that such a framework must meet:

1. The Accord should continue to promote safety and soundness in the financial system and, as such, the new framework should at least maintain the current level of capital in the system;
2. The Accord should continue to enhance competitive equality;
3. The Accord should constitute a more comprehensive approach to addressing risks; and,
4. The Accord should focus on internationally active banks, although its underlying principles should be suitable for application to banks of varying levels of complexity and sophistication.

If we examine these objectives more closely they show first of all that the Committee maintained faith in the established level of eight per cent regulatory capital that had been determined by the 1988 Accord. It is true that the regulatory and supervisory authorities in major financial markets have required around 10% as a minimal level of capitalisation, and that major banks tend to keep around 11% on average to satisfy the concerns of investors. However, an eight percent minimum level was seen as being an appropriate starting point given the generally positive effects of the 1988 agreement. The prevailing belief in the Committee was that, although banking crises had continued to occur throughout the 1990s (most importantly in Japan), the 1988 Accord had increased the overall levels of safety and soundness in the international banking system. Moreover, it is unlikely that any of the Committee members had the stomach to renegotiate the eight per cent mark.

The second objective echoed an objective of the original accord and one that was continuously being called into question during its lifespan. It must be remembered that the prime motivation for the Accord came from US regulators trying to protect the competitiveness of their banks, in particular in the face of Japanese banking dominance. Throughout the 1990s, the Accord was plagued by implementation issues and the question of exemptions (such as the case of commercial mortgages) and the efforts of national regulators to increase the competitiveness of the banks under their authority.

Thirdly, the package aimed at a 'more comprehensive approach to addressing risks', and it was this objective that shaped the new framework as much as anything. As will be explained below, the June 1999 document adopted a multi-faceted and less traditional approach to not only risk-assessment, but also to the overall business of supervising banks.

The final objective, that the new framework should focus on international banks while at the same time providing a basis for application to banks in general, spoke to the increasing legitimacy of the Committee throughout the world's banking systems, not only for internationally-operating institutions.

The package itself was groundbreaking because it put forward a framework for capital adequacy that rested on more than the mere setting of regulatory capital levels. Instead three 'pillars' were proposed in the document (BCBS, 1999c):

> In constructing a revised capital framework, the importance of minimum regulatory capital requirements continues to be recognised. This is the first pillar of the framework. The Committee is now stressing the importance of the supervisory review of an institution's capital adequacy and internal assessment processes as the second pillar. The third pillar, which the Committee has underlined in recent years, is the need for greater market discipline. The Committee believes that, taken together, these three elements are the essential pillars of an effective capital framework.

To recap, the stability and soundness of the international banking system were to be secured by three, interlinked, elements:

1. Capital requirements.
2. Supervisory review.
3. Market discipline.


For several years before the June 1999 announcement, the idea of working with the market, rather than seeking to control or subdue it, had been gaining currency in the Committee's work. The original Accord in 1988, for example, had been promoted using the notion that the market would benefit banks with higher levels of capital. But the Committee had never been as explicit as this in the wording of documents or policy. This was testament to both the growing influence of the banking industry over national regulators and of the rising predominance of the Anglo-Saxon interpretation of efficiency in the area of regulation.

In laying out its ideas for a new capital accord, the Committee acknowledged a number of significant changes in the international banking and financial systems. First, the Committee recognised the growth in economic turbulence in the 1990s and the impact of such international financial upsets on banks in the G-10 countries. Second, the consultative package made explicit reference to financial innovation and particularly to the rise in asset securitisation as a method used by banks to escape the limitations imposed by the original Accord. Third, and most controversially, the Committee acknowledged that banks had developed new forms and methods of risk assessment that ought to be incorporated into the capital adequacy regime.

By far the most innovative element of the new package concerned this last point. The Committee explicitly stated that it was willing to consider the use, by 'some sophisticated banks', of an internal ratings-based (IRB) approach to the setting of capital charges. This would require the use of internal risk-assessment models that would be approved and supervised by national banking authorities. The Committee stated that it 'believes that this will be an important step in the effort to align more closely capital charges with underlying risk' (BCBS, 1999c). Furthermore, the consultative package suggested that it would be willing to look into the effects on capital of 'credit risk mitigation techniques', such as on-balance sheet-netting, collateral guarantees and credit derivatives.

Both of these elements of the 1999 package were essentially concessions to large, international banking organisations of sufficient sophistication to be able to employ such methods. Once again the question of whose interests were being represented on the Committee becomes pertinent.

Nonetheless the document did not only bring forward proposals designed to make life easier for banks. For, in addition to the established focus on credit and market risks, the Committee argued that it was time to 'develop a capital charge for interest rate risk in the banking book for banks where interest rate risk is significantly above average, and is proposing to develop capital charges for other risks, principally operational risk' (BCBS, 1999c). This was a huge blow to the interests of banks who had campaigned against the inclusion of operational risk in the new capital framework since early 1999.

Another innovation of the 1999 package was the proposal to allow banks to use credit ratings set by approved external credit assessment institutions (rating agencies) to classify their claims on sovereign and corporate borrowers. Instead of the simple differentiation between OECD and non-OECD states, the package proposed five risk buckets for sovereign borrowers. For corporate and bank claims the new proposed framework would provide three risk buckets, instead of the simply 100% risk weighting for all corporate debt.

The issue of 'whose standards?' comes up once again on this subject of risk weightings for sovereign countries and private corporations. The Committee proposed using external credit assessments from ratings agencies. This reflected Anglo-Saxon dominance of the Committee because only the US employs a fully-developed and inclusive system of credit ratings and the only firms mentioned in the package were Moody's Investors Service, Standard and Poor's (S&P) and Fitch IBCA. In Europe, although the use of credit rating agencies is on the rise, very few corporations have a credit rating, which would clearly discriminate against European banks, the main lenders to European firms.

Another bone of contention prior to the consultative package had been the sticking point of commercial mortgages that had caused so much ill-will between the US and Germany. A compromise to came in the wording of a clause that read:

> In view of the experience in numerous countries that commercial property lending has been a recurring cause of troubled assets in the banking industry over the past few decades, the committee holds to the view that mortgages do not, in principle, justify other than a 100% weighting of the loans secured. (BCBS, 1999c)

This would seem to suggest that the Germans had lost the battle. However, according to Shirreff (1999, p.24), the inclusion of the words 'in principle' was interpreted by German supervisors 'as an invitation to apply for an exception'. Time will tell if this interpretation is tested in practice.


## Debating the Consultative Package

The Committee, in familiar fashion by now, invited comments on the package by March 31 2000, with the promise of 'more definitive proposals later in the year 2000'.

An actual deadline for approving a new capital adequacy framework, however, was not set at this point in time, as if the Committee expected extensive discussion and controversy over the ideas contained in the consultative package. This proved to be the case as the banking industry responded immediately and vigorously, and other, non-financial actors also took an active role in the public debate, something relatively unheard of in the Committee's prior history. For the Committee's work had by now become an issue of global importance and there was a heightened awareness of the significance of its accords and agreements. In the period up to the end of May 2000, over 200 sets of comments were received by the BCBS.

The main participants in the debate were, of course, the banks themselves and the authorities responsible for their regulation. Over the next few years there would be a constant back and forth between them as banks sought to gain more freedom and regulators defended the original ideas from extensive alteration. A parallel process of debate and negotiation took place among the regulators themselves, each trying to defend their respective national interest or, more accurately, the interests of banks in their territories. A third debate that developed embraced academics and the financial press, as a wider audience became aware of the potential consequences of a re-worked capital accord.

One area in which a healthy dialogue emerged between banks and regulators was that of disclosure. Again an issue where the Committee appeared to be placing an undue amount of faith in market discipline, disclosure and transparency were seen as being the perfect complement to supervision by national authorities. In April of 2000 a new working group was formed in the US, made up of regulators from the Federal Reserve, Office of the Comptroller of the Currency, the Securities and Exchange Commission, and executives of financial firms to determine best practices and methods for improving disclosure (Garver, 2000b). Previously McDonough had commented on the 'urgency of achieving dramatic progress in this area' in a speech he made in Singapore.

This area of convergence between regulators and banks was to prove the exception, however, rather than the rule. Over the next year and a half, a debate raged over the perceived failings of the ideas within the consultative package. Even though the comment period set by the Committee only continued until May of the following year, the international arguments over Basel II continued much longer, and were much more contentious than the Committee had thought.

The first issue that caught the attention of banks was that of external ratings. A major innovation of the Basel consultative package in 1999 was for banks to use credit-rating agencies to help evaluate risk in their credit portfolios, in particular with reference to sovereign debt and corporate loans. Three categories of loans would be created under the new framework. Loans to triple-A rated corporations would require only 1.6% capital while loans to companies rated B-minus or less would require 12%. Several objections were raised to this, not the least of which was that unrated borrowers might well 'get more favourable treatment than lowly rated ones' (*Economist*, 1999b). This was to prevent US banks from gaining an automatic advantage from the new framework. But to grant unrated companies the same risk weight as all but triple- or double-A rated corporations in the US seemed ludicrous to many. For one, it would deter small corporations from ever seeking an official rating.

The reason behind this illogical rule in the proposed framework was political and hearkens back to US-German dispute over the use of rating agencies. Because the Germans were so unhappy over the idea, the US agreed to allow unrated companies to benefit from only a 100% risk weighting. Once in the proposal, Germany would never allow this concession to be eliminated.

The International Swaps and Derivatives Association (ISDA) argued that the new proposals in the consultative package had done little to overcome the problem inherent in the 1988 Accord of lumping too many different risks together. The new framework failed to 'sufficiently differentiate among assets with different probabilities of default' and needed more granularity, ISDA members argued (Garver, 2000). The call for more granularity in the risk weights was echoed by another industry association in April 2000, the Institute of International Finance (IIF). Attacking the consultative package on a number of levels, the IIF called for an increase in the risk categories from three to eight and also called for the Committee to coordinate implementation of changes to the 1988 Accord in conjunction with other international financial supervisors groups (Iyer, 2000).

Banks also argued that their evaluation mechanisms were more accurate than the ratings agencies and that ratings agencies work simply reflected opinion and judgements of the people who worked in those organisations rather than objective evaluations. Shirreff (2000) quotes a managing director at credit risk quantifiers KMV as saying that external ratings 'do not reflect the information that is in market prices, and in fact they do a worse job of detecting credit problems than market prices'. Interestingly, the same source claimed that bank internal ratings were even less accurate.

Most surprisingly, the agencies themselves announced that they were not willing to take on such a task, explained by some as a reluctance to face competition in their domain from new agencies that would inevitably appear due to the increased demand. As *The Economist* (1999c) noted:

> They fear that less rigorous newcomers will nab some of their business. New rating agencies would have to be approved by national regulators. If experience is any guide, they will be sympathetic to domestic rating firms – although regulators counter that markets will penalise companies that opt for generous raters.

Evidence of this fear emerged in June of 2001 when both Moody's and Standard and Poor's sent comments to the Committee calling for clear criteria for approving credit rating agencies (Van Duyn, 2001). S&P's comments in particular exhibited the anxiety that competition would mean lower standards, and called for compulsory disclosure of performance data.

It is interesting to note here that the Committee had obviously developed a strong faith in the ability of the market to discriminate between weak and rigorous standards and that it would work to reinforce healthy practices. By looking to rating agencies to determine the health or otherwise of borrowers and thus set capital charges, the Committee assumed that they had both the resources and the experience necessary to undertake such a task. Once again it is not clear why this should be the case nor from where this faith came. Not even the ratings agencies themselves held similar confidence in their abilities.

As an alternative to the use of rating agencies to determine risk weights, the 1999 consultative package showed that the Committee was willing to consider the use of internal ratings systems by banks. Big banks immediately demonstrated their approval of this idea, although the Committee originally intended this option for no more than 20 of the world's largest banks. Very soon a large number of banks argued that they would be ideal candidates for this form of risk assessment and capital charge setting, some of them anxious not to be seen as not big or sophisticated enough to manage risk independently (*Economist,* 1999c).

This of course changed the calculation involved for the Committee. It had proposed internal risk assessment as an alternative to external ratings or the standard 8% risk weighting but had done so operating on the assumption that only a small number of banks would choose to use them. If, instead, hundreds of banks would apply to use internal models to set capital charges, national supervisors would likely be overworked as they back-tested models for accuracy. This would stretch supervisory resources to the breaking point and jeopardise the capacity of authorities to examine other areas of bank activity.

Another problem relating to supervisory resources was the sheer complexity of many of the risk-management models employed by banks. The question here was not simply which risk assessment models would be acceptable to supervisors, and how many banks should be allowed to employ them. Doubts were raised in 1999 and 2000 as to whether banking authorities could train their personnel to a level where they could adequately evaluate risk models. Such doubts were raised with reference to supervisors in wealthy countries; in many emerging markets it was clear that the problem would be even greater.

The third major bone of contention between the banks and regulators centred on the continuing controversy over the issue of operational risk. Placing a risk premium on the probability of computer failure or the loss of key staff members is not only difficult to quantify, but is also an area in which very little hard data exists to develop models. In its March 2001 comments to the Committee, the ISDA argued that a capital charge for operational risk cannot be standardised, while others in the banking industry more bluntly claimed that operational risk did not even exist (Shirreff, 2000).

Most in the banking industry, however, did accept the validity of the Committee's concern with operational risk and a number of suggestions came forth from the industry as alternatives to a capital charge, including internal systems reform, operational risk insurance, and the building of databases for operational risk experience. Deborah Williams, a financial researcher, even argued that operational risk is ignored by most in the banking market because 'it's such a big problem that nobody wants to talk about it' (*Future Banker,* 2000). Nonetheless, the main thrust of the banking community's complaints were directed against the size of the capital charge foreseen for operational risk. The Committee had suggested that up to 20% of total capital be set against operational risk, an amount that was seen as prohibitive by most banks.

A criticism of the package's proposals that potentially had even broader economic consequences concerned what has come to be known as 'procyclicality'. A commonly heard comment on the new framework was that it would push banks to lend more in boom times, contributing to boom and inflationary tendencies, and less during a recession when credit was most needed. Banks using their internal risk evaluations to determine capital charges would naturally lend more money when credit risk was low (conditions usually seen during periods of economic growth), and less when credit risk was high (conditions usually experienced during a downturn).

## Second Consultative Package

In January of 2001 the Committee published a second consultative package, a revised form of the 1999 package modified in the face of the comments received from banks and regulators around the world. This proposal maintained many of the key elements of the original package, most significantly the emphasis on 'three mutually reinforcing pillars that allow banks and supervisors to evaluate properly the various risks that banks face' (BCBS, 2001a). It was, however, much more detailed than the previous package had been, involving more complexity and more attention to the workings of the various options for setting capital and determining different forms of risk. Made up of more than 500 pages (including the proposal itself and supporting documentation), the second consultative package created a veritable shock wave when it landed on the desks of banks and regulators.

The differences between the new consultative package and the first were several. First, much more detail was given in all areas, particularly Pillars Two and Three, in order to overcome the vagueness of the original proposal. Second, the new proposals set out four instead of three risk buckets for corporate exposures in an attempt to make them 'more closely aligned to the underlying risk' and, for the first time, claims on banks and corporate borrowers could receive a lower risk weighting than those on sovereign entities. Third, two options were laid out for the IRB approach to credit risk management, one a foundation approach, the other an advanced approach. This was designed to allow more banks to access this form of setting capital charges. Fourth, and most controversially, the Committee now chose to focus almost exclusively on the idea of operational risk in Pillar One in its concern with 'other risks', that is risks other than credit and market risk.

Another key difference was that the Committee would now allow national export credit agencies to supplement private credit rating agencies in the provision of external ratings. Many of the comments received on the first consultative package had doubted that the existing agencies would be able to provide sufficient ratings to make the standardised approach to credit risk evaluation work. With national export credit agencies also providing ratings, the Committee argued, there should be no objection to this aspect of the new accord.

A comment period was set until the end of May 2001. Within that time the Committee was to receive over 250 sets of comments from the industry, regulators and academics. Once again the major controversy concerned the IRB approach and the concept of operational risk. Worryingly for the Committee, new issues had been added to the debate.

Whereas in 2000 a consensus on the notion of disclosure had seemed to be emerging, by the middle of 2001 that too seemed mired in a debate between authorities and bankers. Bankers began to argue that the disclosure requirements were too demanding, and that simply gathering the data required would be immensely costly (Helk, 2001). It was also argued that too much information would make it more difficult for market actors to determine what was truly relevant.

A credit charge for derivatives exposure also became a disputed topic in the new package. Called the 'W-factor' and nicknamed the 'who knows why-factor' by many banks, this was seen as being prohibitively expensive for banks, and it was feared that most banks might simply drop out of the derivatives market (Helk, 2001).

Another new area of dispute arose around the issue of claims on small and medium sized enterprises (SMEs). European bankers in particular had been critical of the higher charges set against SME claims as they argued that they were more dependent on SME loans than were banks in the US. Another criticism was that banks would try to orient their lending away from SMEs as a consequence of the higher capital charges, thus stunting credit flow to these businesses, and incurring higher borrowing costs for the sector.

In addition to criticism over the SME capital charges, a growing number of academics and policy-makers (the latter in the developing world) began to question the impact of the proposals for Basel II on LDCs. The Latin American shadow financial regulatory committee (a group of academic regulatory experts) argued that the ideas contained in the consultative package were dangerous for LDCs because, as Liliana Rojas Suarez, a committee member, argued, the new capital framework would be far too complex for developing country supervisors to implement and monitor (Willman, 2001a). An perennial problem for developing country banking authorities, the lack of adequately trained and sufficiently resourced personnel threatened to combine with Basel II to produce a dangerous gap in LDC banking supervision.

A second problem for LDCs arose around the use of external ratings to set capital charges for sovereign borrowers. Under the standardised approach to credit risk, banks would use credit agency ratings to set capital charges. It was argued by some analysts that the use of external ratings would not only likely result in less lending to emerging markets, but would also push lending in the wrong direction. Many recalled the problems of the 1997 Asian crisis, when rating agencies were infamously slow to acknowledge the imminent financial collapse of several economies. Some, such as Griffith-Jones and Spratt (2001), argued that, although some LDCs would benefit from the proposed changes, the use of credit ratings implied a number of very serious problems. First, the existing ratings agencies can be accused of acting in a highly 'procyclical' manner, encouraging more lending to those countries perceived to be doing well. This would result in a slowdown in lending to countries that really needed it. Secondly, the alternative to private credit rating agencies, national export credit agencies, might not be safe from political pressure or truly unbiased in their assessment of LDC credit worthiness.

As for banks who might qualify to use the IRB approach, it was argued that this might lead to the most underdeveloped countries with a history of debt problems and backwards economies effectively being cut off from bank lending because of the prohibitively high capital charge (perhaps over 47%) that would be applied. As Griffith-Jones and Spratt (2001) put it:

> The implications of this are clear: large parts of the developing world will no longer be able to access international bank lending on terms likely to be acceptable. The impact of this is likely to be felt most severely in the lowest rated countries – the very countries most in need of such access.

A further critique in the paper was that the new framework would cause increasing consolidation of the banking industry at the expense of LDC banks, as larger, more sophisticated banks took advantage of their ability to use the IRB approach. A report by Lehman brothers titled *The End of Capital as We Know It* argued that 'the new rules are seen as putting further pressure on smaller- and medium-sized banks to consolidate, while benefiting those global and regional institutions with robust systems already in place' (Golin, 2001). In the face of this Griffith-Jones and Spratt (2001) argued that LDC banks could not compete against developed country banks using the IRB approach and would likely be swallowed up in a series of mergers.

Perhaps most damning, however, was the suggestion that the new framework would increase the frequency of financial crises in the international system, thus completely undermining the goal of the Committee to contribute to the overall safety and soundness of banking worldwide. Procyclicality would lead to increased flow of bank lending to developing countries during periods of emerging market euphoria, such as was seen in the early 1990s in Latin America and the mid-90s in Asia. Although the long-term effects of procyclical lending might turn out to be increased discipline and lower peaks and troughs, the short-term effects threatened to be grossly destabilising.

The seriousness of this criticism was made clear when the parent-institution behind the Basel Committee, the Bank for International Settlements, published its annual report and noted that banks using internal risk assessment methods tend to underestimate risk during boom times (Beattie, 2001). The report indicated that this meant that the Basel II framework might be fundamentally flawed.

But it was the setting of capital against operational risk that was particularly controversial this time around as the Committee had determined three options for its measurement: a basic indicator approach, a standardised approach, and an internal measurement approach. While the third option allowed banks to use internal loss data to determine the correct capital charge for operational risk, the first and second options set the relevant capital charge according to bank income. This would seem to penalise banks receiving higher levels of income, surely a perverse effect of the regulatory process (*Economist*, 2001a). The main problem with the third option was that insufficient data existed at the time to be able to determine expected losses and thus set capital. Even though a number of firms in the market were in the process of collecting figures for losses, commentators noted that it would be years before sufficient amounts of data had been assembled into data banks.

The IIF again weighed into the debate, this time arguing that the 20% figure for operational risk capital was far too high. The body also argued that this figure failed to 'reflect measurable risks' (Willman, 2001c). The IIF also argued that the Committee was trying to move too quickly towards completion of the accord, 'without sufficient market-testing and discussion' (Willman, 2001b).

**Delay and Further Controversy**

The BCBS had intended to publish final drafts of the new capital framework following its meeting in July 2001 but, due to the number of comments and their nature, the Committee made a decision in June to extend discussions over the proposals. The Committee acknowledged the huge interest created by the two consultative packages and agreed with banks that more time was needed to shape the new framework. While reaffirming its belief in the three pillar approach, the Committee did recognise that certain areas needed much more attention. It pointed to three issues in particular:

1. The amount of capital required under the IRB approach.
2. Operational risk.
3. The effect of the proposals on small and medium sized enterprises.

The Committee added another twelve months for discussion and comments, and announced that it would issue a third version of the proposals in early 2002, with a new implementation date of year-end 2005. Banks and regulators alike welcomed the delay and there was almost universal agreement that 'getting it right' was more important that meeting a randomly-set deadline.

Nonetheless, the financial press was becoming increasingly critical of the Basel II process, and some began to question the wisdom of delay. Several articles in the *Financial Times* made the point that further time for comments and discussion meant more time for new issues and controversies to emerge; as John Willman (2001c) put it 'the delay in finalising Basle 2 is likely to increase the number of criticisms rather than diminish them'. *The Economist* (2001b), criticising the procyclical nature of the proposals, made the point that the accord seemed to contradict itself,

> because it is trying to make regulatory capital charges more risk-sensitive while keeping banks as a 'public-good' and a buffer against economic downturns.

> Getting banks to hold more capital and lend more prudently during booms than during busts is like coaxing a cat to put liver in the fridge.

Some publications even began, Cassandra-like, to foretell the doom of the process and the whole capital adequacy framework. An editorial in the August 2001 issue of *Euromoney* argued that:

> two years' hard labour has produced a mess. At the moment Basel II consists of little more than half-written rules and platitudes about the need for sophisticated and proactive supervision.

The influential magazine even went on to conclude:

> Basel has served a useful purpose in a particular historical era. But now it has outstayed its welcome. It should not be reformed. It should be evicted.

Although by 'Basel', the editorial was referring to the capital adequacy system and not the Committee, the commentary was indicative of the discontent felt in banking circles over the perceived bungling of the reform process.

In September of 2001 the banking industry scored two important victories in the battle over Basel II when the Committee announced that the W-factor would be dropped entirely from the framework and that the capital charge for operational risk would drop from 20% to 12% (Cameron, 2001). This capitulation by the Committee was a recognition that the accord was simply unacceptable as it then stood. But its problems were far from over.

A large portion of the problems associated with the proposals had originated in political battles between national regulators and, at a more abstract level, between different philosophies of regulation and supervision. In October 2001, these political tensions re-emerged when German chancellor Gerhard Schroder announced that he would oppose any future European Union banking legislation based on the principles of Basel II. Presumably this also meant that Germany would not accept the Basel II proposals in their present form. Chancellor Schroder 'encouraged German banks not to apply Basel II rules' (Ehrlich and Lebert, 2001), arguing that German small and medium sized enterprises (the *Mittelstand*) would suffer under the new framework. The German economics minister, Werner Muller, repeated the objections a few days later saying that 'the German system of financing the Mittelstand must not be influenced' and that 'Basle II is not acceptable to Germany in its present form' (Ehrlich, Simonian and Willman, 2001).

The BCBS responded almost immediately, posting suggestions on its website for new risk weightings for small companies. Although these were only interim ideas, and the Committee recognised the need for proper testing and revision, the episode demonstrated once again how tortured the Basel II process had become (*Economist*, 2001c), and that Germany was not alone – both Italy and Japan voiced similar fears over the impact of the new framework on SMEs.

The head of the BIS, Andrew Crockett, however, responded more aggressively by calling on BCBS members not to make the process of reform a 'political football' and asked politicians to refrain from interfering in the negotiations and 'resist political pressure arising from national interest' (Beattie, 2002). He argued that one of the strengths of the Committee was that it was removed from the day-to-day demands of national and international politics and focused more on technical issues. Crockett's comments, of course, ignored the real driving force behind the Committee's deliberations and negotiations. Political pressure and particular as well as national interests have always shaped the Committee's work.

Based on these problems the Committee announced in December that the expected new version of the proposals would not appear as scheduled in January 2002, although it did not foresee a significant delay in the eventual implementation of the new framework. The Committee stated that it would focus on three main issues in the coming months:

1. Balancing the need for a risk-sensitive Accord with its being sufficiently clear and flexible so that banks can use it effectively.
2. Ensuring that the Accord leads to appropriate treatment of credit to small- and medium-sized enterprises, which are important for economic growth and job creation.
3. Finalising calibration of the minimum capital requirements to bring about a level of capital that, on average, is approximately equal to the requirements of the present Basel Accord, while providing some incentive to those banks using the more risk-sensitive internal ratings based system.

The first of these issues was a response to many comments in the media that the new framework had become unwieldy and was too complex to be easily and consistently applied. The second point spoke directly to the growing discontent on the part of the German government (and others) that the new capital rules would drastically reduce bank lending to SMEs.

The final point was a response to the complaints of banks that the new framework would mean they would have to reserve much more capital than under the 1988 Accord. According to some estimates, banks had feared that they might have to put aside up to 40% more capital under Basel II. The Committee's statement that it intended to maintain current overall capital levels served to reassure some banks, although others would clearly have to increase capital levels depending on the risk profile of their loan portfolios.

The announcement did little to calm the dispute, controversy and growing pessimism over Basel II and the debate continued at both international and national levels. By the middle of 2002 the process of revision and reform was no more popular in banking circles than it had been before. The BCBS announced that it would launch a Quantitative Impact Study (QIS), the third thus far, by the middle of the year in order that banks might test the impact of the proposals before the Committee came forward with a third consultative package or final draft proposal. The study, known as QIS 3, was seen by the Committee as an essential part of the consultation process and thus of the policy-making procedure. But QIS 3 was not issued in the summer. Instead, the Committee announced in July that its members had 'reached agreement on a number of important issues related to the New Basel Capital Accord' (BCBS, 2002a). In this press release, the Committee announced that QIS 3 would be launched in October 2002 with a completion date of 20 December 2002. Based on the results of the third QIS, the Committee intended to complete Basel II in the fourth quarter of 2003 with an implementation deadline of year-end 2006.

The issues agreed on in the July meeting of the BCBS dealt with many of the key areas of controversy linked to the new framework. As had become the norm by this point, the most important were SMEs, operational risk, procyclicality and overall levels of capital. In a pragmatic response to the increasing disillusionment of the German government with Basel II, the Committee now allowed banks using the IRB approach to distinguish SME borrowers (defined as companies with less than Euro 50 million in annual sales) from other corporate clients and to allocate them a reduced capital charge. The concession was not inconsiderable, and created a significant incentive for banks to lend to SMEs:

> Under the proposed treatment, exposures to SMEs will be able to receive a lower capital requirement than exposures to larger firms. The reduction in the required amount of capital will be as high as twenty percent, depending on the size of the borrower, and should result in an average reduction of approximately ten percent across the entire set of SME borrowers in the IRB framework for corporate loans. (BCBS, 2002a)

After this agreement, the German government seemed placated. The German finance minister, Jochen Sanio, announced that the concession on SME loan capital was the 'breakthrough' that was necessary to propel the Basel II negotiations forward (BAFin, 2002). It seems that, despite Crockett's statements about the apolitical nature of Basel, political wrangling had indeed been successful in gaining a key dispensation for the German economy.

The second crucial area where Committee agreement was reached in July concerned the question of operational risk. On this issue the BCBS reaffirmed its commitment to the notion of a capital charge for this area of risk, but now announced that there would no longer be a floor capital charge for banks using advanced measurement approaches (AMA). This meant that banks would be able to choose their own methodology for determining operational risk (provided it was sufficiently sophisticated and systematic), and no minimum was to be set by the Committee. This was a huge climb-down by the Committee. Initially it had wanted to insist on a 20% minimum level for operational risk - now it was leaving the matter almost entirely in the hands of the banks themselves. In this area of the Basel II process, banks had achieved a major victory in defending their interests. BCBS Chair McDonough later defended the removal of the floor by saying that it had threatened to 'stifle innovation' and that, without it, banks would be 'free to experiment with a great variety of methodologies, without undue constraint on their value to the firm' (McDonough, 2002).

The third concern mentioned in the press release was that of the procyclical effects of the new Accord. The Committee announced that its members wanted to 'address potential concerns about the cyclicality of the IRB approaches' and would require 'a meaningfully conservative credit risk stress test' for each bank. Supervisory authorities would be able to use the results of the tests to make sure that each bank would be adequately capitalised. This however, implied another burden on supervisory authorities, one that many may not be able to shoulder easily.

The fourth, and perhaps most important issue, on which the BCBS pronounced agreement was that of overall capital levels. Since 1988, eight percent had come to be seen and accepted internationally as the minimum level for bank capital (although major financial markets insisted on higher levels) if the system was to be stable and sound. But in the July 2002 press release, the BCBS announced that its members had agreed that:

> Under the new approach, there will be a single capital floor for the first two years following the implementation of the new Accord. The floor will be based on calculations using the rules of the existing Accord. Beginning year-end 2006 and during the first year following implementation, IRB capital requirements for credit risk together with operational risk capital charges cannot fall below 90% of the current minimum required, and in the second year, the minimum will be 80% of this level. (BCBS, 2002a)

This was, quite simply, extraordinary. Throughout the negotiations, the BCBS had determinedly maintained that the new framework should not lead to a reduction in overall capital levels in the international system, and that the 8% minimum set by the original Basel Accord would be the minimum acceptable under the new system of Basel II. Now the Committee seemed to be saying that within two years of implementation, those banks using the foundation IRB approach need only put aside eighty percent of that adequacy level.

At the Twelfth International Conference of Banking Supervisors in Cape Town South Africa in September of 2002, McDonough provided some encouraging words on the subject of Basel II to the assembled supervisory authorities. Pushing aside doubts about the potentially procyclical effects of the Accord, the Committee chair simply claimed that 'stress testing should help banks to maintain adequate capital buffers in advance of potential downturns in the economy' and went on to provide encouraging comments on what G10 supervisors were doing to prepare the ground for the implementation of Basel II – namely evaluating bank readiness, training supervisory staff, and the creation of an Accord Implementation Group within the Committee. What was interesting, however, about McDonough's speech was his comparison of the Basel II negotiation process to a marathon that was far from complete:

> Yet a Chinese proverb reminds us that, 'On a journey of one hundred miles, ninety is but halfway.' I suppose the last miles of any marathon are the toughest to finish.

The wisdom of that proverb is borne out by the tasks ahead of us to complete, and then to implement, the new capital framework. (McDonough, 2002)

These comments suggest that the chair of the BCBS himself had serious doubts about the chances for drawing the negotiation process to a rapid conclusion.

In October 2002 the finally aunched its third Quantitative Impact Study (QIS 3), working with national supervisors in both G10 and non-G10 countries. Banks were asked to submit their findings by the 20th of December 2002. QIS 3, the Committee announced, would be the last impact study before it came out with the final draft of its proposals for industry comment in early 2003.

At congressional hearings in February of 2003, US regulators announced that, contrary to the spirit of the Basel II negotiations, the United States would apply the new rules to only twelve banks, albeit the twelve largest international banks in the country (*Economist*, 2003a). Although the Basel II rules were obligatory only for internationally operating banks, there had been a generally held understanding that Basel member countries would apply the new regime to all banks. The US decision to reduce the coverage of the new Accord is more understandable when it is considered that these twelve banks, plus 'another dozen who are expected to comply voluntarily...comprise 99% of that country's banks' foreign exposure' (*Economist*, 2003b). Later estimates put the number of US banks covered by Basel II at around 20, but the US regulators' announcement brought instant consternation from their European counterparts, who had decided to implement the new regime to all banks on a Europe-wide basis through the EU's third Capital Adequacy Directive (CAD3).

Roger Ferguson, vice-chairman of the board of governors of the Federal Reserve system was quite forthright in outlining US calculations of interest in the decision (*Banker*, 2003):

> When we balanced the costs of imposing a new capital regime on thousands of our banks against the benefits – slightly more risk sensitivity of capital requirements under, say, the standardised version of Basel II for credit risk, and somewhat more disclosure – it did not seem worthwhile to require most of our banks to take that step. Countries with an institutional structure different from ours might clearly find universal application of Basel II to benefit their banking system, but we do not think that imposing Basel II on most of our banks is either necessary or practical.

The US decision was clearly taken in response to increasing pressure from small and community banks, who had been successful in getting their point of view heard in Congress through their representative organisations such as the Independent Community Bankers of America (ICBA), which gave testimony to hearings held by the Senate Committee on Banking, Housing and Urban Affairs in October of 2003. Now that the interest of the US Congress had been awakened, matters promised to be even more complicated, and this served to put further pressure on other Basel members.

In the aftermath of the US decision, several key developing countries, including China and India, announced that they would no longer be forcing their banks to apply Basel II standards. The impact, therefore, of this particular US decision was to weaken the overall impact of the Accord, not only among Basel member countries, but also on the system as a whole.

Worse, however, was to come in late 2003. In October of that year American regulators indicated that they would seek a further impact study to analyse the probable effects of capital charges for expected losses from bad loans, something that was introduced into the Basel II debate in 2001. Recognising the importance of credit card business for US banks, and the risky nature of that business, American authorities began calling for more discussion and studies to be carried out to analyse the situation, and therefore a potentially lengthy delay in applying the new rules. Pressure was also mounting to delay final agreement and implementation of Basel II from groups such as the ICBA who saw that, even though the new Basel rules would not apply to smaller banks, large banks using Basel II guidelines would gain a competitive advantage from lower capital charges for items such as residential mortgages (*PR Newswire*, 2003).

Moreover, pressure was mounting in late 2003 in the US to entirely eliminate the capital charge for operational risk. If successful, this campaign by US banks would signify the total defeat of the Basel Committee on an issue that had once been seen as crucial to the effectiveness of the new regime. Congressional hearings in the US repeatedly featured comments such as those made by Karen Shaw Petrou of Federal Financial Analytics Inc. In June 2003 she bluntly stated before the Senate Committee on Banking, Housing and Urban Affairs (Petrou, 2003) that the 'operational risk-based section of Basel II remains deeply flawed and should be dropped', further claiming that capital charges for operational risk would increase, not reduce, risk.

Divisions also began to emerge among US regulatory authorities. While the Federal Reserve remained committed to the overall project of Basel II, the Office of the Comptroller of the Currency and the Federal Deposit Insurance Corporation began to question the validity of the emerging accord. The Comptroller himself, John D. Hawke Jr., went so far as to stress the limits of the Basel Committee's power, when he said that just because the US is a member of the Committee, 'we did not surrender our discretion to supervise our banking system in the way that we deem most appropriate' (Davenport, 2003).

Such brinkmanship in the Committee alarmed European regulatory authorities and threatened to derail the entire Basel II process. Europeans felt that it was far too late in the reform process to be debating such fundamental questions or to change previously well-established negotiating positions (*Economist*, 2003b). This however only served to strengthen the hand of the US in the Committee. Such challenges by the US achieved their goal. The Committee announced in January 2004 that it would makes changes to a number of elements of the agreement that took into account US concerns, and that the final date for agreement of the accord had been pushed back to mid-2004.

Despite simmering discontent over Basel II in the US Congress and less than complimentary comments from some regulatory authorities in the US and UK in early 2004, the Committee remained on target and committed to its June 2004 deadline, so as to give banks three years to implement the accord. Indeed by May final agreement had been reached and the road was clear for implementation to begin. The document was signed on June 26th 2004.

This did not, of course, mean that all controversy had been resolved. The dispute over the extent of implementation in the United States versus Europe had not been resolved, potentially leaving US banks with a competitive advantage. The Accord was open to criticism for being 'so protean that the central bankers might as well have stayed at home' (*Economist*, 2004). This lack of precision, and openness of interpretation does indeed stand out when one looks at the final version of the Accord. But it must be remembered that the first Basel capital accord was also criticised for being too vague, and it made a definite contribution to the development of the international banking regime. What remains to be seen is how much variance will occur in the national implementation of the rules.

## Basel III: Not If, but When

Even before the Basel II process had been concluded, talk turned in banking circles worldwide to the next reincarnation of the Accord. Such premature conjecture over Basel III, as it would inevitably be called, stemmed from what many viewed as the inherent weaknesses of Basel II and of the need to move in step with the market, something the Committee has consistently tried to do throughout its history.

If we analyse the development of the capital regime from its inception in the late 1980s to the present, we can discern a growing tendency to work with the market in the shaping of capital rules. The various amendments to the 1988 Accord made during the early 1990s had made concessions to banks allowing new items to be counted towards their capital requirements. The Basel II process, after an initial backlash, gave banks increasing flexibility to determine what constitutes adequate levels of capitalisation and which methods to adopt to achieve them. The next step, Basel III, will surely be to allow banks to use their own internal models to decide not only how great are the risks on their books, but how much capital to hold against them. A senior official at the Bank of England, interviewed in late 2002, expressed her certainty that bank risk models would form the backbone of the next stage in the development of the international capital regime.

Again we must ask in whose interest such an innovation would occur. Presumably, at least in the initial stages, only big banks will be able to employ modelling as an alternative to standardized capital ratios. It would clearly bring significant savings as a bank's capital would then exactly match its own estimation of its risk position, likely to be lower than that of a supervisory authority. The key question here is who will supervise the use of such models and thus guarantee that banks are holding sufficient capital to ensure the safety and soundness of the system as a whole.

In December 2003, the newly elected head of the BCBS, Jaime Caruana, emphasised the flexibility of the Basel process and the potential for modifications rather than a move to Basel III. In response to a reporter's question 'Is Basel II a lost cause and Basel III around the corner?', he answered (Robinson, 2003),

> Basel II must be seen as evolutionary. We took a transcendental step. Basel I was static. Now we are saying we want to be next to banking practices so that as they move, the agreement moves. Not necessarily Basel III, but we could have modifications of Basel II. We have used phrases like 'not set in stone'.

## The Significance of Basel II

From its early years, the process of updating the Basel Accord of 1988 has involved political negotiation and bargaining at multiple levels. The Committee has received pressure directly from the banking industry, from national supervisory authorities and from national governments. The interplay of interests at these several levels has defined not only the nature of the reform process but, inevitably, of the new Basel Accord itself.

The road to Basel II involved more actors than ever before in the history of the Committee. It stands as testament to the impact of the original Basel Accord that so many diverse groups have become aware of the importance of its successor. We can thus argue that the policy network of the Committee has expanded because of its own success and that, somewhat ironically, this has further complicated the work of the Committee as it tries to modernise and update its previous achievements. The actors now involved, directly and indirectly, in the policy formulation process includes national regulatory authorities, national governments, developing as well as developed countries, banks, financial industry associations (bank and non-bank), academics, and financial 'watchdog' groups such as the various shadow financial regulatory committees. The utopian picture painted by Andrew Crockett of the technical nature of Committee deliberations, far removed from the hustle and bustle of politics, seems ever more antiquated and distorted.

A second set of concerns that has been seen so often in this book so far is the question of 'whose rules?' and it is again important in this chapter. The question is relevant in a number of senses:

1.  First, we must ask the question with reference to whose rules are being applied, those of authority or those of the market?
2.  Second, which states have been able to push their own interests and perspectives in the new Accord?
3.  Third, which market actors have been most successful in defending and promoting their interests in the reform process?

In response to the first meaning of the question, it is clear to see that the effort to create common international standards for banking supervision increasingly incorporates and reflects market principles. The moves towards market discipline as one of the three pillars of the Basel II framework is only the most obvious policy incarnation of this. The use of external and internal ratings, the consideration of models as acceptable risk-measurement tools, and the overall drive to push banks to shoulder more of the burden (and liberty) of determining how much regulatory capital is appropriate. Basel II has thus not only been an effort to modernise the original Accord and render it more efficient; a central goal has been to shift a large part of the responsibility of regulation to the market itself.

Second, although the Committee tends to focus on the aggregate contribution of its work to systemic stability and soundness, national interests have continued to be a defining factor in the bargaining process. In particular the negotiations over Basel II were shaped by a number of disputes between Germany and the United States over the issues of external credit ratings and loans to SMEs. Although these two states were the most vocal in promoting and defending their respective national interests, the Committee has seen a growing divide between the 'Anglo Saxon' states and the rest. The dominance of the regulatory perspective of the US and UK, though not unchallenged or complete, is perhaps best seen in the emphasis on market discipline and market-based regulation explained in the point above.

The third sense of 'whose rules?' asks which banks have been most effective in gaining representation on the Committee and have consequently benefited in the form of policies that promote their interests. Perhaps unsurprisingly, the big banks have been able to pressure the Committee directly through comments and indirectly through representation to national banking authorities in order to prevent what they have seen as an overly burdensome new capital framework. The latest version of Basel II gives significant concessions to banks using the IRB approach and attaches a greatly reduced importance to the concept of operational risk, which many have argued would disproportionately punish bigger banks using more complex technologies and employing larger numbers of staff. However we must also recognise that smaller banks have been able to influence regulatory authorities to represent their views, particularly in the US.

It must not be thought, however, that this necessarily means that the work of the Committee is flawed. It can be argued, and convincingly so, that by working closely with the market, by embracing the wisdom and experience of banks and their personnel, the Committee has been able to tailor its new framework so that it combines the goals of stability and efficiency. Regulation, it should be remembered, does not have to be a case of suppressing the market; carried out effectively with an eye on the long term effects, regulation can enhance market efficiency at the same time as it reduces the likelihood of systemic crisis. Indeed, by balancing the interests of its members, the Committee has once again engaged in the politics of the possible, thus finding policies that are acceptable to all concerned.

The integrity of the Basel II process and of the BCBS itself, though, has been placed in doubt both by the actions of powerful states such as the US trying to skew the agreement in the favour of their banks, and by the willingness of the Committee to seek industry approval and input for its proposals. The notion of transferring regulation to the banks themselves is evidence of the dubious wisdom of this process. As Avinash Persaud, analyst at State Street Bank, has put it, 'It is a dereliction of duty by the regulators...There is no industry with a longer history of being unable to control its excesses' (Peterson, 2001). When the financial press and even members of the industry itself question the autonomy of the regulatory process, questions must be asked about regulatory capture. The feedback process has resulted in drastic changes to the initial proposals for Basel II that have watered down the Committee's proposals in a number of key areas. It has also produced a framework so complicated and complex that many criticise it as unwieldy. In the words of one member of the Committee:

> as soon as you develop an approach, it's not too long before you hear from the banks complaining about something. So you adjust – at the cost of a more complex calculation for everybody. (*Economist*, 2002)

This capture of the policy formulation process by the very actors who are to be regulated represents one of the biggest challenges to the future effectiveness of the Committee. The 1988 Accord on capital adequacy marked a significant step forward in halting the downward spiral of deregulation and helped to stabilise the international banking system in preparation for what was to be a turbulent decade. That Accord was achieved through bargaining between national authorities, bargaining that, although hard and long and requiring the use of coercive power to achieve a meaningful outcome, was relatively simple compared to the myriad of national and particular interests from member and non-member states. The current and future ability of the BCBS to produce banking standards at the international level will be determined by the willingness of the Committee to take a stand against calls from international banks to reduce their regulatory burden. On the basis of the evidence seen in this chapter, the will of the Committee, or more accurately of its dominant members, to give priority to concerns of safety and soundness over those of the profitability of politically powerful banks seems to be limited. This brings into question both the public responsibility of the Committee and ultimately its ability to legitimise itself through contributing to international financial stability.

**Conclusion**

The balancing of the two goals of efficiency and stability has always been a central task in the business of financial regulation. The modern approach to capital adequacy described in this chapter shows us that the balance has certainly tipped in the favour of the market and efficiency, although not necessarily at the expense of stability. Supporters of Basel II argue that market discipline and the employment of banks' own ratings and risk measurement systems to determine regulatory capital will help to allocate capital much more efficiently and this will result in less market distortions. At the same time banks continue to complain that too much capital is being required of them. This suggests that the Committee has not entirely surrendered to the will of the industry it is trying to regulate.

The road to Basel II was one filled with hazards and warnings, and more than one U-turn, but the agreement was signed in time to allow for implementation of the new capital framework by the end of 2006. Whatever the advantages and problems associated with the new framework, its importance to the global banking system and ultimately the global economy has been demonstrated through an examination of the process that has formulated the coming Accord. What remains to be seen is what will happen after Basel II is finished, accepted and endorsed. How will the market react to the new framework? Which market actors will benefit from the new capital adequacy regime, and which will find their competitiveness compromised. Ultimately, what will Basel III look like when it inevitably emerges as an issue on the negotiating table?

# Chapter 8

# Conclusion

## Introduction

This study has been guided by the principles of international political economy and of political science in its analysis of the development of the Basel Committee for Banking Supervision. It has attempted to inject politics into the purely economic and financial analysis that is undertaken of the Committee, and to assess the importance of the BCBS in the contemporary international system. The interplay of national and particular interests within the Committee and the bargaining that takes place between them have been identified as key elements. The book has argued that to understand the development of the Committee over time, three factors must be considered. First, the evolution of the market in international banking services, and the need to adapt regulation and supervision to changing structures and practices to avoid instability and crisis. Second, the politicised relationship between regulators and the private actors they seek to control, and the ability of banks to pressure national authorities to represent their interests in international negotiations. Third, the exercise of power in the Committee, taking the form of both leadership, and what we have called spoiling behaviour.

The importance of studying the Basel Committee has been shown by highlighting its many contributions to international financial stability and its central role in discussions over the reform of the international financial architecture in the 1990s. But the most significant contribution made thus far by the Committee remains the Capital Accord of 1988 and the capital adequacy regime that has resulted. Current discussions and negotiations over Basel II, and the prospect of future negotiations over Basel III, tell us that this is not only the single most important contribution by the Committee to international banking stability, but it is also by far the most contested and controversial. Moreover, it is the area of Committee work that best exhibits the dynamic interaction between politics and the setting of international banking standards.

Six questions, laid out in the book's introduction, have served as a framework for this study. Having analysed the Committee's development, from its origins in the 1970s to the turn of the century, it is now time to provide some answers to those questions.

## What Success Has the Committee Attained?

Since its inception the primary goal of the Committee has been to protect the health and stability of the international banking system. Thus, if we are to determine the success or otherwise of the Committee, we should evaluate the contributions that it has made to systemic safety and soundness. In other words, what steps has the Committee taken to reduce the probability of a systemic banking crisis, and how can they be seen to have helped both the prevention and management of crisis situations?

Of course an alternative understanding of this question would be to interpret success as the elimination of banking crises. If the goal of the Committee is to protect the system, what better way to do so than by eliminating the crises that threaten it? Banking crises continue to plague national and international policy-makers today, almost thirty years after the creation of the Basel Committee. Some might say, therefore, that the Committee has failed to meet its primary objective.

To define success as narrowly as this however, would not only be rather uninteresting, it would be highly unrealistic. Unless private international banking were to be completely subjected to government control, crises are likely to periodically appear in the international system. As this is highly improbable in the foreseeable future, we are left with the Basel Committee's attempts to coordinate supervisors' work and to develop internationally accepted minimum standards.

The coordination of supervisory standards, demarcation of supervisory responsibility and exchange of information about banking activity was an essential corollary of the new international banking system if persistent crisis was to be avoided, and actual crises to be effectively managed. The Basel Concordat, in its several incarnations, has been a successful attempt to formalise and institutionalise relations between national authorities. The goal that no bank should escape supervision is not only important given the context of international private finance, but also a necessary counter to problems of money-laundering, fraud and terrorist-financing. The course of this project in cooperation has not always been smooth. Indeed the formalisation process has been marked by conflict between authorities, particularly following a breakdown in cooperation and the emergence of a sizeable bank failure having international repercussions. However, by the end of the 20th century the international banking system had been left with an effective regime for supervisory cooperation that determined which national authorities should oversee the operations of the branches and overseas operations of internationally active banks.

Moreover, the Concordat sets standards for ongoing information exchange so that authorities in the G10 states should never be unaware of the presences of problems in the overseas branches of banks operating in their territories. The system, of course, still depends on the compliance of the authorities concerned and their willingness to share information. The decision by the Bank of England in 1990 not to share information about BCCI with its Basel Committee colleagues represented a serious challenge to the spirit as well as the letter of the Concordat.

The subsequent tensions between the US and UK over the BCCI affair were a contributing factor to the improvement of the Concordat.

At the time of writing the Concordat and related agreements on shell-banks and parallel-owned banks stands as a detailed and comprehensive regime to eliminate gaps in the international supervisory net. Banks will, of course, continue to evade supervision, through fair means and foul, but the Concordat has evolved over time to meet the challenges of internationalised private banking.

The other major area of successful cooperation between the Basel members has been the capital adequacy regime. Though its evolution has been even more tortured than that of the Concordat, we can venture that, although some negative effects of the capital regime can be detected (such as procyclicality and poor treatment of credit and country risk) it has also contributed more to the safety and soundness of the international banking system. By establishing minimum levels of bank capitalisation the Committee began to act not only in the manner of an organisation that coordinates supervisory standards, it actually set the standard against which banks throughout the world would fix their capital adequacy ratios. This was no mean feat; the BCBS had never intended to set minimum standards, and the issue of capital adequacy was a particularly sensitive one, being so directly linked with bank competitiveness and profitability. Clearly this was why the negotiations were so difficult and required coercive threats from the US and UK to bring them to conclusion.

The results of the capital adequacy accord tell us more about the success of the Committee. The impact on banking systems in the G10 highlights the success of the Accord. Between 1988 and 1996 the average capital to risk-weighted asset ratio for major banks in the G10 rose from 9.3% to 11.2%. These extra funds set aside against future losses and hard times provided a buffer for big banks against the turmoil of the mid- to late-1990s. Though they were clearly not enough to prevent Japanese banks from going through crises, it can be argued that they protected banks in other countries and even reduced the negative impact of the crisis on Japan's banks.

Furthermore, not only were the ratios imposed throughout the Basel members' banking systems, but they came to be welcomed globally as a minimum acceptable standard. The near-universal acceptance of the Accord demonstrated the perception, at least, that the Committee had done something right. Though the impact, in terms of safety and soundness, on developing-country banking systems is reduced because of the higher levels of economic instability present, the Accord helped to establish the Committee as a body to which all banking supervisors look for leadership.

The successful conclusion of the negotiations leading to a second Basel Capital Accord is another measure of the success of the Committee. Long, drawn-out and highly-controversial talks and bargaining over Basel II were repeatedly threatened with derailment by a combination of political pressure from influential financial actors and the clash of national interests and postures. Yet the flexible, adaptable nature of the Committee allowed an eventual outcome to emerge that was acceptable to all major players in the Committee, although its long-term effects on safety and soundness have yet to be verified.

The expansion of the Committee's influence is the final area by which we should measure the Committee's success. That the Committee has been called on by the leading nations in times of instability to formulate international standards is impressive enough. But the Committee has also come to be seen by supervisors around the world as an authoritative body that sets banking supervisory standards, and looked to for leadership in the area of supervision. This near-universal acceptance amongst supervisory authorities of such an exclusive body should surely be taken as a measure of its success.

This is not to say that the Basel Committee has received such acceptance in academic circles as a legitimate organ of global governance. Concerns exist surrounding the legitimacy of the decision-making progress in the BCBS, as tightly allied as it is to major private financial interests in key countries. Given that the threat of regulatory capture exists, a supplementary line of inquiry relates to the effectiveness of Basel's work. So far as the Committee seems to have made a contribution to safety and soundness in international banking, legitimacy concerns may be downplayed. But if the framework that emerges from the Basel II negotiations, in which private actors played so influential a role, fails to provide higher levels of stability in international banking, the legitimacy of the regime must be called into question.

## How Does the Work of the Committee Interact with the International Banking Market?

The dynamic interaction between the Basel Committee and the market its members oversee should be evaluated on two levels. First in terms of the reactions of the Committee and the banking market to each other, and second how the Committee interacts with private banks in the drawing up of internationally accepted standards. This second level of interaction will be dealt with in greater detail in the flowing section of the conclusion.

First it is worth repeating that the Committee indirectly owed its genesis to the internationalisation of private banking in the post-war period, the breakdown of the Bretton Woods system of restricting private finance and the emergence of the Euromarkets as a phenomenon that linked together all of the major economies' banking systems. The immediate cause for the creation of the Committee was of course the banking crises involving Franklin National and Herstatt banks that hit the system in the mid-1970s. But from the moment of its creation the BCBS has recognised that the nature of an internationalised system of private banking necessitates increased cooperation between national authorities, and cooperation in an institutional setting. In its first efforts to coordinate the actions of supervisors through the Concordat, the Committee demonstrated its intention to contain the negative consequences of internationalised private banking. This goal has never changed throughout the life of the Committee but its approach to solving the problem has certainly evolved.

As the Concordat was tried and tested, the Basel members discovered that it needed frequent evaluation and revision if it was to remain a viable framework for determining supervisory responsibility and ensuring that no bank escaped effective supervision. This was partly due to the high levels of innovation in the market; over time banks have looked to offshore financial centres and complex organisation structures as a way to reduce or evade the impact of supervision on their business. The other major influence for revision came from key members' unwillingness to comply with the spirit of the Concordat.

From building institutional arrangements in order to facilitate supervisory cooperation, in the 1980s the BCBS progressed to the setting of minimum standards for bank capital. Again the intention was to restrain the market, this time by forcing banks to put aside more capital. But at the same time a new motive entered into the Committee's logic, namely that of seeking to rectify imperfections in the competitive landscape, to level the 'playing field' of international banking. In doing so the Committee expressed a desire to work 'with the grain of the market', rather than against it, a tendency that was to become firmly established in the 1990s.

The reaction of the market to the harmonization of capital adequacy standards was two-fold. First, banks moved more assets into areas not covered by the Accord's rulings, and second they lobbied the Committee through national authorities to change the wording of the Accord to allow them to release capital for productive purposes. Over time this was to weaken the Accord significantly and make necessary the negotiation of an entirely new agreement.

The creation of the Joint Forum is a clear example of the tendency of the Committee to match developments in the market. As banking structures became more complex and diverse financial activities became grouped into financial conglomerates, the Committee took the decision to work alongside the IOSCO and IAIS to formulate joint responses to the challenges of cross-sectoral consolidation. Though its contributions thus far have been general in nature, it promises to be a central area of activity for the Committee in the future.

The desire on the part of the Committee to work with the market rather than against it has been exemplified not only by its attempts to reduce competitive inequalities, but more importantly by its efforts to consult widely with the banking community throughout the world as an integral part of the process of forming agreements. The consultative packages that have been emitted by the Committee seek to incorporate the views of the banking industry directly into the policy-making process. Banks give their comments on the consultative packages either to their respective national authorities or directly to the Basel Committee itself. In turn the Committee has sent out modified proposals for consultation, as well as quantitative impact studies to evaluate the potential impact of the new rulings. This process was particularly important during the negotiations towards Basel II.

The dynamic between the Committee and the banks is one that has both positive and negative connotations. We might venture to say, in agreement with banks and the Committee itself, that ongoing consultation produces more workable agreements and more effective supervisory standards. On the other hand, however, the spectre of regulatory capture is not far away, and the notion of the regulated determining the nature of regulation sits uncomfortably with those who have a knowledge of the history of financial crisis and disaster.

## What are the Driving Forces Behind Negotiations in the Committee?

The work of the Basel Committee over the years has been driven by a number of factors, both exogenous and endogenous to the body. Exogenous factors have been primarily responsible for putting issues on the agenda of the Committee, while both exogenous and endogenous factors have determined the outcomes of negotiations. First we must point to the continuous process of change in the banking market, change that is multifaceted itself. The internationalisation of banking spurred the creation of the BCBS, and over the years the Committee has sought to respond to the many innovations in both banking structure and activity. Equally the emergence of new crises and potential trouble spots in international banking have shaped the work of the Committee. Other organs of global governance, such as the G7 and the main IFIs (in particular the IMF) have played a key role in calling on the BCBS to consider certain issues and to contribute to the reform of the IFA.

The issue of national competitiveness was, of course, responsible for the for the arrival of capital adequacy as an item for negotiation. The unilateral moves taken by the US following the onset of the debt crisis in the early 1980s to strengthen American banks' capital positions resulted in pressure on the Congress to bring other states into line in order to reduce the negative competitive impact on US banks.

Once negotiations begin in the BCBS, we can identify a number of dominant factors that have determined outcomes. First we can point to inter-state competition, a traditional focus of international relations. The desire on the part of authorities and governments in the US and Britain to enhance the competitiveness of their national financial centres was clearly a factor in the 1988 Capital Accord. Part of the logic was not only to level the international playing field, but also to impose costs on Japanese, and to a lesser extent, German banks. National economic competitiveness was also a factor in the negotiations for Basel II, as the German government became involved to prevent a negative outcome for SME lending.

More pervasive, though, than inter-state competition has been the protection of domestic interests during negotiations. Negotiations for the original Basel Accord, as well as its successor, saw national authorities defending and promoting their banks and banking systems. US authorities sought the harmonisation of bank capital adequacy standards to reduce the competitive pressures on American banks in the mid-1980s. In the 1990s US and British authorities pushed revisions of the Accord to allow their banks to free up capital. The agreed use of external ratings agencies to help set capital ratios under Basel II was clearly a victory for US banks over their European counterparts.

But it is important that we do not group all banks together. Just as American banks seem to have diverging interests from German and French banks, large banks have very different interests in the Committee's work from smaller banks. Big banks, predominantly those in the US, have pushed their national authorities to pressure the Committee to accept their own evaluations of what constitutes adequate capital, and Basel II will allow large, sophisticated banks to use the IRB approach to determine capital levels is an enormous concession in their favour. In the future, Basel III is likely to see the introduction of banks' own models as a basis for the setting of capital ratios, which, if it happens, will be a victory for big banks in the US and Britain. Although the Committee claims that such moves help to 'align more closely capital charges with underlying risk', it also benefits the large without helping the smaller actors in world banking.

The final factor to consider in the context of BCBS negotiations is the element of ideology. Though it is difficult to quantify, at several points in the development of the Committee the ideological preferences of the two Anglo-Saxon states have driven a new approach to banking supervision. Most importantly for the long-term future of the BCBS, the US and British preference for market discipline in place of traditional forms of regulation has already had and will continue to have a deep influence on the shape of agreements coming out of the Committee.

Though all of these factors have influenced both what is to be discussed in the Committee and what is acceptable to all members, in the final consideration two long-established factors in international relations, namely power and the threat of coercion, have decided much. In the negotiations over the original Basel Accord the threat of closure from London and New York proved enough of a coercive measure to secure Japanese compliance in the agreement. With Japan on board the European members found it impossible to resist any further, even though they had expressed little interest in an international capital regime before, and some had even said such an agreement was unnecessary for their banks. In the negotiations towards Basel II the US used its power in a negative way to 'spoil' the ultimate outcome of the bargaining process and limit the impact of the accord. This spoiling behaviour by the leading state jeopardises the future of the Committee's work and promises to complicate coming negotiations.

### How does the Committee Function as an Organ of Global Governance?

Though the Basel Committee began with limited horizons and goals, it has clearly established itself as one of the central organs in the governance of global banking and finance. As an organ of global financial governance it provides public goods to the system by establishing rules, coordinating cooperative efforts with other institutions, conducting research on international banking, and through its contributions to the process of IFA reform.

The making of rules has always been a foundation of structural power in the international system and the Committee has become the source of internationally accepted rules that are defining the future direction of banking regulation and supervision throughout the world. This is key; not only are the rules applied in the Basel member countries, a considerable contribution to international financial stability as these are the world's leading financial nations, but banking authorities in most states, both developed and developing, are making an effort to adjust their regulatory and supervisory systems to Basel standards. This was seen with the Basel Capital Accord of 1988, the Core Principles of Banking Supervision issued by the Committee in 1997, and finally in the second Basel Capital Accord signed in 2004.

Another form of public good produced by the Committee has been the coordination of supervisory policy with other groups of financial supervisors. First the Committee has been a leader in working with the regional banking supervisors groups throughout the world, an activity that has helped to not only disseminate information on banking supervision to such groups, but has also encourage greater cooperation within them. One regional group in particular, the OGBS, has been an active partner with the BCBS and the importance of collaboration with offshore banking supervisors has been demonstrated in a number of joint projects between the two bodies. Indeed at one point the OGBS, when it decided make membership conditional on independent assessment of supervisory methods and standards, called for Basel to act as an independent observer in this process. Though the BCBS rejected the proposal for fear of encouraging moral hazard, the request shows the prestige given to the Committee by the OGBS.

The BCBS has also acted in a leadership role in the Joint Forum, pulling together banking supervisors with their counterparts in insurance and securities supervision. A necessary corollary to the growth of complex financial conglomerates, the Joint Forum holds the potential for significant cooperation between supervisory groups. To date the Committee has pushed the issues of regulatory capital and supervisory techniques.

Basel's commitment to research and study of the international banking system was established as a primary motive at the creation of the Committee. The original intention was to generate impartial studies on international banking for Basel members, but the numerous studies rapidly began to circulate widely among supervisors from non-member states as well. Through the organisation's website these studies are now available to an even wider public, and can be used by both supervisors and banks alike.

The final area in which the Committee has provided public goods is connected to its contributions to the process of reform of the international financial architecture. The publication of its *Core Principles for Effective Banking Supervision* has already been discussed. Another, ongoing effort is to be seen in the Financial Stability Institute, created jointly by the Basel Committee and the BIS in 1999. The FSI provides technical assistance to banking supervisors from around the world to improve their supervisory techniques and helps keep them abreast of developments in the market. This further level of institutionalisation of Basel's outreach to the global community of banking supervisors lays the foundation for continued and growing influence, especially with regards to authorities in LDCs.

## How does the Committee Relate to the Other Organs of Global Economic Governance?

Having established the Basel Committee as a body that contributes to global governance, it is important that its relationship to other institutions is examined. As noted in this book, at several points in its history the Committee has taken policy direction from the dominant institutions of international cooperation. Founded as a sub-committee of the Bank for International Settlements, the BCBS has operated as a semi-autonomous body, and has not been given strict guidance on desirable areas of cooperation by its parent institution. While a large part of the work of the Committee has originated with the concerns of supervisory authorities in Basel member states, in recent years the Committee has come to be recognised by other organs of global economic governance as an important and useful partner in applying common rules in the world economy and in preventing and managing crises.

The Group of Seven/Group of Eight has perhaps been the single most important international source of policy direction for the Committee. During the financial crises of the mid- to late 1990s, the G7 called on the BCBS to formulate a response to the growing problems of banking crises in developing countries. As seven of the Committee's members are also G7 participants, it was natural for them to turn to the Committee as an authoritative source for a knowledge-based response to the problems of the international banking system. The G7 has also called on the BCBS to work with IOSCO and the IAIS to develop common approaches to financial supervision across the three sectors through the Joint Forum. The G7 has also supported the work of the Basel Committee to counter money laundering and the channelling of finance to terrorist organisations jointly with the Financial Action Task Force, a body created by the G7 in 1989. Thus we can say that Basel's contribution to the ongoing process of reform of the IFA has been shaped and directed by the G7.

It would be wrong, however, to attribute to the G7 overall control of the Committee. On its two most important issues of cooperation, the Concordat and the Basel Capital Accord, the G7 had no connection either to the process of negotiation or to the original idea for cooperation in these areas. Instead we should conceptualise the relationship as one in which the G7 can intervene in the business of the Committee when it sees fit, although this is only likely to happen during periods of systemic instability.

Because of the near-complete overlap in membership (with the exception of Spain), the Group of Ten is another organ of global economic governance to which the BCBS is connected. Created in 1962 by those countries who agreed to participate in the General Arrangement to Borrow in the IMF, the G10 continues to work on financial issues, studying the international financial system and drawing policy conclusions. As such it partly shares a policy-space with the BCBS; for example, its January 2001 report on consolidation in finance borrowed from the ongoing work of the Joint Forum and the Basel Committee examining the consolidation of the financial sector.

The IMF and World Bank have come to recognise the value of the Committee's work in recent years and have incorporated Basel standards into their reviews of member country financial systems. Of particular importance have been the Basel Core Principles which have become the basis for financial supervisory review by the Bretton Woods institutions.

A final point worth noting in this section is the deepening relationship between Basel and IOSCO and the IAIS. As a triumvirate in the Joint Forum they form the backbone of emerging standards of governance for an international financial system that has undergone significant structural change over the past twenty years. Though the three institutions have developed to different levels of organisational complexity and cooperation among their respective members, and though they are still a long way from having harmonized supervisory standards in the three financial sectors, the Joint Forum holds the potential to develop into one of the most important sources of financial governance at the international level.

**What is the Future and What Challenges Lie Ahead for the Committee?**

The first priority for the Basel Committee in the near future is, of course, to implement Basel II. The signing of the agreement in June of 2004 was a significant achievement, but the implementation of the Accord will show whether or not it has a differential impact on the member states and their banks. Moreover, the disagreements between key member states during the negotiation process showed that the collaborative spirit in the Committee is under considerable strain and this needs to be remedied before any meaningful agreements can be negotiated in the future.

Even before the new capital framework was complete, thoughts had turned to the next step, as noted in chapter seven. Basel III promises to be another hotly contested area of negotiation, as big banks will push to use their own internal models to determine appropriate capital levels. The debate will turn on whether authorities are convinced that models provide enough capital to cover banking risks. At the moment, supervisors believe much more work needs to be done to make models safer, but there is a feeling that banks will soon be able to provide enough reassurance to authorities that their models work equally as well as a standardised approach.

Beyond Basel III the Committee will inevitably be faced with more banking and financial crises that will require revisions of the Concordat and new ways of ensuring implementation of the Core Principles. The BCBS will also face continuing change in the financial industry, with increasing consolidation and innovation that will test the strength of current agreements. It is perhaps unavoidable that the Committee will fail to prevent the development of new threats to systemic stability, but it has shown an ability over the years to respond rapidly and effectively to such threats once they arise.

The biggest challenge to the effectiveness of the Basel Committee in the future will come not from new developments in the market, but rather from the ability of market participants to influence the agenda and outcomes of negotiations. The Committee must face up to the problem of regulatory capture by the biggest private actors in international banking, particularly institutions in the United States, if it is to maintain both legitimacy and effectiveness. A similar problem emerges with the seeming dominance of Anglo-Saxon approaches to banking supervision in recent years. Continental European and Japanese authorities will feel that their interests and preferences are not being completely catered for the Committee, something that could threaten the long-term viability of cooperation in the BCBS. The rivalries that emerged in the Basel II negotiations between the US and Germany over the treatment of SME loans and the use of external ratings agencies were resolved after lengthy discussions and the threat by the German government to abandon Basel II if the American position remained unchanged. Such brinkmanship, though apparently required at the time, cannot be conducive to the long-term health of cooperation in the Committee.

## Domestic Politics and State Preferences in the Committee

Throughout the life of the Committee, but particularly during the negotiations over the capital adequacy regime, we can see the significance of the influence exercised by private financial actors over regulatory authorities. In the case of the most powerful country, the United States, this occurs directly in the relationship between the authorities and banks, but also indirectly in the pressure exerted by private financial actors on legislators during Congressional hearings.

The internationalisation of US standards on capital adequacy seen in the 1980s is a story already well-known in political economy circles. US banks, seeking to minimize the impact on their international competitiveness from new capital adequacy standards, pressured Congress and regulators to seek harmonized standards at the international level. The story of Basel II, however, shows this dynamic in even greater detail. US financial actors have influenced their negotiators at every stage of the bargaining process to alter the wording and content of the agreement to give them greater flexibility in determining capital levels and to limit the scope of the accord. Large banks have managed to obtain the right to use internal risk models to determine necessary capital, giving them a significant advantage over banks not qualifying for this option. At the same time, pressure from smaller, community banks has meant that the US will only apply the final accord to a limited number of banks. This stands in stark contrast with the Europeans, who are using Basel II as the basis for CAD3, regulations that will apply to banks throughout the European system. This is not to say that European regulators have not engaged in similar behaviour. German (and other European) authorities insisted on a more favourable risk-weighting for SME loans, which make up a more substantial portion of European bank business.

We also see the importance of the relationship between private actors and the authorities at the level of the Committee itself. The BCBS has consistently sought input from banks, other financial firms and academics in its work, often incorporating concerns from these actors into revisions to the accord. It would, of course, be an exaggeration to claim that this process of consultation has a comparable impact when compared to that of negotiations between regulators and their constituencies at the national level, but the institutionalisation of the process over time has helped to establish the authority and acceptance of the Committee in banking circles.

## Power, Leadership and Spoiling Behaviour

The dominance of the United States in the arena of international finance, shown so often in other studies, and the importance of its main supporter state, the United Kingdom, emerge as determining factors in explaining bargaining and outcomes in the Basel Committee. The ability of the United States to obtain international agreements that reflect its interests and those of its banks has been the single most important factor in determining outcomes in the Committee.

The structural power of the US, in particular, has been crucial. The 1988 Accord demonstrated the willingness of the US to threaten unilateral or bilateral (with the UK) closure in order to forge an agreement that would internationalise US standards and thus redistribute the costs of increased bank capital levels. This has been seen again during the negotiations towards Basel II, with the US using its power in a more negative way, unilaterally reducing the scope of the accord in response to pressures from domestic actors.

The difference in these two examples of US exercise of power is informative. In the first it can be claimed that the US demonstrated leadership in the governance of international banking, albeit in a way that promoted US interests at the expense of those of other states. This leadership produced notable advances in the international regime for banking safety and soundness. This 'happy coincidence', if you will, between US interests and those of the system as a whole, provides us with a clue as to the prerequisites for US leadership behaviour.

In the second example, however, we can observe that when the interests of powerful US domestic actors are at odds with those of a stricter international regime, the US is more likely to engage in 'spoiling' behaviour, reducing the scope and potential effectiveness of international standards. The more negative exercise of US power in this case not only reduced the scope of the agreement, but also encouraged other important actors, including the important developing country financial regulators of China and India, to decide to delay implementation of the accord.

## Final Thoughts

The Basel Committee on Banking Supervision has risen from modest beginnings in the post-Bretton Woods turmoil of the 1970s to its current position as the single most important source of banking policy coordination in the international system. It has taken on diverse topics in its studies and agreements, and has expanded its influence beyond its own members and beyond banking into other sectors of finance. It is recognised by the leading nations and by the other IFIs as an essential piece in the jigsaw of global financial governance.

However the Committee has not risen to this elevated position in a political vacuum. Its development and success have been marked by political conflict as much as by changes in the banking industry and international financial system. Though frequently viewed as a body of banking supervisory experts engaged in lofty and esoteric discussions over financial stability, it is clear that the clashes between national and particular interests have played a determining role in shaping the outcome of attempts to coordinate policy. This, then, places the study of the Committee firmly within the bounds of political science and international political economy. Looking to the future, political scientists and political economists must continue to study the Committee alongside economists and banking experts for it is only by examining the interplay between the interests of market actors and the imperatives of national authorities that the future development of the Committee will be fully understood.

# Appendix I

# Regional Supervisors Groups

Arab Committee on Banking Supervision
Caribbean Banking Supervisors Group
Association of Banking Supervisory Authorities of Latin America and the
  Caribbean
Eastern and Southern Africa Banking Supervisors Group
EMEAP Study Group on Banking Supervision
Group of Banking Supervisors from Central and Eastern European Countries
Gulf Cooperation Council Banking supervisors' Committee
Offshore Group of Banking Supervisors
Regional Supervisory Group of Central Asia and Transcaucasia
SEANZA Forum of Banking Supervisors
Committee of Banking Supervisors in West and Central Africa

# Chairs of the Basel Committee

| | |
|---|---|
| 2003-? | Mr. Jaime Caruana (Governor of the Bank of Spain) |
| 1998-2003 | Mr. William J. McDonough (Chief Executive Officer, Federal Reserve Bank of New York) |
| 1997-1998 | Mr. T. de Swaan (Executive Director of De Nederlandsche Bank) |
| 1993-1997 | Dr. T. Padoa-Schioppa (Deputy Director of the Bank of Italy) |
| 1991-1993 | Mr. E. Gerald Corrigan (President of the Federal Reserve Bank of New York) |
| 1988-1991 | Mr. H.J. Muller (Executive Director of De Nederlandsche Bank) |
| 1977-1988 | Mr W.P. Cooke (Associate Director, Bank of England) |
| 1974-1977 | Sir George Blunden (Executive Director, Bank of England) |

# Bibliography

Adams, James R. and Douglas Frantz (1993), *A Full Service Bank: How BCCI Stole Billions Around the World*, Pocket Books, New York.

Akyuz, Yilmaz (2002), ed., *Reforming the Global Financial Architecture*, Zed Books, London.

Armijo, Leslie Elliott (2002), ed., *Debating the Global Financial Architecture*, SUNY Press, Albany.

BAFin (2002), 'Durchbruch bei Basel II', Bundesanstalt fur Finanzdienstleistungsaufsicht (German Finance Ministry), press release, 10th July 2002.

Baldwin, David A. (1985), *Economic Statecraft*, Princeton University Press, Princeton.

Bank of England (1988), 'Implementation of the Basle Convergence Agreement in the United Kingdom', BSD/1988/3, Bank of England Banking Supervision Division, October 18th 1988.

*Banker, The* (2003), 'Latest US move sets the pace for the world', August 1, 2003.

Banuri, Tariq and Juliet B. Schor (1992), eds., *Financial Openness and National Autonomy*, Oxford University Press, Oxford.

Bardos, Jeffrey (1987), ' The Risk-Based Capital Agreement: A Further Step Towards Policy Convergence', *Federal Reserve Bank of New York Quarterly Review*, 26, Winter 1987/88.

BCBS (1982), *Report on International Developments in Banking Supervision*.

BCBS (1983), *Principles for the supervision of banks' foreign establishments*, Basel Committee Publications No. 2, May 1983.

BCBS (1988), *International Convergence of Capital Measurement and Capital Standards*, Basel Committee Publications No. 4, July 1988.

BCBS (1990), *Information Flows Between Banking Supervisory Authorities (Supplement to the Concordat)*, Basel Committee Publications No. 7, April 1990.

BCBS (1991), *Amendment of the Basel capital accord in respect of the inclusion of general provisions/general loan-loss reserves in capital*, Basel Committee Publications No. 9, November 1991.

BCBS (1992), *Minimum Standards for the supervision of International Banking Groups and their Cross-Border Establishments*, Basel Committee Publications No.10, July 1992.

BCBS (1993), ' The prudential supervision of netting, market risks and interest rate risk', Preface to Consultative Proposal by the Basel Committee on Banking Supervision, April 1993.

BCBS (1994), *Amendment to the Capital Accord of July 1988*, Basel Committee Publications No. 12, July 1994.

BCBS (1995a), *Basel Capital Accord: treatment of potential exposure for off-balance-sheet items*, Basel Committee Publications No.18, April 1995.

BCBS (1995b), *The Supervision of Financial Conglomerates*, Report by the Tripartite Group of Bank, Securities and Insurance supervisors, Basel Committee Publications No.20, July 1995.

BCBS (1996a), *Amendment to the capital accord to incorporate market risks*, Basel Committee Publications No.24, January 1996.

BCBS (1996b), *The Supervision of Cross-Border Banking*, Basel Committee Publications No. 27, October 1996.

BCBS (1996c), 'Press Release on Market Risk', 10th December 1996.

BCBS (1997), *Core Principles for Effective Banking Supervision (Basle Core Principles)*, Basel Committee Publications No. 30, September 1997.

BCBS (1998), *Survey of disclosures about trading and derivatives activities of banks and securities firms 1997*, Basel Committee Publications No. 44, November 1998.

BCBS (1999a), *Sound Practices for Banks' Interactions with highly-Leveraged Institutions*, Basel Committee Publications No. 46, January 1999.

BCBS (1999b), *Recommendations for Public Disclosure of Trading and Derivatives Activities of Banks and Securities Firms*, Joint reports by the Basel Committee on Banking Supervision and the Technical Committee of the "IOSCO", Basel Committee Publications No. 48, February 1999.

BCBS (1999c), *A new capital adequacy framework*, Basel Committee Publications No.50, June 1999.

BCBS (1999d), *Best Practices for Credit Risk Disclosure*, Basel Committee Publications No. 53, July 1999.

BCBS (1999e), *Sound Practices for Loan Accounting and Disclosure*, Basel Committee Publications No. 55, July 1999.

BCBS (1999f), *Recommendations for Public Disclosure of Trading and Derivatives Activities of Banks and Securities Firms*, Basel Committee Publications No. 60, October 1999.

BCBS (1999g), *Core Principles Methodology*, Basel Committee Publications No. 61, October 1999.

BCBS (1999h), *Trading and Derivatives Disclosures of Banks and Securities Firms*, Joint report by the Basel Committee on Banking supervision and the Technical Committee of the "IOSCO", Basel Committee Publications No. 64, December 1999.

BCBS (2000a), *Banks' Interactions with highly Leveraged Institutions: Implementation of the Basel Committee's Sound Practices Paper*, Basel Committee Publications No. 68, January 2000.

BCBS (2000b), *Best Practices for Credit Risk Disclosure*, Basel Committee Publications No. 74, September 2000.

BCBS (2001a), *The New Basel Capital Accord*, Consultative Document, January 2001.

BCBS (2001b), *Compendium of documents produced by the Joint Forum*, July 2001.

BCBS (2001c), *The Joint Forum Core Principles Cross-Sectoral Comparison*, November 2001.

BCBS (2001d), *The Joint Forum Risk Management Practices and Regulatory Capital Cross-Sectoral Comparison*, November 2001.

BCBS (2002a), 'Basel Committee reaches agreement on New Capital Accord Issues', press release, 10 July 2002.

BCBS (2004), 'Continued progress toward Basel II', press release, 15 January 2004.

Beattie, Alan (2001), 'Risk assessment in the spotlight', *Financial Times*, 11th June 2001.

Beattie, Alan (2002), 'BIS hits back over banking standards', *Financial Times*, 8th March 2002.

Belloni, Bertrand & Jorge Niosi (1988), *The Decline of the American Economy*, Black Rose Books, Montreal.

Bhagwati, Jagdish (1991), *The World Trading System at Risk*, Princeton University Press, Princeton.

BIS (1991), *61st Annual Report*, June 1991.

BIS (1998), 'BIS Institute for Financial Stability', Press release, 12th March 1998.

Block, Fred (1977), *The Origins of International Economic Disorder*, University of California Press, Berkeley.

Bryant, Ralph (1987), *International Financial Intermediation*, The Brookings Institution, Washington.

Cameron, Doug (2001), 'Basle committee gives in to bankers' pressure', *Financial Times*, 28th September 2001.

Casson, Mark, (1990) 'Evolution of multinational banks: a theoretical perspective', in Geoffrey Jones, ed., *Banks as Multinationals*, Routledge, London.

Cerny, Philip G. (1993), *Finance and World Politics*, Elgar Publishing Limited, Aldershot.

Cohen, Benjamin J. (1986), *In Whose Interest?* Yale University Press, New Haven, Conn.

Coulbeck, Neil (1984), *The Multinational Banking Industry*, Croom Helm, London.

Cox, Robert (1987), *Production, Power and World Order: Social Forces in the Making of History*, Columbia University Press, New York.

Currie, Antony (1998), 'Squeezing more into tier one', *Euromoney*, December 1998, pp.47-50.

Dale, Richard (1984), *The Regulation of International Banking*, Woodhead-Faulkner, Cambridge.

Davenport, Todd (2003), 'A regulatory middle ground on Basel II?', *The American Banker*, December 2003.

Dougherty, James E. & Robert L. Pfaltzgraff, Jr. (1990), *Contending Theories of International Relations*, Harper & Row, New York.

Drucker, Peter F. (1986), 'The Changes in World Economy', *Foreign Affairs* 64, 4, Spring 1986.

Drucker, Peter F. (1993), *Post-Capitalist Society*, Harper Collins, New York.

Duffy, John J. (1987), 'Capital Rules will fortify Banks', *American Banker*, 20th January 1987.

*Economist* (1991a), 'Living, and dying, by the rule-book', February 15th 1991.

*Economist* (1991b), 'Speedy winners', October 26th 1991.

*Economist* (1991c), ' Thoroughly modern safety-net', October 26th 1991.

*Economist* (1991d), 'Deep in bad debt', November 2nd 1991.

*Economist* (1991e), 'The cooks spoil the broth', November 30th 1991.

*Economist* (1991f), 'A loan sale to the rescue?', November 30th 1991.

*Economist* (1992a), 'Whipping boys', May 23rd 1992.

*Economist* (1992b), 'Crash Landing', June 6th 1992.

*Economist* (1992c), 'Over the hills and far away', July 11th 1992.

*Economist* (1993), 'Hold the bouquets, please', July 31st 1993.

*Economist* (1994a), 'The capital handicap', February 26th 1994.

*Economist* (1994b), 'Japan's bankers breach the wall', November 26th 1994.

*Economist* (1995), 'Walking Wounded', January 7th 1995.

*Economist* (1999a), 'Basle brush', May 1st 1999.

*Economist* (1999b), 'Basle bust-up', October 16th 1999.

*Economist* (1999c), 'Bank rules in disarray', November 27th 1999.

*Economist* (2001a), 'Capital cushion fight', June 9th 2001.

*Economist* (2001b), 'Basel postponed', June 30th 2001.

*Economist* (2001c), ' The Basel perplex', November 10th 2001.

*Economist* (2002), ' The good tailors of Basel', February 23rd 2002.

Edwards, Franklin R. and Hugh T. Patrick (1992), eds., *Regulating International Financial Markets: Issues and Policies*, Kluwer Academic Publishers, Boston.

Ehrlich, Peter and Rob Lebert (2001), 'Schroder balks at bank plans', *Financial Times*, 31st October 2001.

Ehrlich, Peter, Haig Simonian and John Willman (2001), 'Germans warn over banking capital rules', *Financial Times*, 1st November 2001.

Eichengreen, Barry (1999), *Toward a New International Financial Architecture: a Practical Post-Asia Agenda*, Institute for International Economics, Washington, D.C.

*Euromoney* (2001), 'It's time to scrap the Basel system', August 2001.

Evans, Peter B., Harold K. Jacobson, Robert D. Putnam (1993), eds., *Double-Edged Diplomacy: International Bargaining and Domestic Politics*, University of California Press, Berkeley.

FDIC (1997), *History of the Eighties – Lessons for the Future*, Federal Deposit Insurance Corporation, Washington, D.C.

FSF (2003), 'Ongoing and Recent Work Relevant to Sound Financial Systems', note by the FSF Secretariat for the FSF Meeting on 10 September 2003.

*Financial Times* (1998a), 'This year's Basle models', February 2nd 1998.

*Financial Times* (1998b), 'Bankers seek new Basle formula', March 24th 1998.

*Financial Times* (1998c), 'Harassed regulators try to draw the line', April 4th 1998.

*Financial Times* (1998d), 'More equity', April 8th 1998.

*Financial Times* (1998e), 'Top banks' capital cushion shrinks', July 6th, 1998.

Funabashi, Yoichi (1988), *Managing the Dollar: From the Plaza to the Louvre*, Institute for International Economics, Washington, D.C.

*Future Banker* (2000), 'Risk management: Serious Treatment for Operational Risk', May 11th 2000.

G7 (1996), *Finance Ministers' Report to the Heads of State and Government on international monetary stability*, http://www.g7.utoronto.ca/summit/1996lyon/finance.html

G7 (1998), *Strengthening the Architecture of the Global Financial System*, http://birmingham.g8summit.gov.uk/docs/finmin.fri.shtml

G10 (2001), *Report on Consolidation in the Financial Sector*, January 2001.

Galbraith, John Kenneth (1955), *The Great Crash, 1929*, Houghton Mifflin, Boston.

Galbraith, John Kenneth (1993), *A Short History of Financial Euphoria*, Whittle Books, USA.

Gardner, Richard (1980), *Sterling-Dollar Diplomacy in Current Perspective: The Origins of International Economic Order*, Columbia University Press, New York.

Garten, Jeffrey E. (1998), *The Big Ten: The Big Emerging Markets and How They Will Change Our Lives*, Basic Books, New York.

Garver, Rob (2000a), 'Banks Say Basel Capital Plan Lumps Too Many Risk Categories Together', *American Banker* 04/04/2000.

Garver, Rob (2000b), 'In Rare Partnership, Banks, Regulators Tackle Risk', *American Banker* 04/28/2000.

GAO (1991), , 'International Banking: Implementation of Risk-Based Capital Adequacy Standards', GAO/NSIAD-91-80, United States General Accounting Office, Washington, D.C.

Germain, Randall D. (1997), *The International Organization of Credit*, Cambridge University Press, Cambridge.

Goldstein, Morris (1997), *The Case for an International Banking Standard*, Institute for International Economics, Washington, D.C.

Golin, Jonathan (2001), 'Basel 2 and its likely impact on Asia's banks', *FinanceAsia.com*, www.financeasia.com/articles/630CEECD-3DC7-11D5-81CB0090277E174B.cfm, 17th July 2001.

Goodhart, C.A.E., Philipp Hartmann, David Llewellyn, Liliana Rojas-Suarez, Steven Weisbrod (1998), *Financial Regulation: Why, how and where now?*, Routledge and Bank of England, London.

Graham, George (1996), 'Capital: Bank regulators refuse to change rules', *Financial Times*, 11th December 1996.

Graham, George (1997), 'New banking standards set for approval', *Financial Times*, 22nd September 1997.

Graham, George (1999a), 'Banks Angered By Regulators' Plan for Operational-Risk Provision', *Financial Times*, 5th March 1999.

Graham, George (1999b), 'German Objections Hold Up Banking Reform by International Regulatory Committee', *Financial Times*, 5th April 1999.

Graham, George (1999c), 'German-U.S. Rift slows Talks On Reforms of Banking's Basle Accord', *Financial Times*, 13th May 1999.

Griffith-Jones, Stephany and Stephen Spratt (2001), 'Will the proposed new Basel Capital Accord have a net negative effect on developing countries', Institute of Development Studies, University of Sussex.

Gruson, Michael and Wolfgang Feuring (1991), 'The New Banking Law of the European Community', *The International Lawyer* **25**(1), Spring 1991.

Guitian, Manuel (1992), *Rules and Discretion in International Economic Policy*, International Monetary Fund, Washington D.C.

Haraf, William S. and Rose Marie Kushmeider (1988), *Restructuring Banking and Financial Services in America*, American Enterprise Institute for Public Policy Research, Washington.

Helk, Anja (2001), 'Basel – what next?', *Euromoney*, August 2001.

Helleiner, Eric (1994) *States and the Reemergence of Global Finance*, Cornell University Press, Ithaca.

IMF (1993), 'Revised Basle Concordat on Bank Oversight Clarifies the Division of Supervisory Roles', *IMF Survey*, July 11 1983.

Iyer, Savita (2000), 'IIF Report Proposes More Changes to Basel', *Bank Loan Report*, 04/24/2000.

Jackson, Patricia, Craig Furfine, Hans Groeneveld, Diana Hancock, David Jones, William Perraudin, Lawrence Radecki & Masao Yoneyama (1999), *Capital Requirements and Bank Behaviour: the impact of the Basle Accord*, Basel Committee on Banking Supervision Working Paper No.1, April 1999.

Johnson, G.G. and Richard K, Adams (1983), *Aspects of the International Banking Safety Net*, IMF, Washington.

Johnson, R.B. (1983), *The Economics of the Euro-Market*, MacMillan Press Ltd., London.

Jones, David (2000), 'Emerging problems with the Basel Capital Accord: Regulatory capital arbitrage and related issues', *Journal of Banking and Finance*, 24 (2000), 35-58.

Kahler, Miles (1985), 'Politics and International Debt: Explaining the Debt Crisis', *International Organization*, **39**, Summer 1985.

Kahler, Miles (1986), ed., *The Politics of International Debt*, Cornell University Press, Ithaca.

Kahler, Miles (1993), 'Bargaining with the IMF: Two-Level Strategies and Developing Countries', in Evans, Peter B., Harold K. Jacobson, Robert D. Putnam (1993), eds., *Double-Edged Diplomacy: International Bargaining and Domestic Politics*, University of California Press, Berkeley.

Kaiser, Karl, John Kirton and Joseph P. Daniels (2000), eds., *Shaping a New International Financial System: challenges of governance in a globalizing world*, Ashgate Publishing Company, Aldershot.

Kane, Edward J. (1977), 'Good intentions and unintended evil: The case against selective credit allocation', *Journal of Money, Credit, and Banking*, **9**(1), (Feb. 1977), pp. 55-69.

Kane, Edward J. (1988), 'How market forces influence the structure of financial regulation' in William S. Haraf & Rose Marie Kushmeider, eds., *Restructuring Banking and Financial Services in America*, American Enterprise Institute for Public Policy Research, Washington, D.C.

Kapstein, Ethan B. (1989), 'Resolving the regulator's dilemma: international coordination of banking regulations', *International Organization*, **43**(2), Spring 1989.

Kapstein, Ethan B. (1991), 'Supervising International Banks: Origins and Implications of the Basle Accord', *Princeton Essays in International Finance*, no.185, December 1991.

Kapstein, Ethan B. (1992), 'Between Power and Purpose: central bankers and the politics of regulatory convergence', *International Organization*, **46** (1), Winter 1992.

Kapstein, Ethan B. (1994), *Governing the Global Economy: International Finance and the State,* Harvard University Press, Cambridge, MA.

Kenen, Peter B. (2001), *The International Financial Architecture: what's new? What's missing?*, Institute for International Economics, Washington, D.C.

172      *Governing Global Banking*

Kester, C. and T. Luehrman (1992), 'The Myth of Japan's Low-Cost Capital, *Harvard Business Review*, May-June 1992.

Kindleberger, Charles (1973), *The World in Depression: 1929-39*, University of California Press, Berkeley.

Kindleberger, Charles (1978), *Manias, Panics and Crashes: A History of Financial Crises*, Basic Books, New York.

Kindleberger, Charles (1989), *International Capital Movements*, Cambridge University Press, Cambridge.

Kindleberger, Charles & Peter H. Lindert (1978), *International Economics*, Richard D. Irwin, Inc., Homewood, Illinois.

Kirton, John (1995), ' The Diplomacy of Concert: Canada, the G-7 and the Halifax Summit', *Canadian Foreign Policy*, **3** (Spring), pp. 63-80.

Lake, David (1983), 'International Economic Structures and American Foreign Economic Policy, 1887-1934', *World Politics*, **35**, July 1983.

Lake, David (1993), 'Leadership, Hegemony, and the International Economy: Naked Emperor or Tattered Monarch with Potential?', *International Studies Quarterly*, **37**, 1993.

Lindblom, Charles (1977), *Politics and Markets*, Basic Books, New York.

Lindgren, Carl-Johan, Gillian Garcia, Matthew I. Saal (1996), *Bank Soundness and Macroeconomic Policy*, International Monetary Fund, Washington, D.C.

Llewellyn, David T. (1989), 'The strategic dilemma of world banking: Competitive implications of the Basle Capital Conference Provisions', *Retail Banker's Management Review*, Spring/Summer 1989.

Llewellyn, David T. (1992), 'Bank Capital: The strategic issue of the 1990s', *Banking World*, January 1992.

Lombra, Raymond and William Witte (1982), eds., *The Political Economy of International and Domestic Monetary Relations*, Iowa State University, Ames.

Maisel, Sherman (1981), *Risk and Capital Adequacy in Commercial Banks*, University of Chicago Press, Chicago.

McDonough, William (2002), 'Completing the journey to the New Basel Accord', speech given to the Twelfth International Conference of Banking Supervisors, Cape Town, South Africa, 18th September 2002.

McKinnon, Ronald I. (1984), *An International Standard for Monetary Stability*, Policy Analyses in International Economics, No.8, Institute for International Economics, Washington.

McKinnon, Ronald I. (1993), *The Order of Economic Liberalization: Financial Control in the Transition to a Market Economy*, The Johns Hopkins University Press, Baltimore.

Moffitt, Michael (1983), *The World's Money*, Simon and Schuster, New York.

Nabors, Robert and Thomas Oatley (1998), 'Redistributive Cooperation: Market Failure, Wealth Transfers, and the Basle Accord', *International Organization*, **52**(1), Winter 1998, pp. 35-54.

Norton, J.J. (1989), 'The work of the Basle Supervisors Committee on Bank Capital Adequacy and the July 1988 Report on 'International Convergence of Capital Measurement and Capital Standards', *The International Lawyer*, **23**(1), Winter 1989.

Nye, Joseph (1991), *Bound to Lead: The Changing Nature of American Power*, Basic Books, USA.

O'Brien, Richard (1992), *Global Financial Integration: The End of Geography*, Royal Institute of International Affairs, London.

Odell, John S. (1982), *U.S. International Monetary Policy: Markets, Power and Ideas as Sources of Change*, Princeton University Press, Princeton.

Pauly, Louis W (1988)., *Opening Financial Markets: Banking Politics on the Pacific Rim*, Cornell University Press, Ithaca.

Pauly, Louis W. (1993), 'Multinational Enterprises and Global Capital Markets', in U.S. Congress, Office of Technology Assessment, *Multinationals and the National Interest: Playing by Different Rules*, OTA-ITE-569 U.S. Government Printing Office, Washington, DC, September 1993.

Pauly, Louis W. (1997), *Who Elected the Bankers? Surveillance and Control in the World Economy*, Cornell University Press, Ithaca.

Peek, J. and E. Rosengreen (1993), 'Bank Regulation and the Credit Crunch', Federal Reserve Bank of Boston, Working Paper No.93-2, February 1993.

Peterson, Michael (2001), 'Basel gives banks the whipping hand', *Euromoney*, March 2001.

Polanyi, Karl (1957), *The Great Transformation: the political and economic origins of our time*, Beacon Press, Boston.

Porter, Tony (1993), *States, Markets and Regimes in Global Finance*, St. Martin's Press, New York.

Porter, Tony (2000), 'The G-7, the Financial Stability forum, the G-20, and the Politics of International Financial Regulation', paper prepared for the International Studies Association Annual Meeting, Los Angeles, California, March 15, 2000.

Porter, Tony and Duncan Wood (2002), 'Reform without Representation? The International and Transnational Dialogue on the Global Financial Architecture', in Leslie Elliott Armijo, ed., *Debating the Global Financial Architecture*, SUNY Press, Albany, pp. 236-56.

PR Newswire (2003), 'ICBA to agencies: ensure competitive equality under Basel II', November 5, 2003.

Putnam, Robert D., and Nicholas Bayne (1984), *Hanging Together: The Seven Power Summits*, Harvard University Press, Cambridge, Mass.

Putnam, Robert D. (1988), 'Diplomacy and Domestic Politics: The Logic of Two-Level Games', *International Organization*, **42**(3) (Summer 1988), pp. 427-460.

Quinn, Brian Scott (1975) *The New Euromarkets* London: MacMillan Press Ltd., 1975.

Quinn, Brian Scott (1992), speech given to the *Financial Times* Conference on "International Banking", London, 25th February 1992.

Quinn, Brian Scott (1992), 'Regulating global financial markets: problems and solutions', in Edwards, Franklin R. and Hugh T. Patrick, eds., *Regulating International Financial Markets: Issues and Policies*, Kluwer Academic Publishers, Boston.

Rapkin, David (1990), *World Leadership and Hegemony*, Lynne Reinner, Boulder.

Robinson, Karina (2003), 'An aficionado for the fine print', *The Banker*, December 2003.

Roosa, Robert (1967), *The Dollar and World Liquidity*, Random House, New York..

Schuijer, Jan (1992), *Banks Under Stress*, OECD, Paris.

Scott, Hal S. and Shinsaku Iwahara (1994), *In Search of a Level Playing Field: The Implementation of the Basle Capital Accord in Japan and the United States*, Group of Thirty, Washington.

Shirreff, David (1999), 'Too far, too fast?', *Euromoney*, August 1999.

Shirreff, David (2000), 'Basel's big exam', *Euromoney*, May 2000.

Simmons, Beth A. (2001), ' The International Politics of Harmonization: The Case of Capital Market Regulation', *International Organization*, **55**(3), Summer 2001, pp. 589-620.

Singer, J. (1987), 'The Behavioral Science Approach to International Relations Theory', *International Organization*, Summer 1987.

Snidal, Duncan (1985), 'The Limits of Hegemonic Stability Theory', *International Organization*, **39**(4), Autumn 1985.

Spero, Joan (1980) *The Failure of Franklin National Bank*, Columbia University Press, New York.

Strange, Susan (1986), *Casino Capitalism*, Basil Blackwell Inc., Oxford.

Strange, Susan (1988) *States and Markets*, Basil Blackwell Press Inc., New York.

Strange, Susan (1987), 'The persistent myth of lost hegemony', *International Organization*, **41**(4), Autumn 1987.

Strange, Susan (1998), *Mad Money: when markets outgrow governments*, University of Michigan Press, Ann Arbor.

Stubbs, Richard and Geoffrey Underhill, eds. (1994), *Political Economy and the Changing Global Order*, McClelland & Stewart, London.

Sundararajan, V. & Tomas J.T. Balino (1991), eds., *Banking Crises: Cases and Issues*, International Monetary Fund, Washington, D.C.

Swary, Itzhak and Barry Topf (1992), *Global Financial Deregulation: Commercial Banking at the crossroads*, Blackwell Publishers, Cambridge, Mass.

Swary, Itzhak (1980), *Capital Adequacy Requirements and Bank Holding Companies*, University of Michigan Press, Ann Arbor.

Tait, Nikki (2003), 'Bank of England set for its day in court', *Financial Times*, November 11, 2003, p. 16.

Underhill, Geoffrey R.D. (1997), *The New World Order in International Finance*, St. Martin's Press, New York.

US Congress (1993), *Multinational and the National Interest: Playing by Different Rules*, Office of Technology Assessment, OTA-ITE-569, U.S. Government Printing Office, Washington.

US Senate (1983), Committee on Banking, *Proposed Solutions to the International Debt Problem*, 98th Congress, 1st session, April 11th, 1983.

US Senate (1992), *The BCCI Affair*, report to the Committee on Foreign Relations, United States Senate, December 1992, 102d Congress 2d Session Senate Print 102-140.

Van Duyn, Aline (2001), "Agencies lobby Basle Committee on ratings disclosures", *Financial Times*, 1st June 2001.

Volcker, Paul A. and Toyoo Gyohten (1992) *Changing Fortunes: The World's Money and the Threat to American Leadership*, Times Books, New York.

Wachtel, Howard (1986) *The Money Mandarins*, Pantheon Books, New York.

Wagster, John D. (1996), 'Impact of the 1988 Basle Accord on International Banks', *The Journal of Finance*, **51**(4) (Sep. 1996), pp. 1321-1346.

Walker, Marcus (1999), 'Punch-up in Basle', *Euromoney*, May 1999.

Willman, John (2001a), 'Basle banking rules criticised', *Financial Times* 18th June 2001.

Willman, John (2001b), 'Basle accord to be delayed', *Financial Times* 25th June 2001.

Willman, John (2001c), 'Devil in the detail makes it necessary to delay', *Financial Times* 25th June 2001.

Wood, Duncan (1996), *From Bretton Woods to Basle: Authority-Market Relations in the International Banking System*, PhD dissertation, Queen's University, Kingston, Ontario.

Wood, Duncan (2000), 'The G7, International Finance, and the Developing Countries', in Karl Kaiser, John Kirton and Joseph P. Daniels, eds., *Shaping a New International Financial System: challenges of governance in a globalizing world*, Ashgate Publishing Company, Aldershot.

# Index

Voluntary Foreign Credit Restraint
   (VFCR) 33-34, 44
White, Harry Dexter 26, 32
W- Factor 138, 141
Waltz, Kenneth 14
World Bank 4, 25, 26, 27, 106, 108, 161

x3 Amendment 126

Young Committee 24

Zwick Report 1967 35